22 Sept 17
7/11
4/3

PCH

Get **more** out of libraries

Please return or renew this item by the last date shown.

You can renew online at www.hants.gov.uk/library

Or by phoning 0300 555 1387

Hampshire
County Council

PREFACE

Family law can be a fascinating topic; it is so infinitely varied in the different issues that may be encountered, whether in the examination room or in practice.

Each family is different and it is a challenge to try to use the law to achieve a practical solution to the problems encountered.

As a student of family law you must ensure that you master the basic legal concepts that are to be your tools for study, for examinations and, hopefully, for your future practice.

Statute law features strongly in family law, and you must be familiar with the statutory provisions that govern the various areas of the syllabus. Students frequently complain about the wealth of case law that they are exposed to; it may be comforting to remember that cases in the main part merely illustrate how the statutory principles have operated in relation to a particular family. Since each family is different, cases should be regarded as providing guidance, rather than absolute rules, and help to put issues into perspective.

I have tried where possible to refer to the same basic cases when illustrating the answers to the problems. I do this in the hope of providing some comfort to those who have become exasperated by the volume of the subject.

Family law can be an enjoyable and rewarding topic to study and I hope this book will be of use, not only in your revision and question answering technique, but also in providing you with an enthusiasm for the subject

Finally, I would like to thank Liz Rodgers for her help and my husband Paul and family for their support.

Rachael Stretch
April 2006

CONTENTS

TABLE OF CASES

Note: Where recent cases have not been widely reported, it is possible to read the judgment on the ECJ website. Go to www.curia.eu.int, select 'Proceedings' and 'case law'. Use the case number to search for the case you want to read.

TABLE OF STATUTES

CHAPTER 1

NULLITY OF MARRIAGE

▌INTRODUCTION

Many family law syllabuses begin by looking at the rules on who can marry and how that marriage should be conducted. As part of this, they often consider nullity even though in the 'real world' the number of nullity petitions is very small, less than 300 petitions per year. In any case, nullity is still essential, for those who wish to end, their marital obligations, but who are opposed for religious or social reasons to divorce. It is also possible to end a marriage within one year of it taking place if nullity proceedings succeed.

Some courses will focus on the conflict of laws or foreign element to nullity, and the following questions are a mixture of those containing entirely English nullity issues and those containing a foreign element. Cases which involve a foreign element require you to be familiar with the concept of domicile since it affects a person's capacity to marry, and with the lex loci which governs the formal requirements of marriage that must be complied with. Other courses may concentrate on the grounds for nullity and the limitations on who can marry. In this respect the development of the law on transsexuals and marriage from *Corbett v Corbett (1970)* to the Gender Recognition Act 2004 will be important as will be the law's rejection of homosexual marriage (*Wilkinson v Kitzinger and others (2006)*) and the introduction of civil registration of homosexual partnerships in the Civil Partnership Act 2004.

Nullity proceedings may be brought under Matrimonial Causes Act 1973 s 11 in respect of void marriages and MCA 1973 s 12 in respect of voidable marriages. You should ensure that you are familiar with all the grounds for presenting a petition under these sections, and whether there are any bars to the granting of the decree. The different consequences of void and voidable marriages must also be mastered. In relation to civil partnerships, the Civil Partnerships Act 2004 s 49 contains the reasons why such a partnership will be void and s 50 of that Act contains the reasons why a civil partnership will be voidable.

Void marriages under *MCA s 11* are fundamentally flawed from the outset and students must be able to identify the appropriate part of s 11:

- *s 11(a)* deals with marriages that are invalid under the Marriage Acts 1949 and 1970. This is because the parties are within the prohibited degrees of

1

relationship, or either is under 16, or certain formalities are not complied with;

- *s 11(b)* deals with marriages that are void because either party is already validly married;

- *s 11(c)* deals with marriages that are void because the parties are not respectively male and female;

- *s 11(d)* renders polygamous marriages with an English domiciliary void.

Section 12 deals with marriages that are merely voidable. This means that the marriage is valid unless and until a nullity decree is obtained. Unlike void marriages only the spouses can petition for nullity.

- *s 12(a)* deals with the incapacity of either party to consummate the marriage;

- *s 12(b)* covers the respondent's wilful refusal to consummate the marriage;

- *s 12(c)* renders a marriage voidable on the basis of mistake, duress, unsoundness of mind, or otherwise;

- *s 12(d)* enables a marriage to be ended if either party was suffering from a mental disorder such as to make them unfit for marriage;

- *s 12(e)* deals with marriages where the respondent is affected by venereal disease in a communicable form;

- *s 12(f)* renders a marriage voidable if the respondent is pregnant by another person;

- *s 12(g)* will be added by the Gender Recognition Act 2004 and will make a marriage voidable once one of the spouses has obtained an interim Gender Recognition Certificate;

- *s 12(h)* will be added by the Gender Recognition Act 2004 and will make a marriage voidable on the grounds that petitioner did not know that the respondent had changed their gender under the Gender Recognition Act 2004.

There are no bars or defences to a petition based on s 11 (void marriage). However, in relation to petitions under s 12 (voidable marriages), there are three bars in *s 13*:

- *s 13(1)* contains the bar of statutory approbation;

- *s 13(2)* provides a bar once three years have passed for petitions based on s 12(c), (d), (e) or (f);

- *s 13(3)* provides a bar of knowledge to petitions based on s 12(e) or (f).

Question 1

Jane, an Englishwoman, went to Ruritania to work, and there she met and married Fred, a Ruritanian man with whom she had fallen in love. He told her that although the law of his country allowed him to take more than one wife, he felt that she was so special he would never do so. After a few months Jane tired of his adoring, but boring company and decided to return home. She soon forgot about Fred and began to form a relationship with Tarzan, who had been briefly married to Jane's mother. Jane's mother had died two years previously and shortly after meeting, Jane and Tarzan married. However, after the ceremony Jane could not bring herself to have sexual intercourse with Tarzan, as she is tormented by the thought of his relationship with her mother.

Advise Jane on the validity of her marriages.

Answer plan

Begin by examining the validity of the marriage to Fred:

- consider if both parties had capacity;
- this depends on where they were domiciled at the time of marriage;
- the effect of the polygamous, or potentially polygamous, nature of the marriage.

Then consider the validity of the marriage to Tarzan:

- consider capacity;
- problem of prohibited degrees;
- problem if Jane is already validly married to Fred.

Consider also the possibility that the marriage is voidable:

- non-consummation (incapacity or wilful refusal?)

Answer

In advising Jane on the validity of her marriages, it will be necessary to examine the first marriage to Fred, which took place in Ruritania. For this marriage to be valid, both parties must have had capacity to marry and the relevant formalities must have been complied with.

Turning to the issue of capacity, English case law has determined this by reference to two different tests. Cases such as *In the Will of Swan (1871)* have judged the validity of the marriage by examining whether the parties had capacity to marry by reference to the law of the 'intended matrimonial home'. This has the advantage of requiring only one jurisdiction to be examined, and treats marriage on a par with other contracts by examining its validity according to the jurisdiction the marriage has the closest connection to. It is the test most likely to render a marriage valid. However, the intended matrimonial home test is vague and uncertain, and problems may be encountered if the parties do not go on to set up a matrimonial home in the jurisdiction.

The second test requires the parties to have capacity by reference to the law of their respective domiciles before they married. This is the test favoured by the Law Commission as being more certain, and it viewed testing the validity of marriage by reference to something existing at the time of the marriage preferable to testing the validity by reference to something that can only really be established after the marriage takes place. Applying this test in the present case it must be established that each party to the marriage had capacity to marry according to the law of their ante-nuptial domicile, *Sottomayer v de Barros (No 1) (1877)*.

Fred was domiciled in Ruritania. Ruritania was clearly his permanent home: *Whicker v Hume (1858)*. Thus Fred would seem to have capacity to marry Jane, although it is arguable whether Jane had capacity to marry Fred. She begins with an English domicile. However, when she goes to Ruritania to work, she may have obtained a Ruritanian domicile of choice. To establish this it would be necessary for her to have made Ruritania her permanent home, that is, established a physical presence of a lasting nature, with an intention to make it her permanent home. This intention must be positive and demonstrate a fixed and settled intention to remain; mere indifference on Jane's part would not suffice (*Winans v AG (1910)*). In going to Ruritania to work, Jane's intentions are not clear. If she intended this as a temporary or transient measure then there is insufficient determination to acquire a domicile of choice. However, if on meeting Fred, Jane decides that she should settle in Ruritania then she may have acquired a Ruritanian domicile of choice.

If Jane is domiciled in Ruritania at the time of her marriage to Fred then she will also have capacity to marry, notwithstanding the potentially polygamous nature of the marriage, as Ruritanian law allows polygamy. It is assumed that the requisite formalities of Ruritanian law, which is the lex loci, have been complied with, and so the marriage will be valid: *Herbert v Herbert (1819)*.

There is, however, a strong possibility that Jane was still domiciled in England at the time of her marriage to Fred, in which case her capacity must be judged according to English law. Lord Penzance in *Hyde v Hyde (1866)* defined marriage as 'the voluntary union of a man and a woman for life to the exclusion of all others' and this definition has formed the basis of the English law rules on capacity. To be able to contract a valid marriage, an English domiciliary must be over 16 (which it is assumed Jane and Fred are); not within the prohibited degrees of relationship, (which again appears to cause no difficulty here); not already married; and the marriage must not be polygamous. This is the aspect of the marriage that requires greater examination.

Section 11(d) of the Matrimonial Causes Act 1973 provides that a marriage that is polygamous is void. This means that the marriage is treated as a complete nullity, and there is no need to obtain a nullity decree unless financial provision is to be sought under s 23 or 24 of the Act. In the instant case the marriage is not actually polygamous, but it has the potential, given Fred's domicile, to become polygamous. In *Hussain v Hussain (1982)* a marriage between a man and a woman in Pakistan which permitted polygamy was nevertheless held to be valid, as the woman had the Pakistani domicile and could not take a second husband, and the man had an English domicile and could not take a second wife, thereby rendering the marriage monogamous. This would not apply to the marriage between Jane and Fred, as the roles are reversed and Fred could still, in theory, take another spouse. Thus the marriage between Jane and Fred, whilst not actually polygamous, is potentially so. Until the provisions of the **Private International Law (Miscellaneous Provisions) Act 1995** *(PIL (MP) A)* came into force in 1996, s 11(d) MCA 1973 had the effect of making a potentially polygamous marriage by an English domiciliary void. This somewhat discriminatory rule was the subject of criticism by the Law Commission in their report on polygamous marriages, which thought that the rule as relating to potentially polygamous marriages was harsh. Accordingly *s 5* of the *PIL (MP) A 1995* amended s 11(d) to make marriages that were only potentially polygamous valid. The Act has retrospective effect, *s 6(1)*, but it does not retrospectively validate a potentially polygamous marriage if a party to that marriage has gone on to celebrate a later valid marriage, *s 6(2)*.

In Jane and Fred's case, we are not told when their marriage took place. If it took place after the provisions of the PIL (MP) A 1995 were in force, then it is valid. If it took place before this date, then it may still be valid, provided neither party has gone on to celebrate a subsequent valid marriage.

It therefore seems that if Jane was domiciled in England the first marriages status will depend upon when it took place and the status of any second marriage, whereas if she were domiciled in Ruritania it would be valid. English law will not refuse to recognise valid polygamous marriages for public policy reasons: *Mohammed v Knott (1969)*. The second marriage will be valid if both parties have capacity by the law of their ante-nuptial domiciles and have complied with the requisite formalities. Both Tarzan and Jane are domiciled in England at the time of the marriage and are male and female and above the age of 16. There is, however, a potential problem given that for a short while Tarzan was married to Jane's mother. There would be an absolute prohibition on Jane marrying Tarzan if he were her natural or adoptive father; likewise if she had at any stage been a child of the family whilst Tarzan was married to her mother: *Marriage Act 1949 Sched 1*. However, if Jane had never been treated by Tarzan as a child of the family and Tarzan's relationship with Jane's mother had occurred when Jane was no longer living at home, then provided that Tarzan and Jane are both over 21 they will be able to marry: **Marriage (Prohibited Degrees) Act**

1986. However, an additional problem may be encountered if the first marriage to Fred was valid. English law requires both parties to be single, and if one or more of them is already married then the subsequent marriage is a nullity: *MCA 1973 s 11(b)*. If the marriage to Fred was valid then the marriage to Tarzan will be void. However, if the marriages to Fred and Tarzan took place before the provisions of the PIL (MP) A 1995 came into force then the marriage to Fred is void as potentially polygamous, and the marriage to Tarzan will be valid. This is because the retrospective nature of the provisions does not operate if there has been a second valid marriage according to the law at the time it was celebrated.

There are possible grounds for arguing that the marriage between Jane and Tarzan is voidable for one of the reasons in MCA s 12 . It does not seem that the marriage has been consummated. Jane's attitude has ensured that there has been no complete and regular intercourse (*D v A (1845)*) once the marriage has taken place. Premarital intercourse does not suffice for consummation. It is then necessary to consider whether this is due to incapacity to consummate or wilful refusal.

Either party can petition on the basis that there is some physical or psychological reason preventing consummation (*D v D (1982)*). Here it would seem that Jane has psychological problems that are preventing intercourse. In order for the decree to be granted these reasons must exist at the date of the petition and the date of the hearing (*Napier v Napier (1915)*), but there must also be no practical possibility of intercourse (*S v S (1962)*). In the instant case it is not clear what, if anything at all, can be done to help Jane; neither is it apparent that she wishes to be helped to overcome the problem. If it is felt that there is a possibility of intercourse should Jane accept help which would not expose her to too great a risk, then Jane's refusal to seek such assistance may amount to a wilful refusal to consummate. This would be a settled and definite decision without just cause (*Horton v Horton (1947)*), and would give Tarzan the opportunity to petition for nullity.

A voidable marriage is valid unless and until it is dissolved by way of nullity decree (*De Renville v De Renville (1948)*), unlike the void marriage. Therefore, Jane should seek a nullity decree in respect of her marriage to Tarzan.

Question 2

Jasmine's parents settled in England from Ruritania, and Jasmine was born and grew up in England. She was introduced on her Sixteenth birthday to Jafar, a Ruritanian domiciliary, who had come to England to go through an arranged marriage with Jasmine. Two weeks later, Jasmine reluctantly went through a ceremony of marriage with Jafar. On their wedding night Jasmine was horrified to find that Jafar was a drug addict, and she refused to have sexual intercourse with him until he gave up his drug habit. A few months later, Jasmine left Jafar and went through a ceremony of marriage with Aladdin in a registry office using false names so that her father would not find out and prevent the marriage. In disgust, Jafar returned to Ruritania to visit relatives. Ruritanian law allows polygamy, and Jafar married Asha, a 14-year-old Ruritanian girl, who returned to England with him. Jafar's drug addiction has rendered him impotent and so after two years he and Asha adopt a child. Jafar now wishes to end his relationship with Asha.

Advise Jasmine and Jafar on the validity of their various marriages.

Answer plan

First, consider the validity of the marriage between Jasmine and Jafar:

- check the domicile of both parties;
- consider the provisions of MCA s 11 on void marriages as they apply to the parties;
- also examine whether the marriage is voidable under s 12 for non-consummation or duress;
- consider the bars in s 13.

The marriage between Jasmine and Aladdin must then be considered on two bases:

- First, if the marriage to Jafar is valid, then the marriage to Aladdin is void under s 11(b).
- Second, if the marriage to Jafar was void, then the issue of formalities under s 11(a) must be considered.

Finally, the marriage between Asha and Jafar is affected by the validity of the marriage to Jasmine:

- if the marriage to Jasmine is valid, then consider capacity to enter into a polygamous marriage;
- also consider voidable marriage under s 12 for non-consummation and the bar of statutory approbation;
- if the marriage to Jasmine is void, then the marriage to Asha is valid, and the only possibility is a s 12 voidable marriage.

Answer

The first marriage between Jasmine and Jafar is of crucial importance in determining the validity of the subsequent marriages.

The capacity of Jasmine and Jafar to contract a valid marriage is determined by reference to the law of their ante-nuptial domiciles: *Sottomayer v de Barros (No 1) (1877)*. Jasmine was born in England and grew up here. Her domicile at birth, her domicile of origin, is that of her father at the time of her birth, which, since he had settled in England, was an English domicile. At 16 Jasmine is capable of acquiring an independent domicile (**Domicile and Matrimonial Proceedings Act 1973 s 4**), but it would seem that at the time of marriage she possesses an English domicile. Jafar had a Ruritanian domicile, but on coming to England he may have acquired an English domicile of choice. This will be the case if he has established a lasting physical presence in England coupled with a fixed and settled intention to remain and make England his permanent home: *Winans v AG (1910)*. Jafar has come here to marry Jasmine and he has remained after the marriage, but if this is merely the result of indifference and apathy it may be that he has retained his Ruritanian domicile: *Ramsay v Liverpool Royal Infirmary (1930)*.

If Jafar has an English domicile at the time of the marriage then it would seem that both he and Jasmine have capacity to marry. Lord Penzance's definition of marriage in *Hyde v Hyde (1866)* as 'the voluntary union of a man and a woman for life to the exclusion of all others' forms the basis of the English rules on capacity. If a party lacks capacity then the marriage would be void under MCA 1973 s 11. Here both Jasmine and Jafar are over 16, man and woman, single, and not within the prohibited degrees. Since Jafar has an English domicile the marriage is not polygamous or potentially so; therefore the provisions of s 11(d) do not apply.

It would then be necessary to ensure that the marriage had complied with the requisite formalities of English law, which is the lex loci in this case: *Herbert v Herbert (1819)*. The facts mention a ceremony of marriage without specifying where this took place. English law requires marriages to comply with certain procedural requirements, and those that do not comply with the provisions of *s 25* of the *Marriage Act 1949*, for Anglican weddings, and *s 49* for other marriages, will be void: *MCA 1973 s 11(a)*. If the wedding complied with the requirements of the Marriage Act it will be valid; if not it will be void. A void marriage is regarded by the law as a complete nullity and there would be no need to obtain a nullity decree, unless financial provision was sought.

If Jafar had a Ruritanian domicile, then he would have the capacity to contract a polygamous or potentially polygamous marriage. However, if the marriage took place in England, English law, which is the lex loci, only permits marriages in a monogamous form. The earlier discussion as to the formalities would also apply in the event of Jafar being domiciled in Ruritania.

If the marriage is not void, it may be voidable by reference to the provisions in s 12 of the Matrimonial Causes Act 1973. It is likely that the marriage has not been consummated, given Jasmine's timely discovery of Jafar's addiction. There has been no complete and regular intercourse: *D v A (1845)*. However, it is not clear whether this is because Jafar is already impotent, and therefore physically incapable, or whether Jasmine is psychologically unable to consummate: *D v D (1982)*. It seems that Jasmine is revolted by Jafar, rather than she being unable to consummate and there is no practical possibility of this being achieved: *S v S (1962)*. If there is incapacity then either party may petition, either on the basis of their own or the other's incapacity: *Harthan v Harthan (1949)*.

There is also the possibility that a petition could be presented on the basis that there is a wilful refusal to consummate by the respondent: MCA 1973 s 12(b). At first glance, it appears that Jasmine is refusing to consummate the marriage, but in *Horton v Horton (1947)*, it was stressed that the refusal needed to be a settled and definite decision reached without just cause. It is obvious that Jasmine has made a positive decision (*Potter v Potter (1975)*), but it could be argued that she has just cause. Drug addicts may be more prone to certain kinds of disease and their behaviour may be more erratic and violent than the normal individual. Indeed, by drawing an analogy with the cases involving non-consummation because of refusal to arrange a religious ceremony, it could be argued that Jafar's refusal to give up his drug habit is wilful refusal on his part, thereby enabling Jasmine to petition: *Kaur v Singh (1972)*.

The other possible basis for nullity would be to rely on the provisions of MCA 1973 s 12(c) which give grounds for nullity if there was no valid consent through duress, mistake, unsoundness of mind or otherwise. Jasmine's marriage to Jafar was an arranged marriage, and although this is not sufficient in itself to amount to duress (*Singh v Singh (1971)*), if there is extreme pressure on Jasmine the reality of consent may be destroyed. The traditional view of duress was that it involved fear to life, limb or liberty: *Szechter v Szechter (1971)*. There does not seem to be such threats in the instant case; it is more the pressure to conform to family expectations. If Jasmine still had a choice, then there will be no duress. However, in *Hirani v Hirani (1982)* it was recognised that a young, vulnerable girl may be under such extreme pressure from her family to conform that in reality her free will has been overborne. This would be applicable in the instant case if Jasmine had led a sheltered existence with no real friends or way of supporting herself should she be ostracised by her family.

If the marriage is voidable, then it is valid unless a nullity decree is obtained: *De Renville v De Renville (1948)*. Therefore it will be necessary if one of the grounds in s 12 is used for a petition to be presented. Although there is no time bar to petitions based on non-consummation, those based on duress must be brought within three years of the marriage: MCA 1973 s 13(2).

If the marriage of Jasmine and Jafar is valid or if voidable and no nullity decree was obtained before Jasmine married Aladdin, then the marriage to Aladdin is void since *MCA 1973 s 11(b)* requires neither party to be already validly married. Jasmine is domiciled in England, as is Aladdin, and therefore this would govern their capacity to marry: *Sottomayer v de Barros (No 1) (1877)*.

If, however, the marriage to Jafar is void, then there is no need to obtain a decree, and Jasmine would have capacity to marry Aladdin. The marriage would have to comply with the formalities prescribed by English law, the lex loci: *Herbert v Herbert (1819)*. In the instant case, the registry office wedding took place without the requisite parental consent for Jasmine but *s 48* of the *Marriage Act* provides that this does not render the marriage invalid. A marriage is void if celebrated in the absence of the formalities in s 49 for registry office weddings but the use of false names does not mean that the parties have knowingly and wilfully married without due notice: *Puttick v AG* (1980). Therefore the marriage will not be void by reason of *MCA 1973 s 11(a)*. Consequently the validity of the marriage between Jasmine and Aladdin depends upon the validity of Jasmine's earlier marriage to Jafar.

Jafar's subsequent marriage to Asha needs to be considered assuming that the first marriage to Jasmine was valid and then, alternatively, that the first marriage was void. If the first marriage was valid then it is necessary to examine Jafar's and Asha's capacity to enter into their marriage by reference to the law of their ante-nuptial domiciles. Asha is clearly domiciled in Ruritania at the time of the wedding and has capacity to enter into a polygamous union. However, it is not clear what Ruritanian laws are regarding age of marriage. There is no evidence that she has concealed her age, so it is assumed that Ruritania permits marriage for girls of 14. Jafar had a Ruritanian domicile of origin which he may have lost if he acquired an English domicile of choice on his marriage to Jasmine. On returning to Ruritania to visit relatives, it may be argued that the English domicile was lost and that his Ruritanian domicile of origin revives. This would then permit him to contract a polygamous marriage with Asha. However, if at the time of the marriage he had an English domicile, then the marriage to Asha will be void, as s 11(d) prohibits the making of a polygamous union by an English domiciliary anywhere in the world.

If the marriage to Asha was valid according to the requirements on capacity, it would also be necessary to establish that Ruritanian formalities were complied with. Assuming this to be the case, English law would not refuse to recognise a valid polygamous marriage contracted overseas on public policy grounds (*Mohammed v Knott*); likewise if the girl was 14 and marriage at this age was allowed by the law of her domicile.

It will then be necessary to consider whether there are grounds for arguing that the marriage is voidable under one of the provisions in s 12. Obviously Jafar's impotence gives the possibility of non-consummation through incapacity. Either side may petition on this basis (*Harthan v Harthan (1949)*); based on their own or the other's incapacity. However, in Harthan, it was suggested that a petitioner could not rely on his own incapacity if he knew of it at the date of the marriage. Therefore, Asha could rely on s 12(a) but Jafar could not if he knew of his problem at the relevant time. Petitions based on non-consummation may be presented at any time, although the bar of statutory approbation under s 13(1) may apply. This prevents petitioners who knew that they could have the marriage avoided from succeeding if they have behaved in such a way as to lead the other to believe that they would not do so, and it would be unjust to grant the petition. The petitioner must know that they have the legal right to petition (*Slater v Slater (1953)*) and there must be behaviour from which it can be argued that there would be injustice to grant the petition (*Pettit v Pettit (1962)*). In the instant case, Asha and Jafar have adopted a child: in *W v W (1967)* this amounted to approbation; whereas in *D v D (1982)*, since there was no injustice, the petition was granted. Without more information on the knowledge of the parties and the discussions leading to the adoption it will be difficult to know how this would finally be determined.

If the marriage to Jasmine was void, then the marriage to Asha is monogamous if Jafar has an English domicile at the date of the marriage: *Hussain v Hussain (1982)*. If, however, Jafar has a Ruritanian domicile then the marriage is potentially polygamous, but since this is acceptable by the law of his ante-nuptial domicile, English law will recognise the marriage. The same issues on the age of Asha and the possible use of s 12 apply as previously discussed.

Question 3

Kate was a journalist covering a civil war in the depths of Africa. There she met a fellow English journalist, Leo, with whom she fell instantly and madly in love. They wanted to marry but were in the midst of heavy fighting and were unable to make the journey to the nearest city. They exchanged marriage vows in front of Mike, a missionary who was hoping to become a priest. Both Kate and Leo were captured by rival factions in the civil war, and Kate assumed Leo had been killed when she did not hear from him again. Kate met another journalist, Nick, in the prisoner of war camp she was held in and, finding she was pregnant by Leo, agreed to marry Nick so that her child would have a father. The marriage was intended by both as a companionship-only relationship, as neither wished to have intercourse with the other. After Kate's baby was born, Nick found he looked on Kate with increasing affection, and wanted her to be more than his housekeeper. However, Kate refused to have intercourse with him, and Nick has now met Olive, with whom he hopes to have a proper marriage.

Advise Nick.

Answer

In advising Nick on his ability to marry Olive it will be necessary to examine the validity of his marriage to Kate, which in turn is affected by the validity of the marriage between Kate and Leo. It is proposed that the first marriage to be discussed will be that of Kate and Leo.

The capacity of Kate and Leo to contract a valid marriage is to be judged by the law of their ante-nuptial domicile: *Sottomayer v de Barros (No 1) (1877)*. Both Kate and Leo have English domicile and do not appear to have acquired a domicile of choice in Africa. They are present there as part of their job to report on the civil war. It would seem that neither of them has the intention to make this their permanent home: *Winans v AG (1910)*.

The English law rules on capacity are based on Lord Penzance's definition of marriage as 'the voluntary union for life of a man and a woman to the exclusion of all others': *Hyde v Hyde (1866)*. Thus s 11 of the MCA 1973 requires the parties to be over 16, of opposite sex, not within the prohibited degrees, and not already married. It would therefore seem that Kate and Leo have capacity to marry.

It is also necessary that a valid marriage complies with the formal requirements of the lex loci, the place where the marriage is taking place: *Herbert v Herbert (1819)*.

However, in the instant case, Kate and Leo do not appear to have complied with any formalities prescribed by local law. Indeed, in a civil war situation, it may be virtually impossible for them to do so. The English law will nevertheless recognise such marriages if it is not possible to comply with local law because of insurmountable difficulties, provided that the English common law formalities have been complied with: *Taczanowski v Taczanowski (1957)*. This requires the parties to declare that they take each other as man and wife to the exclusion of all others and these vows must usually be exchanged before an ordained minister. This concept has been criticised as artificial, especially where the parties have no connection with England, but it might operate to make the ceremony between Kate and Leo a valid marriage. However, Mike is not an ordained minister, and this may mean that the marriage is invalid unless it can be argued that, in the circumstances, this missionary was the best person available to lend an air of formality as in *Wolfenden v Wolfenden (1945)*.

If the marriage is void through lack of compliance with the formalities, then there is no need to seek a nullity decree unless financial provision is sought under the Matrimonial Causes Act. If however, the marriage is valid, then it may have been possible for Kate to seek dissolution of her marriage by seeking to rely on the presumption of death. This would enable her to apply if she could show that no one who should have heard from Leo has done so in the past seven years and if the period exceeds seven years then the presumption that Leo is dead will operate, thereby entitling Kate to a dissolution of her marriage: MCA 1973 s 19.

If the marriage between Kate and Leo was void or had been dissolved before the marriage to Nick, then it would appear that both Kate and Nick would have capacity to marry according to the law of their domiciles. English law would be applied, since their capture and detention in prisoner of war camps could not result in them acquiring a domicile of choice. Section 11 of the MCA 1973 would require them to be both over the age of 16, of opposite sex, not within the prohibited degrees, and not already validly married. Even if they had capacity to marry, they must comply with the formalities required by the place where the marriage took place, the lex loci. It is not clear where the marriage took place and it is therefore assumed that either the necessary formalities were complied with or it was a situation where the doctrine of the English common law marriage would provide validity.

If, however, Kate's marriage to Leo was still valid then the subsequent marriage to Nick is void since s 11(b) requires neither party to be lawfully married. Likewise s 11(d) prevents an English domiciliary from entering into a polygamous union anywhere in the world, even if the local law permits polygamy.

If the marriage to Nick is valid then it may still be voidable by reference to the provisions of MCA 1973 s 12. It would seem that the marriage has not been consummated; there has been no complete and regular sexual intercourse (*D v A (1845)*). However, there does not appear to be any incapacity; just an initial decision that the relationship would be platonic, followed by Kate refusing to alter the status quo. This may be evidence of a wilful refusal to consummate the marriage, thereby rendering the marriage voidable under MCA 1973 s 12(b). In *Horton v Horton (1948)* it was held that there needed to be a settled and definite decision by the respondent reached without just cause. Initially there was a mutual understanding, and the status quo cannot be regarded as a refusal by either party: *Potter v Potter* (1982). However, when Nick tries to alter the situation and Kate refuses, then this may give the necessary definite decision on Kate's part, although it would still be necessary to examine whether her refusal was without just cause. They had agreed at the outset that theirs was to be a platonic relationship: would it be unreasonable for her to refuse to alter the nature of the relationship? Much might depend on how old the couple were with a young couple, the court are more likely to hold a refusal unreasonable, whereas obiter comments suggest that in the case of elderly couples a companionship arrangement might not be voidable: *Morgan v Morgan (1959)*. Since Kate has had a child she cannot be too old and it is likely that her refusal is unreasonable.

Kate was also pregnant by another man at the time of her marriage to Nick, and this can be the basis for a petition under s 12(f) pregnancy per alium. However, s 13(3) provides a bar to petitioning if Nick was aware of this fact at the time of the marriage. This seems likely given that he did not want intercourse with Kate initially, and so the petition would only succeed on the basis of non-consummation.

In conclusion, if Nick's marriage to Kate is void, then he is free to marry Olive. A void marriage is treated as if it never existed and no nullity decree is required. If, however, the marriage to Kate is merely voidable, then Nick must ensure that he obtains a nullity decree before marrying Olive.

Question 4

Frances is a law student who hates men. She is a very keen campaigner for homosexual rights and arranges to 'marry' Bernadette in a registry office as a publicity stunt. For the ceremony, Frances dresses up in a morning suit and signs her name in the male way, as Francis, to trick the registrar into carrying out the ceremony. After the ceremony Bernadette confesses to Frances that she had been born male, but had undergone a sex change operation. Frances is horrified and immediately leaves Bernadette. Sometime later, Frances suffers from serious clinical depression, and wanders the streets until she is befriended by Diego, an illegal immigrant. Frances agrees to marry Diego so that he can remain in the United Kingdom, and they are married in an Anglican church. Frances uses the surname by which she has been known for the past 10 years, but this is different from her surname as a child.

Advise the parties on the validity of the various marriages.

Answer plan

Again, take each marriage in turn and consider its validity.

The 'marriage' between Frances and Bernadette: is it void?

- consider the capacity of the parties;
- the problem of s 11(c) – male and female;
- no real problem about formalities.

Is it voidable?

- non-consummation through incapacity or wilful refusal;
- possible bar of approbation;
- mistake.

If no nullity decree is obtained, then this could affect validity of marriage between Frances and Diego:

- Is this void because already validly married (s 11(b))?
- use of false names – formalities;
- possibility of voidable marriage due to lack of consent or mental defect.

Answer

The marriage between Frances and Bernadette will be valid if both parties had capacity to enter into the marriage, and if the appropriate formalities were complied with. It seems that both Frances and Bernadette are domiciled in England at the date of their marriage, and so it is English law that will govern their capacity to marry. Section 11 of the MCA 1973 requires the parties to be over the age of 16, not already married and not within the prohibited degrees of relationship. None of these would appear to cause problems in relation to the marriage of Frances and Bernadette. However, s 11 also requires the parties to be male and female (*Wilkinson v Kitzinger and others (2006)*). In the instant case, it is clear that Frances is female, despite her dressing and posing as a male. It is the biological composition that determines a person's male or female categorisation: *Corbett v Corbett (1970)*. Corbett was based on medical knowledge and attitudes of the time. Whilst English law still seems opposed to homosexual marriages, there has been a realisation that the position of transsexuals may require reconsideration, *ST (Formerly J) v J (1998)*. However in that case the court upheld the traditional view that transsexuals could not alter their biological sex determined at birth. Bernadette would appear to physically resemble a female and would have the external appearance of a female.

However, English law does not adopt the more liberal views of some other countries that gender can be determined by choice or physical appearance. Therefore, although Bernadette may resemble a woman, and wish to be treated as one, Bernadette remains a male in the eyes of the law. Consequently the marriage that was intended by the parties to be a sham, given that they believed it to involve two females, in fact is a valid union between male and female.

There may be grounds for declaring the marriage void if the requisite formalities have not been complied with, but this is unlikely given that the marriage took place in a registry office. Section 11(a) would render such a marriage void if it failed to comply with *s 49* of the *Marriage Act 1949*. The false names would not amount to a failure to give due notice: *Puttick v AG (1980)*, and the mode of dress of the parties is not a ground for annulment.

A marriage may be voidable under the provisions of s 12, but this does not have the same effect as if the marriage was void. A void marriage is a complete nullity and there is no need to obtain a decree in respect of it before a party can remarry. However, a voidable marriage is valid until a nullity decree is obtained: *de Renville v de Renville (1948)*.

Clearly, the marriage has not been consummated, and this would seem to be a practical impossibility, given Bernadette's sex change operation. Either party could petition, in theory, on the basis of this incapacity to have complete and regular intercourse: *D v A (1845)*. Bernadette must have known that consummation was impossible, and following *Harthan v Harthan (1949)*, it may be argued that she (he) cannot rely on an incapacity that they were aware of at the time of the marriage. This would give Frances the option of petitioning on the basis of non-consummation, and there is no time bar under s 13 to such a petition. There is a defence of statutory approbation, which would require knowledge on the part of the petitioner that it was open to her to have the marriage dissolved. Clearly, Frances must have realised that the marriage could not be consummated, since she thought Bernadette was a woman, and as a law student she probably realised that this gave her grounds for an annulment. However, there is not really any behaviour by Frances that could illustrate that she led Bernadette to believe that Frances would not seek an annulment. After all, the marriage was intended as a publicity stunt, and there has been no real relationship to show that it would be unjust to grant the petition.

There is also the possibility of arguing that there was no valid consent to the marriage because of mistake: MCA 1973 s 12(c). The mistake in this case is very fundamental. Both parties thought they were taking part in a publicity stunt, but the difficulty is that they also seem to be well aware that they are taking part in a marriage ceremony. It could be argued that Frances is merely mistaken as to the attributes of Bernadette, which is insufficient to render the marriage voidable: *Puttick v AG (1980)*. The parties do not consider, mistakenly, that they are contracting a marriage, and this does give possible grounds for annulment, since there is a mistake as to the nature of proceedings, although proceedings must be brought within three years of the marriage: MCA 1973 s 13(2).

If the marriage is valid and no nullity proceedings are brought, then this will have profound implications for the validity of France's marriage to Diego.

Section 11(b) renders a marriage void if either of the parties is already validly married, and this would mean that Frances' marriage to Diego would be a nullity. If, however, the marriage to Bernadette is void or has been ended by a nullity decree, then it is necessary to consider the effect of the false names used for the church wedding. Section 11(a) renders a marriage void if it is celebrated in breach of certain formal requirements of the Marriage Acts. Since this marriage took place in church, the false names will affect the validity if they have been used to conceal identity (*Small v Small (1923)*) rather than to assist identification (*Dancer v Dancer (1948)*). The situation with Frances could arguably be said to fall within the category of cases where the name helps identify the party rather than hiding their true identity. In addition, the marriage is only void if both parties enter into it knowingly and wilfully. Thus the difference in name will not affect the validity of the marriage.

Frances' mental condition may mean that the marriage is voidable either under s 12(c) because there was no true consent through Frances' unsoundness of mind, or under s 12(d) because her mental disorder was such to make her unfit for marriage. More needs to be known about the extent of Frances' mental condition, as it will only be extensive rather than temporary mental disorder that renders her unfit for marriage: *Bennett v Bennett (1969)*.

If Diego, being an illegal immigrant, has such insufficient understanding of English that he has mistaken the nature of the ceremony, then he may petition under s 12(c) on the basis of mistake: *Valier v Valier (1925)*. However, given that the marriage has been entered into for its immigration consequences, this seems unlikely.

Question 5

[T]he biological sexual constitution of an individual is fixed at birth (at the latest), and cannot be changed, either by the natural development of organs of the opposite sex, or by medical or surgical means. The respondent's operation, therefore, cannot affect her true sex.

Per Omrod J *Corbett v Corbett (1971) P 83*

Critically examine whether this is still an accurate description of English law?

Answer plan

The quote is from *Corbett v Corbett* (1970), the leading case establishing the refusal of English law to allow transsexual to marry in their new sex. Answers should explain how the law has developed. They should include the influence of European case law and the effect that the Gender Recognition Act 2004 will have.

The approach in *Corbett v Corbett*

- According to Corbett how is gender to be defined?
- Transsexuals and consummation.
- Corbett is applied as the leading case.
- The European Court allows national jurisdictions a wide margin of appreciation.
- The decision of the European Court of Human Rights in Goodwin.
- Bellinger v Bellinger.

The Gender Recognition Act 2004

- Gender Recognition Certificate.

Answer

According to the Matrimonial Causes Act 1973 s. 11(c), parties to a marriage should be male and female. This requirement has caused problems for transsexuals because unless a transsexual can marry in her acquired gender, her options for marriage are likely to be significantly limited. The leading case for a long time has been that of *Corbett v Corbett* (1970) which is quoted in the question. In this case the petitioner was seeking nullity from his marriage to male to female transsexual. The High Court agreed that the marriage was void. It stated that a person's gender was determined by their biology, that is by the chromosomal, the gonadal and the genital tests, and because by these tests the respondent was a man, her marriage was void. The court in *Corbett* also stated that, in any case, a marriage involving male to female transsexual would be voidable because she would be unable to consummate her marriage as a woman. Whether transsexuals can consummate in their new gender is a less significant argument though as in any case, consummation is merely a grounds for a voidable marriage.

The approach in Corbett was for a long time upheld by both the English and the European Courts. For example in *Cossey v UK (1990)*, Caroline Cossey's claim to be recognised in her new gender and to be able to marry was rejected and the approach of the English courts was upheld by the European Court. For a long time, the

European Court of Human Rights viewed the extent to which the acquired gender of transsexuals was recognised to be a matter for national appreciation, allowing individual countries to take different approaches to reflect the different degrees to which transsexualism was accepted by their population. For English law, this changed with the European Court's decision in *Goodwin v UK (2002)*. In this case, the European Court decided that denying transsexuals the right to marry was a breach of Article 12 of the European Convention of Human Rights, and that it was no longer appropriate for a person's gender to be determined purely by reference to biological conditions present at their birth.

Whilst the European Court was deciding the *Goodwin* case, the English courts were hearing the claims of Mr and Mrs Bellinger for their marriage to be declared valid. The Court of Appeal in *Bellinger (2002)* was sympathetic to Mrs Bellinger but the majority upheld the decision in *Corbett* that a person's gender was fixed at birth. In his dissenting judgement, Thorpe argued that the law should be changed to take account of changes in social attitudes towards transsexuals and developing medical knowledge. Mrs Bellinger appealed to the House of Lords where despite the decision in *Goodwin* she was unsuccessful. The House of Lords decided that the issue was too important to be decided by a court and that reform would have to come from Parliament. This has now happened through the *Gender Recognition Act 2004*.

The *Gender Recognition Act 2004* will enable transsexuals to apply to a gender recognition panel for a certificate recognising their change of gender. This certificate will enable them to marry in their new gender. Perhaps controversially, the Act does not require a transsexual to have undergone surgery before (s)he can obtain a certificate. The reason for this is that if surgery were needed for a gender recognition certificate, an individual who, for medical reasons, was unable to have a full sex change would, perhaps unfairly, be prevented from being recognised in their new gender. Instead a person must show that they have lived for two years in their acquired gender and intend to live in that gender for the rest of their live. If a person is married in their original sex, they can only obtain an interim gender recognition certificate. This interim certificate will make the marriage voidable and once the marriage is dissolved, it can be converted to a full certificate. The Act will not apply retrospectively and individuals like Mrs Bellinger will still find that their existing marriages are void.

The UK approach is interesting because it does not base a person's gender on their biology. It will be possible for an individual to have the sexual characteristics of a man, but be registered by the Gender Recognition Panel as a woman. Furthermore, the fact that a person has to intend to live in their acquired sex does suggest that gender recognition is based, at least in part, on a person's psychological commitment to their new sex. This is a significant development from the approach adopted in *Corbett*.

CHAPTER 2

DIVORCE

INTRODUCTION

Divorce questions frequently feature on examination papers, either as a whole question or linked with other issues. Divorce is increasingly common, with recent statistics showing that around one in three marriages end in divorce. The law regarding divorce is in confusion. The Family Law Act 1996 would have fundamentally altered the way in which divorces would be obtained, and abolished the concept of fault-based divorce. The Act was radical, but will now not be implemented. In 1997 the new Labour Government indicated they would implement the divorce provisions of the Act (that is, Pt II, ss 2–21) after successful pilot schemes, probably in 2000. However, in 1999, the Lord Chancellor's Department stated that implementation was to be delayed and in 2001 the Government announced that it was abandoning the divorce reforms. The pilot schemes had not been viewed as a success, and had proved costly and not necessarily any less antagonistic than the Matrimonial Causes Act (MCA) 1973 procedure.

In practice, the vast majority of divorces are uncontested, but examination questions tend to concentrate on whether the basis for divorce exists. Students should ensure that they have a good knowledge of the rules concerning divorce; these are not questions that can be skated over superficially.

THE MATRIMONIAL CAUSES ACT 1973

Remember that there is only one ground for divorce, that of irretrievable breakdown of marriage: MCA 1973 s 1(1). This must be evidenced by one of the five facts in s 1(2).

Section 1(2)(a) provides for the granting of a petition based on the respondent's adultery and the petitioner finding it intolerable to live with the respondent:

- remember the definition of adultery and the difficulties of proving that it has occurred;
- the requirement of intolerability is subjective and does not have to result from the adultery;

- consider the effect of any continuing cohabitation.

Section 1(2)(b) allows divorce if the respondent has behaved in such a way that the petitioner cannot reasonably be expected to live with him/her:

- do not use the label 'unreasonable behaviour' – it is incorrect. It is the prospect of continued cohabitation that must be unreasonable;
- check that there has been behaviour by the respondent;
- look at the characters of the individuals involved;
- then examine whether they can reasonably be expected to live together – this is an objective test.

Section 1(2)(c) contains the fact of two years desertion by the respondent:

- there needs to be a separation, that is, withdrawal from married life;
- this needs to be without the consent of the petitioner;
- and last for a two year duration;
- remember the possibility of constructive desertion;
- consider the effect of cohabitation.

Section 1(2)(d) deals with two years living apart and the respondent consents to the granting of the petition:

- need for two separate households;
- Requirement for one party at least to recognise that the marriage was at an end, although this does not need to be communicated;
- separation of two years;
- positive consent to granting of petition;
- effect of cohabitation;
- possible delay through s 10, financial provision.

Section 1(2)(e) allows divorce on a no-fault basis, even without consent, if there has been five years living apart:

- physical separation into two households;
- mental element of one spouse recognising the marriage is at an end;
- duration of five years;
- effect of cohabitation;
- possible bar under s 5 if grave financial or other hardship;
- possible delay through s 10.

Remember also that no petition can be presented within one year of marriage.

THE FAMILY LAW ACT 1996

Divorce procedure was set out in *Part II*. This is not in force and there are no plans for it to be implemented. The ground for divorce was still the irretrievable breakdown of marriage, and this was to be demonstrated by a statement by one or both of the parties that they believe that the marriage has irretrievably broken down. The initial marital statement could only be lodged with the court after at least three months after one or both parties had attended an information meeting. Fourteen days after the statement is lodged, the period of reflection and consideration would begin. This would last for a minimum of nine months, although it can be extended by another six months. Once the period for reflection and consideration had ended, then either or both parties could apply for a divorce or separation order. The court would then make the order unless the arrangements for the future are unsatisfactory, or unless one of the parties raises the hardship bar in *s 10*. No application for a divorce order could be made within one year of the marriage: *s 7(6)*.

ENDING CIVIL PARTNERSHIPS UNDER THE *CIVIL PARTNERSHIP ACT 2004*

The Civil Partnership Act 2004 introduces the possibility for homosexual and lesbian couples to register their relationships. Chapter 2 of the Act sets out the reasons why a civil partnership may be dissolved. Dissolution under the *Civil Partnership Act 2004* largely corresponds to divorce under the Matrimonial Causes Act 1973. The only ground for dissolution is that the partnership has broken down irretrievably. This is shown by proving one of the facts in *section 44(5)*:

- That the respondent has behaved in such a way that the petitioner can not reasonably be expected to live with respondent.
- That the applicant and the respondent have lived apart for a continuous period of at least two years immediately preceding the making of the application and the respondent consents to a dissolution order being made.
- That the applicant and the respondent have lived apart for a continuous period of at least five years preceding the application.
- That the respondent has deserted the applicant for a continuous period of at least two years preceding the making of the application.

Question 6

Fred and Wilma married 10 years ago, and were initially very happy. However, Fred started to go out with his friends every Saturday night, leaving Wilma at home with their daughter, Pebbles. Fred frequently returned home drunk, waking Wilma and Pebbles with his raucous singing. One Saturday, Fred crashed his car, returning home after a night in the pub, and was severely injured and left with permanent paraplegia. Wilma visited Fred every day whilst he was in hospital, but when he returned home she realised that the marriage was effectively at an end. Wilma continued to cook for Fred, and she would help bathe and dress him. She did not tell Fred of her feelings, but she began to have an affair with a neighbour, Barney. Wilma told Barney that she would never leave Fred whilst he still needed her, but five years after the accident Wilma moved out of the matrimonial home, to live with Barney, taking Pebbles with her. Wilma said that Fred's depression and irritability had proved too much for her, and she could no longer cope with the strain of looking after him. Fred has refused to consider divorce, saying that he needs Wilma to look after him and that he misses Pebbles.

Advise Wilma as to whether she has any basis for divorce under the present law.

Answer plan

Present law

Ensure that you mention the one ground of divorce, irretrievable breakdown.

Check that a petition can be presented, which it can, given the duration of the marriage. Examine:

- *s 1(2)(a)* – adultery and intolerability (unlikely on the facts)
- *s 1(2)(b)* – behaviour (problem of Fred's condition; consider their characters; is it reasonable to expect them to continue to live together?)
- *s 1(2)(c)* – desertion (unlikely)
- *s 1(2)(d)* – two years living apart (physical separation; mental element; duration; Fred's consent – seems unlikely)
- *s 1(2)(e)* – five years living apart (physical separation; mental element; duration possible s 5 application)

Answer

At present, there is one ground for divorce, namely that the marriage between Fred and Wilma has broken down irretrievably: MCA 1973 s 1(1). However, in order to establish irretrievable breakdown, Wilma must establish one of the five facts in s 1(2) of the MCA 1973: *Richards v Richards (1972)*. From the facts of the question, it seems clear that the marriage has broken down irretrievably; despite Fred's unwillingness to divorce, there seems little realistic prospect for the couple's marriage to revive.

A petition for divorce may only be presented after one year of marriage (MCA 1973 s 3(1)), and since this marriage has lasted 10 years, Wilma can petition, provided she can establish one of the five facts.

There is no evidence that Fred has committed adultery, indeed his condition may make it impossible for him to achieve the penetration required for there to be voluntary sexual intercourse with another woman: *Dennis v Dennis (1955)*. Section 1(2)(a) of the MCA 1973 provides that a petition may be presented on the basis that the respondent has committed adultery and that the petitioner finds it intolerable to live with the respondent. Although it is quite clear that Wilma has had voluntary sexual intercourse with Barney, she cannot petition on the basis of her own adultery. Instead this may be relied on by Fred if he were to cross-petition, with the additional requirement of intolerability having to be satisfied. The test for intolerability is subjective – does this petitioner find it intolerable to live with this respondent? – and there is no need for the adultery to be the cause of the intolerability: *Cleary v Cleary (1974)*. In the instant case, it appears that Fred wishes to continue to live with Wilma, and so the intolerability does not exist, although if he later finds Wilma's attitude offensive, then the fact may be established: *Goodrich v Goodrich (1971)*.

Fred would be precluded from relying on the adultery if he had continued to live with Wilma for a period in excess of six months following his discovery of the last adulterous liaison: *MCA s 2(1)*.

A more realistic option for Wilma is to use the fact in MCA 1973 s 1(2)(b) that the respondent has behaved in such a way that the petitioner cannot reasonably be expected to live with the respondent. First, she will need to establish that there has been some behaviour on Fred's part: a mere state of affairs is insufficient (*Katz v Katz (1972)*). Fred's physical condition may cause difficulty if he is merely handicapped; there would need to be a significant strain on Wilma for her petition to succeed: *Thurlow v Thurlow (1975)*. If Fred had become difficult, bad tempered or violent, then Wilma's chances of success would increase. It is also possible to maintain a petition based on several incidents, each insufficient in itself, but which have a cumulative effect: *Livingstone-Stallard v Livingstone-Stallard (1974)*. Wilma may be able to argue that Fred's Saturday nights out with his friends, his drunkenness, and his disturbing of her and their child amounted to intolerable behaviour. In addition, his action in driving whilst drunk was behaviour that led to his present incapacity.

Once some kind of behaviour has been established, it is then necessary to look at the character of the individual concerned (*Ash v Ash (1972)*), and examine whether it would be reasonable to expect them to continue to live together: *Livingstone-Stallard v Livingstone-Stallard (1974)*. Applying that to Wilma and Fred, it could be contended that the strain of looking after Fred, who has been severely incapacitated through his own negligence, is too much for Wilma. Against this it could be argued that Wilma has been having an adulterous relationship with Barney, she has continued to share the same house with Fred for a number of years, stating that she would not leave him, and, although cohabitation of more than six months is not an absolute bar under s 2(3) to a successful petition based on behaviour, it does seem that her unwillingness to remain is based more on her developing romance with Barney rather than Fred's behaviour. Nevertheless, in reality it is likely that Wilma would bring her divorce petition using the special procedure. This would mean she would be unlikely to face much opposition or questioning and there would be little examination of whether Fred's behaviour really justified a divorce.

It is unlikely that Fred could cross-petition based on Wilma's behaviour, as adultery per se or desertion must be pursued as separate facts: *Morgan v Morgan (1973)*.

The fact of two years desertion by the respondent in s 1(2)(c) is very rarely relied on and is fraught with technicalities. First, Wilma would need to establish the fact of separation, that is, a withdrawal from married life: *Price v Price (1970)*. There does not have to be a living apart in separate places; it is enough that a couple live under the same roof but in two separate households, (*Hopes v Hopes (1949)*). In Fred and Wilma's case, they do not have intercourse, but other aspects of married life are shared, and this would probably preclude desertion: *Le Brocq v Le Brocq* (1964). In addition, Wilma would have to show that Fred intended to desert her, and that this was without her consent. Both seem very unlikely to succeed, since the arrangement has to some extent been forced upon them by circumstances and the home scenario seems to be controlled by Wilma.

It may be more realistic to examine the facts based on separation, namely s 1(2)(d) and (e). Both require the petitioner to establish separation in that the parties have lived apart. Living apart is explained in s 2(6) by reference to whether the husband and wife live with each other in the same household. If they do, then they are not living apart. In Fred and Wilma's case, they have been living in two households once Wilma left to live with Barney. However, there is still the possibility that they lived apart prior to this, whilst in the same house. Although it will not suffice to show merely that there was no intercourse between them (*Mouncer v Mouncer (1972)*), if it can be shown that they did not share any married life, then they may be treated as living apart (*Fuller v Fuller (1973)*). From the facts, it is clear that Fred and Wilma did have some shared life, but Wilma could try to argue that her case is like Fuller v Fuller in that this shared life was in a different capacity of nursemaid/patient and not husband/wife. However, this case is distinguishable from Fuller, in that in Fuller the wife's boyfriend lived in the same household and it was clearly recognised by all parties that the marriage was at an end. Unfortunately for Wilma, no third party was present in the household apart from Pebbles, and Fred did not realise that Wilma no longer cared for him as a spouse.

In addition to living apart, the petitioner must show that at least one of the parties recognised that the marriage was at an end, even though this does not need to be communicated: *Santos v Santos (1972)*. Clearly this could not have existed until Fred returned home from the hospital, but Wilma may have difficulty establishing this if Fred contests the petition. She did not inform anyone of that conclusion, although, when she told Barney of her unwillingness to leave Fred, she may have communicated the conclusion that the marriage was at an end.

To petition under s 1(2)(d), Wilma needs to show two years living apart, and that the respondent consents to the granting of the decree. Given Fred's attitude, it is unlikely that Wilma will be able to provide the court with Fred's positive consent to the granting of the divorce.

Therefore, the only other option open to Wilma would seem to be the fact of five years separation in s 1(2)(e). As discussed earlier, there needs to be the fact of five years living apart, coupled with Wilma's recognition that the marriage was at an end. This necessitates the finding that Fred and Wilma were living apart whilst still in the same house, something that is not without difficulty. If this were to fail, Wilma would need to wait for five years after leaving Fred before she petitioned.

Regardless of when her petition based on s 1(2)(e) is presented, Fred may oppose the granting of the decree if the dissolution of the marriage would cause him grave financial or other hardship, and in all the circumstances it would be unjust to dissolve the marriage: *MCA s 5(1)*.

Fred's argument would be based on the loss of Wilma's care and the fact that he misses Pebbles. The court is required to look at all of the circumstances of the case, including the conduct of the parties, their interests and the interests of any children or other persons: *s 5(2)*. It is unlikely that the court would dismiss the petition as Fred's hardship arises from the breakdown of the relationship with Wilma, not the granting of a divorce: *Parghi v Parghi (1973)*. Even if there is no divorce, he will still not have Wilma's care, as she is now having a relationship with Barney. Since both Fred and Wilma seem to be young, and Wilma is involved in another relationship, the court might consider that justice demands the divorce be granted to give Wilma the freedom to start a new life, as in *Parker v Parker (1972)*. There is no evidence that Fred would suffer grave financial hardship on divorce, and therefore he is unlikely to succeed in his use of s 5.

Question 7

H and W married six months ago after a brief courtship. From the outset, the relationship was fraught with problems. W had led a very sheltered life and found some of the sexual practices H forced her to undergo extremely repugnant. H responded by claiming that W was very cool towards him, unaffectionate and sexually inhibited. W began to shop frequently, often spending enormous amounts of money on luxury items, despite the fact that she and H were not well off. Whilst out shopping past week, W saw H emerging from a restaurant with his arm around X, his secretary. H had been working late recently, and W accused him of an adulterous affair with his secretary. H was furious at this, denied any impropriety and slapped W across the face.

Advise W, who wishes to obtain a divorce.

Answer plan

At the outset, mention the bar on petitioning for divorce within one year of marriage in MCA 1973 s 3(1). The only possibility would be nullity or judicial separation immediately.

Then go on to consider divorce:

- irretrievable breakdown as the only ground – s 1(1)
- evidenced by one of the five facts – in s 1(2)
- examine s 1(2)(a)

  – adultery and intolerability
  – difficulty in proving
  – effect of cohabitation

- consider s 1(2)(b)

  – behaviour and unreasonable to expect her to continue living with him
  – repugnant sexual practices
  – violence
  – examine their characters and the objective test for the reasonableness of cohabitation
  – the effect of continued cohabitation
  – possible cross-petition by H based on W's behaviour – both sexual and financial

- reject possibility of desertion
- explain possibility of waiting and petitioning under s 1(2)(d) or (e)

Answer

In order for W to petition for divorce under the present law, the marriage between her and H must have lasted for at least one year. Section 3(1) of the MCA 1973 imposes an absolute bar on the presenting of petitions for divorce within one year of marriage, regardless of the hardship or injustice to the petitioner. Therefore W cannot petition for divorce until the expiry of one year from the date of the marriage, although incidents within that period may be relied on to support the petition: MCA 1973 s 3(2).

If W wishes to end her marriage immediately, then the only possibility would be to petition on the basis of nullity, that is, her marriage to H is void or voidable. However, there seems to be no evidence in the facts of the question to suggest that any of the grounds in s 11 for void marriages or s 12 for voidable marriages exist.

It is possible for W to present a petition for judicial separation within one year of marriage. This does not end the marriage, but does terminate the obligation to cohabit: *MCA s 18*. Judicial separation may be sought on proving any of the five facts in MCA s 1(2), although there is no need to prove irretrievable breakdown under MCA s 1(1): *MCA 1973 s 17*.

After the expiry of one year from the date of the marriage, W can then petition for divorce on the ground that the marriage has broken down irretrievably: MCA 1973 s 1(1). This concept of irretrievable breakdown must be established by proving one of the five facts in MCA s 1(2): *Richards v Richards (1972)*. In the present case, proof of one of the five facts would give rise to the presumption that the marriage had broken down irretrievably and it seems unlikely that the couple could be reconciled.

The first possible fact that W could rely on is that of adultery and intolerability in MCA s 1(2)(a). As the petitioner, W would need to establish that H has committed adultery and that she finds it intolerable to live with him.

Adultery may be defined as voluntary sexual intercourse between persons of the opposite sex, at least one of whom is married to another. W will need to establish that H had sexual intercourse with his secretary; sexual behaviour that does not amount to intercourse is insufficient to establish adultery (*Sapsford v Sapsford (1954)*). H clearly denies that there has been intercourse and therefore W is faced with the difficulties of proving that intercourse took place.

Circumstantial evidence of inclination and opportunity may be used: *Farnham v Farnham (1925)*. It seems unlikely that H had the opportunity to indulge in intercourse in the restaurant, even if he did have the inclination. Likewise, the recent excuse of working late is very flimsy evidence, since W does not even know whether the secretary was present or not. Adultery is a serious accusation to make, and the courts have always insisted on strong evidence to support such a weighty accusation: *Serio v Serio (1983)*. W may therefore experience difficulty in establishing that H had voluntary intercourse with his secretary.

If intercourse can be established, W must then show that she finds it intolerable to live with H. The test is subjective and the intolerability does not have to be caused by the adultery: *Cleary v Cleary (1974)*. Thus W could rely on H's sexual practices and his response to her accusation as supporting her claim of intolerability.

The facts do not disclose whether W has ceased to live with H, or whether they are still living together. Periods of cohabitation that total six months or less may be ignored when a petition is presented on the basis of adultery: *MCA 1973 s 2(1)*. However, if W continues to live with H for a period in excess of six months from the last act of adultery complained of, then the petition will fail.

Another option open to W is to petition relying on the fact in s 1(2)(b) that the respondent has behaved in such a way that the petitioner cannot reasonably be expected to live with him. In the present case, H has insisted on sexual practices that W finds embarrassing and degrading. There is no detailed evidence as to what these practices are, and there seems to be a conflict in evidence between W who objects to the practices and H who feels that W is sexually inhibited, given her sheltered upbringing. Behaviour must be some action or conduct by one spouse that affects the other and is referable to the marriage (*Katz v Katz (1972)*), and it may be that if H's actions are really perverted, then this will constitute behaviour such that W cannot reasonably be expected to live with him. However, W could also argue that H's lack of understanding, his taunts and his forcing her to do something she finds repugnant constitute behaviour.

It would also be possible for W to include in her petition the violent response of H, but H would probably argue that this was a one-off incident after extreme provocation, and so should be excluded. H's relationship with his secretary, if not adulterous, could also be used by W to support her petition if it was more than merely platonic, or if H were flaunting this friendship to try to force W to be more sexually accommodating, since such relationships can be very destructive: *Wachtel v Wachtel (1973)*. Cumulative incidents can be included in a petition even if each individual incident would be insufficient, since their total effect can be examined: *Livingstone-Stallard v Livingstone-Stallard (1974)*.

It would then be necessary to look at the character of the petitioner and respondent (*Ash v Ash (1972)*), and ask if it would be reasonable to expect these individuals to live together. This approach combines a subjective and objective approach: *Livingstone-Stallard v Livingstone-Stallard (1974)*. Whether it is reasonable to expect W to live with H, given their totally different characters and attitudes to sex, is arguable.

Cohabitation is not a bar to petitions based on behaviour (*MCA s 2(3)*), but it is important for W to remember that the longer she lives with H, the weaker her argument that it is unreasonable for her to have to do so becomes.

It is highly likely that H would defend a petition based on behaviour, and W should be advised of the possibility that H will cross-petition based on her behaviour. H may well cite her unaffectionate nature, but since this is a state of affairs rather than deliberate behaviour (*Pheasant v Pheasant (1972)*), he will need more to support his petition. A complete and deliberate refusal to have any kind of sexual intercourse might well be behaviour, but her unsatisfactory sexual performance would not be (*Dowden v Dowden (1977)*). In addition, H might want to cite W's financial irresponsibility in spending large sums of money on luxury items which the family finances could not afford. Such behaviour might well, if very extreme, result in it being unreasonable to expect H to live with W (*Carter-Fea v Carter-Fea (1987)*), especially if H was financially prudent, yet faced debt and financial ruin because of W's habit.

There is no evidence in this case that either party is in desertion, nor have they been living apart as two separate households as required for s 1(2)(d) and s 1(2)(e). Obviously, if W cannot succeed in her petition based on adultery or behaviour, then she must begin to live apart from H, and, after two years, petition for divorce with his consent under s 1(2)(d) or, if H refuses consent, she will have to wait for five years before petitioning under s 1(2)(e).

Question 8

X and Y were married seven years ago, when they were both 50, but, unknown to Y, X's hobby was the keeping of reptiles, including a snake. Y was terrified of the snake and threatened to leave if X did not get rid of the snake. X was very fond of his snake, and felt Y was being unreasonable in forcing him to choose between her and his snake. X refused to get rid of the snake, offering instead to confine it to the spare room, but six months later Y stormed out of the matrimonial home. X did not hear from Y for several months, and only heard of her whereabouts when he was contacted by a mental hospital where Y was a patient. X visited Y frequently in hospital, but Y was suffering from insane delusions about snakes. After six months in hospital, Y was discharged to be cared for in the community but refused to return home to X whilst he had the snake.

X and Y have not lived in the same house for the past six and a half years, and X now wishes to divorce Y. Y is opposed to the divorce as she is concerned about her financial situation should she lose her widow's pension on X's death.

Advise X on his position under the present law.

Answer plan

Restate the one ground for divorce, namely irretrievable breakdown, and the requirement for it to be evidenced by one of the five facts. Consider each of these in turn:

- reject adultery – s 1(2)(a)
- consider behaviour – s 1(2)(b)
  - Exactly what has Y done that can amount to behaviour?
  - Refusal to live with the snake may not be such that it was unreasonable to expect him to live with her!
  - cannot rely on desertion
  - problem of mental illness
  - reasonableness of cohabitation
  - possible cross-petition
- examine desertion in detail (s 1(2)(c)):
  - factual separation
  - problem of visits and cohabitation
  - need to show X had intention to desert and difficulty of mental illness
  - lack of consent by petitioner and effect of ultimatum
  - without just cause
  - for two year period
- then consider living apart – for two years (s 1(2)(d)) and five years (s 1(2)(e)):
  - two separate households
  - recognition by one party that marriage at end
  - if two years, need X's consent – unlikely
  - if five years, no consent
  - problem of s 5 – grave financial and other hardship
  - possible postponement under s 10

Answer

If X wishes to petition for divorce now, he must establish the one ground for divorce in *MCA 1973 s 1(1)*; that the marriage has broken down irretrievably. Since his marriage to Y has lasted longer than one year, he is not prevented from presenting his petition by the bar in *MCA 1973 s 3(1)*. However, the petition must do more than allege irretrievable breakdown; it must also specify which one of the five facts in *MCA 1973 s 1(2)* X is relying on as evidence of irretrievable breakdown. Whilst the circumstances of the present case do seem to indicate that this marriage has little future prospect, it is necessary to show that one of the five facts can be established, or else the petition will fail: *Richards v Richards (1972)*.

There is no evidence that either party to the marriage has committed adultery and so it is unnecessary to consider the application of *MCA 1973 s 1(2)(a)*. The next fact, contained in *s 1(2)(b)*, is that the respondent has behaved in such a way that the petitioner cannot reasonably be expected to live with her. X will need to point to some behaviour by Y, and there may be difficulty in doing this. The first thing mentioned in the question is Y's insistence that X removes his snake from the house. Whilst X's distress at losing his pet is understandable, a snake is not something that many people would feel easy living with. Much might depend on the kind of snake, how large it is, and the way in which it is confined, if at all. It is clear that Y knew nothing of X's passion for his snake before they married, and if X is so absorbed in the snake, this may be evidence of X's behaviour rather than Y's!

Y's simple desertion cannot be evidence of behaviour (*Morgan v Morgan (1973)*) and there would also be problems if X were to try to rely on Y's illness or mental condition. Behaviour needs to be some action or conduct by one spouse that affects the other and is referable to the marriage: *Katz v Katz (1972)*. The development of a mental illness by Y, after she left the matrimonial home, is somewhat problematic, especially since the nature of the illness may suggest that it was precipitated by X and his snake. The courts often take the view that marriage involves a certain amount of give and take and understanding for a spouse's illness (*Thurlow v Thurlow (1975)*), and X would probably need to refer to stressful incidents committed by Y in her illness, rather than just her unhappy condition. If her delusions resulted in violence, as in Thurlow, or caused him considerable distress as in Katz, then he might succeed, but this is doubtful.

The nature of Y's behaviour must be such that, taking into account the issues and personalities of the parties (*Ash v Ash (1972)*), it is not reasonable to expect X to live with Y (*Livingstone-Stallard v Livingstone-Stallard (1974)*). It could be argued that a snake-loving husband cannot reasonably be expected to live with a snake-hating wife!

It would be open to Y to defend X's petition based on behaviour, and she could always cross-petition on the basis of X's behaviour. He has constantly failed to assuage her fears of the snake, and indeed, it could be argued that his love and relationship with the snake have been destructive and his deliberate refusal to give the snake away despite his wife's genuine fear is behaviour that makes it unreasonable to expect her to live with him. From the facts, Y does not want a divorce, but, if one appears to be inevitable, it may be that she will seek one on the basis of X's behaviour.

Another possibility available to X is to petition on the basis of Y's desertion of him for a period of two years prior to the presenting of the petition under *MCA 1973 s 12(c)*. This fact is very rarely relied on in practice and has a number of technical requirements.

First, X must establish that there has been factual separation in that there has been a withdrawal from married life: *Pulford v Pulford (1923)*. When Y left X, she withdrew from married life, and they have not cohabited together since. X's visits to the hospital probably do not count as periods of living a married life, since they were out of his concern for Y, and there is no evidence that she was in any way responding to him. If, however, there were brief resumptions of married life during these visits, the reconciliation provisions in *MCA 1973 s 2* provide that such periods totalling six months or less shall be disregarded.

It is then necessary to establish that Y had the intention to desert. At the time she left X, it seems that Y, although distressed, was not insane and her mental illness developed later. If this is so, then she had the intention permanently to desert X, unless she just intended to storm out to teach X a lesson and force him to remove the snake. Subsequently, Y has become mentally ill, and at common law her desertion would cease when she developed the incapacity: *Crowther v Crowther (1951)*. This has been affected by *MCA 1973 s 2(4)*, which provides that the court can treat the period of desertion as continuing through the period of mental incapacity if the evidence is such that had Y not been incapable, the court would infer that her desertion continued. From the facts, there is no evidence that Y had changed her mind, and so the likelihood is that she would still have the intention to desert even during her period in hospital. It is quite clear that on her discharge, she has no intention of returning to X whilst the snake remains in the house, and so she would continue in desertion.

If, however, at the time of leaving X, Y was suffering from delusions about the snake, then her capacity to form the intention to desert is questionable. In *Perry v Perry (1964)* it was suggested that the respondent be judged on the basis that the delusions were true, and therefore if she has delusions that her husband and the snake would harm her, then she may not be held to have formed the intention to desert. In such a case, X will need to establish at what point Y ceases to suffer from the delusions and is capable of forming the intention to desert.

X must then establish that he did not consent to the desertion; if he did then it is more appropriate to use *s 1(2)(d)* (two years living apart and consent), or *s 1(2)(e)* (five years living apart). The problem X faces here is that Y left only after he refused her ultimatum for staying. A petitioner who refuses a respondent's reasonable offer of reconciliation cannot rely on desertion: *Gallagher v Gallagher*

(1965). Much will depend on whether Y's offer of staying with the snake removed was reasonable, in which case she is not in desertion, as in *Slawson v Slawson (1942)*. It is by no means clear that X can establish that Y is in desertion; indeed, it may be that if he has refused her reasonable offer of reconciliation, which he will be in desertion (*Hall v Hall (1960)*).

If X can show that he did not consent to Y's desertion, then he must finally establish that Y deserted without just cause. The same problem concerning X's relationship with the snake and the fear it caused Y is encountered. Indeed, if it could be said that X's behaviour in refusing to remove the snake, despite the terror it caused his wife, is grave and weighty (*Lang v Lang (1953)*), and has caused Y to leave, this would thereby place X in constructive desertion.

If desertion can be established, it must be for a continuous period of at least two years immediately prior to the presenting of the petition. In X and Y's case, they separated shortly after their marriage seven years ago, and have not really resumed married life since. It seems likely that the two year period is satisfied, notwithstanding what was said previously regarding the period of Y's mental illness.

It is clear from the facts of the case that the couple have been living apart for a considerable time. There have been two separate households (*MCA 1973 s 2(6)*), but it will be necessary to show that one party formed the conclusion that the marriage was at an end, even though this was not communicated to the other: *Santos v Santos (1972)*. Looking at X, it is not clear when, if at all, he reached this conclusion. Initially, he offers to confine the snake to ensure Y does not leave; he also visits Y whilst she is in hospital. It may be that on Y's discharge, it becomes clear to X that the marriage has ended, but there is no evidence of this. X did not mention it to anyone, make a note, nor is there evidence of a relationship with anyone else. If Y were to defend this case, she might well contend that X never recognised the marriage was at an end, and this could cause X difficulty in establishing that he did to the court's satisfaction.

If living apart can be established, it seems clear that X and Y have lived apart for at least two years. However, Y seems unlikely to consent to the granting of the divorce as required in *s 1(2)(d)*. This would necessitate X relying on the fact of five years living apart in *s 1(2)(e)*. It seems that the couple have lived apart since shortly after their marriage, which is longer than five years, but again the problem of recognition of the ending of the marriage (*Santos*), may mean that the five year period is not yet established. If it is, then X does not need Y's consent to the divorce, although she may be able to prevent or postpone the divorce through the use of *s 5* or *10* of the *MCA 1973*.

Section 5 of the MCA provides that a respondent may oppose the granting of a divorce on the grounds of grave financial or other hardship, and that, in all the circumstances of the case, it would be wrong to dissolve the marriage. Y has expressed concern about her financial situation if the divorce were to be granted. Hardship is defined to include the loss of the chance of acquiring any benefit (*s 5(3)*), and here Y is concerned at the possible loss of a widow's pension. At present, on divorce, the ex-wife would lose her entitlement to a widow's pension. This would not cause grave financial hardship if only the state widow's pension were lost, as this would be replaced by income support or a retirement pension: *Reiterbund v Reiterbund (1975)*. However, if on X's death his widow would be provided with an occupational pension, then this might cause grave financial hardship if it were lost. Much will depend upon Y's personal financial position, since if she has independent means or wealth she is unlikely to be prejudiced. In *Archer v Archer (1999)*, the 53-year-old wife risked losing £18,000 per annum on her 55-year-old husband's death if the divorce were granted. However, she had a house valued at £200,000 and her own investments of £300,000, and therefore would not suffer grave hardship through the divorce. If, however, she is in difficult financial circumstances, then grave hardship may be established: *Dorrell v Dorrell (1972)*. She is now in her late 50s and is the kind of wife that s 5 was designed to protect, in that a widow's pension is not a remote possibility, but something that might realistically accrue to her if married, but be denied to her on divorce: *Mathias v Mathias (1972)*.

Under **Pensions Act 1995** *s 166*, part of one partner's private pension can be earmarked for the benefit of the other partner. However, this would only be of benefit on the retirement of the partner with the pension. The more radical option of splitting X's pension fund between him and Y has been made possible by the pension sharing provisions of the **Welfare Reform and Pensions Act 1999**. This would arguably remove any argument that the divorce would cause grave hardship.

If such a defence is raised, then X may be able to obtain his divorce if he can put forward reasonable proposals that would compensate Y for the loss of pension, such as the provision of an annuity, or insurance policy (*Parker v Parker (1972)*). In the circumstances, if X cannot adequately compensate Y, then the court may consider, in all the circumstances, including the conduct of X, that it would be wrong to dissolve the marriage.

Even if Y does not seek to rely on s 5, she may seek to postpone the granting of the decree based on either s 1(2)(d) or (e) until the court has considered her financial position. Section 10 of the MCA 1973 provides that on such an application the court must look at all of the circumstances of the case, including the age, health, conduct, needs and resources of the parties. The decree will not be made absolute until the court is satisfied that either no financial provision for Y will be made, or that the financial provision made by X is reasonable and fair or the best that can be made in the circumstances. Therefore, it is important for X to be prepared to outline his proposals for financial provision for Y, if any can be made.

Question 9

H and W have been married for 30 years, and are now both aged 60. H is a successful businessman and has, for many years, been involved in Freemasonry. H and W have become increasingly estranged over the years, especially since their daughter, J, grew up and left home. When J left home, W joined some adult education classes and has become increasingly involved in women's rights and radical politics. H finds this embarrassing and has had to endure many taunts from his friends about his wife getting 'out of control'. W has become increasingly assertive and will not cook H's meals or wash and iron his clothes, arguing that she is no longer his slave.

W frequently makes jokes about H's involvement with the Freemasons and has refused to accompany H to the annual Freemasons' social event, 'Ladies' Night', saying that it is derogatory to women. This is too much for H who told her to 'shape up or get out'. W responded by changing the locks on the doors to the matrimonial home, whilst H was out at work, to teach him a lesson. W made H wait on the doorstep for two hours before throwing him the new keys. H moved back in, but W refuses to cook and clean for him, and H now wishes to divorce W. W is unwilling to consider divorce as she does not wish to upset her elderly mother, C, who is a staunch Catholic and vehemently opposed to divorce. C has threatened to disinherit any of her children who divorce.

Advise H on whether he can obtain a divorce under the present law in the MCA 1973.

Answer plan

Mention irretrievable breakdown as sole ground for divorce, and requirement for it to be evidenced by one of five facts:

- no evidence of adultery (s 1(2)(a)):
- behaviour (s 1(2)(b)):
  - what constitutes behaviour?
  - look at character
  - consider reasonableness of cohabitation by Livingstone-Stallard test
- desertion (s 1(2)(c)):
  - difficult given no complete withdrawal
- living apart (s 1(2)(d)):
  - two separate households do not exist as yet

> - unlikely W would consent after two years
> - living apart for five years (s 1(2)(e)):
>   - need separation
>   - five years duration
>   - no need for consent
>   - problem – s 5 – grave financial or other hardship
>   - possible postponement – s 10

Answer

H can petition for divorce if he can show that his marriage has broken down irretrievably: *MCA 1973 s 1(1)*. This must be evidenced by one of the five facts in *s 1(2)* (*Richards v Richards (1972)*), since irretrievable breakdown in isolation is insufficient to obtain a divorce. The marriage between H and W has obviously encountered difficulties; however, the facts must be such that one of the five facts in *s 1(2)* can be established.

The marriage is of a lengthy nature, and so the bar on presenting petitions within one year of marriage contained in *MCA 1973 s 3(1)* does not apply. However, in lengthy marriages, it is not uncommon for the parties to encounter disagreement and dispute without necessarily providing evidence of a fact supporting irretrievable breakdown.

There is no evidence in this case of either H or W committing adultery, and therefore *s 1(2)(a)* is inapplicable. However, there is a need to consider s 1(2)(b) whereby a petition may be presented on the basis that the respondent has behaved in such a way that the petitioner cannot reasonably be expected to live with them. H needs to be aware that presenting a petition on this ground can cause a cross-petition from the respondent alleging behaviour on the part of the petitioner.

Initially, H will need to specify exactly what constitutes behaviour on W's part. In *Katz v Katz (1972)*, behaviour was defined in terms of action or conduct by one spouse that affects the other and is referable to the marriage. It seems that H has been upset by W's new-found interests, and by the jokes made by his friends. It seems harsh to argue that W's desire to gain new interests has somehow constituted behaviour towards H. Many women find the need for new horizons as they grow older and their children leave home. The fact that H feels threatened or embarrassed by this cannot fairly be attributable to W. If, however, W's new interests were very extreme, causing her completely to isolate herself from H, then this might constitute behaviour. She has refused to do any cooking or cleaning for H, and this seems to be a deliberate decision by her. It is not apparent whether both she and H work, or whether only H does; such a factor will determine the reasonableness of the expectation of contribution. W has also begun to ridicule H's involvement with Freemasonry, and has refused to accompany him on one particular occasion. Again, it is unclear whether the ridicule is good natured joking in private or cruel jibing in public. It seems that W has not withdrawn from all social activities with H, but merely the one 'Ladies' Night' that her conscience found unpalatable. W's changing of the locks was behaviour, albeit of a joking nature, but it is by no means clear that H will succeed on this fact.

Then it will be necessary to show that, given the individual parties' characters and conduct (*Ash v Ash (1972)*), it is unreasonable to expect H to live with W. This is a partly subjective approach, and, according to Bagnall J in Ash v Ash:

> a violent petitioner can reasonably be expected to live with a violent respondent...and if each is equally bad, at any rate in sinister respects, each can reasonably be expected to live with the other.

Applying this to the present case, H seems to be a dedicated chauvinist whilst W seems to be an equally trenchant feminist. There could be an argument that these two extremes could never be expected to live together.

The reasonableness of the expectation of contribution is judged objectively, the so called 'jury test' in *Livingstone-Stallard v Livingstone-Stallard (1974)*. Here the parties have had a long marriage, and the readjustment that naturally occurs as the parties adapt in later years will cause problems in most marriages. The disagreements in the instant case may not be so extreme that it is not reasonable to expect H to live with W. The changing of the locks was to teach H a lesson after his ultimatum, not a vindictive exclusion of a blameless spouse. Incidents can have a cumulative effect (*Livingstone-Stallard v Livingstone-Stallard (1974)*), but seen in totality it seems that H will have difficulty in establishing behaviour. It seems to be the classic case of 'six of one, half a dozen of the other'.

The fact of desertion in s 1(2)(c) will be difficult to establish for H. The fact of desertion is established by showing a withdrawal from married life: *Pulford v Pulford (1923)*. W has refused to cook or clean for H, but seems willing to talk to him and share aspects of family life. There is a distinction between desertion and gross neglect or chronic discord (*Hopes v Hopes (1949)*) and in the instant case there is not complete separation, just disharmony.

The fact that H and W are not truly living apart as two households will also make any petition under s 1(2)(d) or (e) unlikely to succeed. The fact that the relationship is strained is insufficient to show the parties are maintaining two households: *Mouncer v Mouncer (1972)*. However, if H were to move out or cease to share any common life, then he could petition for divorce after two years with W's consent. This does not seem likely to be forthcoming, in which case H would need to establish five years living apart, in terms of physical living apart coupled with his recognition that the marriage was at an end: *Santos v Santos (1972)*.

In such a situation, W may seek to prevent the divorce by relying on MCA 1973 s 5. It could be argued that the granting of the divorce would cause her grave financial or other hardship, and that in all the circumstances it would be wrong to grant the petition. W wishes to avoid upsetting her elderly mother who, for religious reasons, is opposed to divorce. There is no evidence to show whether W herself is opposed to divorce for religious reasons and in any case, the court will look for strong evidence of social ostracism before refusing the petition, as in *Banik v Banik (1973)*. The mere fact that divorce is frowned upon would be insufficiently grave to justify opposing the divorce: *Parghi v Parghi (1973)*.

However, W can also argue that divorce would cause her grave financial hardship. This could include the loss of any benefit that the respondent might acquire if the marriage were not dissolved: *MCA 1973 s 5(3)*. This was designed to cover the possible loss of widow's pensions, etc, which could be a severe hardship for a woman of W's age: *Mathias v Mathias (1972)*. It is not clear whether this covers the potential loss of inheritance from a third party. The section is widely drafted and could potentially cover it, but it would seem harsh to H to deny him a divorce because of the possible reaction of his elderly mother-in-law. The court is instructed to look at all of the circumstances of the case, including the conduct of the parties and their interests and those of any children or other persons: *MCA 1973 s 5(2)*. If H can make some sort of attempt to mitigate any possible financial hardship for W, then he may be allowed his divorce (*Parker v Parker (1972)*), and since he is a successful businessman it seems likely that he could purchase some kind of annuity or set aside some lump sum to offset the loss of any widow's pension, and possibly any inheritance if that is a valid consideration.

Even if W does not invoke s 5, then she may well use the provisions in MCA 1973 s 10 to postpone the divorce being made absolute. Where petitions are presented on facts in s 1(2)(d) or (e), the respondent can apply to the court for consideration of her financial position: *s 10(2)*. In such a situation, the court will not award a decree absolute unless no financial provision is to be made, which is unlikely in this case, or unless the financial provision is reasonable and fair or the best that can be made in the circumstances: *MCA 1973 s 10(3)*. After such a long marriage, and given H's standing as a businessman, W is likely to be entitled to financial provision. Therefore H should be prepared to present a clear explanation to the court of the financial provision he is proposing: *Grigson v Grigson (1974)*.

Question 10

Kathy was a devout Christian, and devoted a great deal of her time to charitable works, including prison visits. On one visit to the prison, she met John, who had been convicted of rape and attempted murder. John impressed Kathy with his charm and repentance, and soon she fell in love with him. They were married whilst John was still in jail, some eight years ago, but with Kathy's help John was released early five years ago. Immediately on his release, John's personality changed and he shouted obscenities at Kathy, forcing her to perform degrading sexual acts, but stopping short of actual intercourse. He then hit Kathy, who has been too frightened to tell anyone of what happened. John disappeared and since then there have been numerous reports linking John with rapes throughout the country, but nothing has been heard of him since an incident three years ago, when the victim shot her attacker, who fitted John's description. The attacker had been badly wounded, as much blood was found at the scene and nearby. DNA tests reveal that the blood is almost definitely John's.

Kathy does not want to divorce John, for religious reasons, but is most anxious to know what can be done to end her marital obligations to him.

Advise Kathy.

Answer plan

In this question, the petitioner does not want divorce, and so you should consider the other options, namely nullity, judicial separation, presumption of death, and dissolution of marriage.

Consider if the marriage is void under *MCA s 11*. Explain effect – but no evidence on facts of marriage being void.

Then examine *s 12* provisions for voidable marriages:

- *s 12(a) and (b)*
  - Has the marriage been consummated?
  - incapacity or wilful refusal?
- *s 12(c)*
  - Is there lack of consent?
  - only a mistake as to attributes of partner – insufficient
  - unlikely that John did not understand nature of ceremony
- *s 12(d)*
  - mental disorder – on part of John, so as to make him unfit for marriage
- *s 12(e)* – venereal disease, and *s 12(f)* – pregnancy per alium is inapplicable

Consider possible bars in s 13 – approbation and time. Then go on to examine judicial separation which is obtainable by proving one of the five facts in

MCA s 1(2), but without the marriage being ended, merely the obligation to cohabit:

- s 1(2)(a) – adultery
    - evidence of the rapes
    - subjective test of intolerability
- s 1(2)(b) – behaviour
    - easily established

Consider also possibility of applying to have John declared dead and the marriage dissolved:

- absence not long enough for seven year presumption to operate
- will need to bring evidence to suggest why dead

Answer

Since Kathy is adamantly opposed to the idea of divorcing John, it is necessary to consider the other options available to her if she wishes to end her marital obligations towards John. There are three possibilities, namely nullity, judicial separation, and presumption of death and dissolution of marriage.

Nullity proceedings are available in respect of void marriages by reference to the grounds in *MCA 1973 s 11* and in respect of voidable marriages by reference to the grounds in MCA 1973 s 12. A void marriage is one that suffers from such a basic defect that it is treated as a complete nullity. In the eyes of the law, the marriage never existed, and technically there is no need for a decree to be sought. However, if a decree is obtained the courts have power to grant ancillary relief, which may be desirable if there are any family assets to be dealt with. It also provides certainty. Kathy may petition for nullity under *s 11* even after the death of John, but she must establish one of the fundamental defects in *s 11*.

The first ground is that the marriage is not valid within the *Marriage Acts of 1949* and *1970*, in that the parties are within the prohibited degrees of relationship, either party is under the age of 16, or the parties have knowingly married in disregard of certain formal requirements. There is no evidence of any such defect in Kathy and John's case, nor is there any evidence of the other *s 11* grounds that either party was already lawfully married, that they were not respectively male and female, or that the marriage was actually or potentially polygamous.

The other possible way of obtaining an annulment is by relying on the s 12 provisions for voidable marriages. A voidable marriage is treated as valid unless and until it is voided. This means that a nullity decree is a necessity in order to end Kathy's obligations, but it is only possible for her to petition for nullity during John's lifetime.

The first two grounds in *s 12(a)* and *(b)* require the marriage not to have been consummated. Consummation is one act of complete and regular intercourse after the marriage: *D v A (1845)*. It is unclear whether Kathy and John had the opportunity to have sexual intercourse whilst John was in prison. If they did not do so, then the incident after John's release does not amount to consummation. There must be full penetration of the vagina by the penis; sexual activities other than this do not suffice (*W v W (1967)*). If the marriage has not been consummated, then the reason for this must be examined. *Section 12(a)* requires incapacity to consummate on the part of the petitioner or the respondent. There is no evidence that Kathy or John is incapable of consummating the relationship; rather it seems that John has deliberately chosen not to. This may be evidence of wilful refusal to consummate by John, thereby enabling Kathy to petition. In *Horton v Horton (1947)*, it was necessary to show 'a settled and definite decision come to without just cause', and such a situation would seem to be indicated here by John's treatment of Kathy and his immediate departure.

Section 12(c) of the *MCA 1973* makes a marriage voidable through lack of consent through mistake, duress, unsoundness of mind, or otherwise. In Kathy's case, she could try to argue that she made a mistake about John's reformed character. However, mistake must be as to the nature of the ceremony (*Mehta v Mehta (1945)*) or the identity of the party, but a mistake as to a quality of the party does not render the marriage voidable (*Puttick v AG (1979)*).

The facts seem to indicate that John is unbalanced, to say the least, but in order for the marriage to be invalid it must be shown that at the time of the ceremony he was suffering from such an unsoundness of mind that he could not understand the nature of the ceremony (*Sheffield City Council v E and Another (2004)*). This rarely succeeds, and, in the present case, John seems to have exploited the prospects that marriage brings in terms of early release, and, therefore, was unlikely to have satisfied the test of unsoundness of mind.

There is no evidence of duress or any other factor to vitiate consent, and there is no evidence of the grounds in *s 12(e)* (venereal disease) or *s 12(f)* (pregnancy per alium). The only other option available to Kathy is to rely on *s 12(d)* and argue that although John was capable of consenting to the marriage, he was suffering at the time from a mental disorder, within the meaning of the Mental Health Act 1983, of such a kind or extent as to be unfit for marriage. The test is whether the party was capable of carrying out the ordinary duties and obligations of marriage (*Bennett v Bennett (1968)*), and, despite his criminal tendencies and cunning, it would seem that John was not suffering from some such disorder.

If the petition is presented on the basis of non-consummation, then the possible bars to the granting of the decree need to be considered. Kathy has not behaved in any way to lead John to believe that she would not annul the marriage and so statutory approbation does not apply: *MCA 1973 s 13(1)*. There are no time bars to petitions based on non-consummation, although a petition based on any other ground must be presented within three years of the marriage: *MCA s 13(2)*. The only possible waiver of this time limit is a discretionary one if at any time the petitioner has been suffering from a mental disorder. Kathy's wedding took place eight years ago, and since she has never suffered such a defect, she could not petition on any basis other than s 12(b) (wilful refusal to consummate).

If the marriage has been consummated, then Kathy's other option is to seek a decree of judicial separation. The decree does not end the marriage, but it does end the duty to cohabit: *MCA 1973 s 18(1)*. This would mean that Kathy could apply for ancillary relief, but she would be prevented from inheriting from John, should he die intestate after the granting of the decree.

There is no need to establish that the marriage has irretrievably broken down, but the petitioner must establish one of the five facts in MCA s 1(2). John has committed rape, and this will amount to adultery since he has voluntarily had sexual intercourse with a woman whilst he was married to Kathy. Section 1(2)(a) further requires the petitioner to show that she finds it intolerable to live with the respondent, and there is little doubt, given what has happened, that this subjective test can be satisfied. The intolerability need not arise from the adultery (*Cleary v Cleary (1974)*), and therefore John's treatment of Kathy will help satisfy the fact in s 1(2)(b). In addition, there is little doubt also that John has behaved in such a way that it is not reasonable to expect Kathy to continue to live with him: MCA s 1(2)(b). Therefore Kathy will be able to obtain a decree of judicial separation.

There is the additional possibility here that John may be dead. The forensic and identification evidence seems to indicate that he was shot and badly wounded, and as nothing has been heard of him by friends, relatives, or victims of his crimes, it may be possible to apply to the court for a decree of presumption of death and dissolution of marriage: *s 19 MCA*. *Section 19(1)* provides that any married person who has reasonable grounds for supposing that his or her spouse is dead may present a petition to the court to have the spouse presumed dead and the marriage dissolved. *Section 19(3)* provides a presumption that a person is dead if he or she has been absent for seven years or more, but this does not apply to John. Therefore, Kathy will need to provide the court with details as to why she believes John to be dead. She seems to have made enquiries about him (*Bullock v Bullock (1960)*), and despite a huge police search for him, he has not been found. His last known appearance was in circumstances to suggest he had been fatally wounded and so Kathy could succeed in her application under *s 19*. If she does, and John reappears, then the decree nisi will be rescinded, but if the decree has been made absolute, the marriage remains ended.

Therefore, it can be seen that despite her unwillingness to divorce, Kathy has several options available to her to end her obligations towards John.

Question 11

The present procedures for ending a marriage fail both the parties and society, generally. Something radical must be done.

Discuss.

Answer plan

- look at irretrievable breakdown and the need to prove one of facts;
- no-fault divorce facts;
- fault-based facts – not commonly used;
- bitterness inherent in present system;
- Booth Committee, Law Commission and Government proposals;
- conciliation and its role – criticisms and reforms.

Answer

A marriage may end in divorce if one of the parties successfully presents a petition alleging that the marriage has irretrievably broken down (MCA 1973 s 1(1)), and proves this by establishing one of the five facts in MCA 1973 s 1(2). Very few petitions are contested (less than 1%), and the vast majority of divorces are granted by way of the special procedure whereby the petition is read and approved without oral hearing. However, for many couples, divorce is a bitter process, and does not end their problems, but merely leads to further dispute and antagonism. It is therefore necessary to examine the current divorce procedures and see how far, if at all, they serve the parties' and society's interests.

Historically, marriage has been regarded as an institution that should be firmly supported and not undermined by the State. However, increasing numbers have found their marriages intolerable and have sought an end to their marital obligations. Initially, it was only possible to divorce a partner who could be shown to be at fault. This inevitably leads to bitter accusations about past indiscretions and conduct and is hardly conducive to civilised conduct after the divorce. This bitterness can have repercussions on the welfare of any children as well as the parties' willingness to co-operate in other matters, such as financial agreements.

Despite much opposition, especially from vocal clergy, the Divorce Reform Act 1969 introduced the concept of a no-fault divorce. This is now to be found in s 1(2)(d) and (e) of the MCA 1973, namely divorce after two years separation with the respondent's consent to the granting of the petition, and five years separation if there is no such consent. The idea behind a no-fault divorce is that it would reduce bitterness and antagonism and improve the ongoing relationship between the parties and their children. However, the provisions of s 1(2)(e) have been objected to by those who opposed the idea of an 'innocent' spouse being divorced against his or her wishes.

The *Matrimonial Causes Act 1973* does not provide for a completely no-fault divorce system, and it retains fault-based facts of adultery, behaviour and desertion. Despite the availability of no-fault divorce, more than 80 per cent of petitions allege adultery or behaviour, which enables immediate divorce and obviates the need to live apart for a lengthy period. Thus, in reality, no-fault divorce exists in less than one-fifth of cases, and the requirement of physical separation is often difficult to achieve for families on low incomes. Presently, therefore, most divorces do involve the petitioner alleging fault on the part of the respondent. This encourages petitioners to rake over incidents in the past, often exaggerating them, in order to obtain a speedy divorce. This can increase the respondent's resentment, lead to cross-petitions, antagonism and lasting conflict that can be very damaging to the welfare of the children.

Once it is recognised that divorce is inevitable in many cases, good divorce law should ensure that it provides an effective method of ending marriages that have not worked with the minimum of bitterness, leaving the parties in a position where future co-operation in financial matters and the upbringing of the children can be achieved. The present law does not do that because of the tendency for most divorces to be fault-based. In 1985, the Booth Committee on Matrimonial Causes Procedures recommended that all divorce should be fault-free, since the fault element increases bitterness and stops sensible discussion about crucial future issues. The only basis of divorce should, according to the Committee, be irretrievable breakdown of marriage without specifying any further facts. This has been criticised, but in reality the lack of investigation in the special procedure adopted by the courts for most divorces means that this could be happening already if the parties agree not to contest the petition. There is little evidence that fault-based divorce reduces the divorce rate or saves marriages from failure and from society's point of view the bitterness of fault-based divorce spills over into ancillary matters and children issues, which are costly in terms of legal aid and human misery.

The Law Commission reported in 1990 (The Ground for Divorce) and agreed that the way forward lay in no-fault divorce. Its report suggested that irretrievable breakdown without any further fact should be the basis of divorce. Once a person felt that their marriage had broken down, they should be able to lodge a sworn statement in court to that effect. The Law Commission thought that a joint application could also be made, and that, once this had happened, the parties should be given an information pack outlining what should happen next and the need to sort out financial arrangements and arrangements for the children. Mediation would be available to assist the parties to reach agreement on these matters, and then after 11 months it would be open to either party to apply for a divorce stating that the marriage had in fact irretrievably broken down. Thus, the important practical issues would be sorted out before the divorce was granted, and hopefully the no-fault nature of proceedings would ensure the minimum of bitterness. The Law Commission wanted the court to retain the power to refuse divorce on the basis of grave financial or other hardship. Critics argued that this would further undermine the institution of marriage, make divorce easier to obtain and could lead to parties instigating proceedings as a threat thereby setting the process in motion. There would also be no method of ending a marriage sooner than 12 months, and the statistics presently show that many petitioners prefer not to wait once they have decided the marriage is at an end.

The Lord Chancellor published a Green Paper on divorce reform at the end of 1993, which mirrored the Law Commission's view that the way ahead might well be no-fault divorce on the basis of irretrievable breakdown. A period of reflection once the initial application was made was considered a good idea. There has been considerable public debate on this matter, with opinion divided upon whether the proposals would make divorce too easy and undermine marriage. Most commentators felt, however, that reform was long overdue and hoped that the provisions of the *Family Law Act 1996* were going to address the problems of the past.

Further criticism of the present system concerns the enormous financial cost of protracted litigation for the public purse, and there are those that have suggested that legal aid should be withdrawn in contested divorce cases and ancillary relief applications. Others suggest that it should only be available if the parties agree to conciliation.

Mediation is a process whereby an impartial and trained individual meets with the parties and encourages them to reach an agreement on areas of dispute such as financial provision and arrangements for the children. This hopefully reduces bitterness, saves costs and has an important role in making divorce less traumatic and adversarial. Mediation may take place in court, and in 1971 a Practice Direction allowed courts to refer cases to the court's welfare office if it was thought he could help with the process. Initially, pilot schemes were established, but have spread throughout the country and allow emotional and possibly confrontational issues to be handled in a constructive manner. Criticisms have been made, in that the parties often feel under pressure to reach an agreement in a short time, and it is very important that the parties are legally represented and kept fully informed. The Law Commission and the Green Paper did not suggest making mediation compulsory in all divorces, as it is its voluntary nature that ensures co-operation and a willingness to reach agreement.

Out of court mediation schemes also exist whereby trained personnel offer assistance to parties to reach agreement independently of the court system. Some people believe that these schemes are more successful since they are not so involved in the legal process and can be used before the parties' positions become too entrenched. However, there has been concern that such schemes can be dominated by the more forceful partner and that information may be withheld.

The *Family Law Act 1996* tried in statutory format to provide a mechanism which recognised that divorce was a social reality, but at the same time tried to get the couple concerned to properly consider whether their relationship was at an end. The no-fault concept attempted to reduce bitterness if divorce was to occur, but the information meetings and period for reflection and consideration were designed to encourage parties to think about reconciliation. Assistance was provided to parties by giving information about organisations helping resolve difficulties, as well as funding for conciliation services and marriage support services.

The Act also sought to reduce bitterness and encourage future co-operation by requiring the couples to seek to negotiate their own arrangements regarding finance and their children where possible. The option of mediation was available in the hope that expensive adversarial litigation could be avoided. However, the pilot schemes have shown that the Government's expectations for mediation have not been met. Fewer than one in 10 couples were prepared to mediate rather than litigate, and the vast majority felt better protected by lawyers. Mediation can be expensive and time-consuming, and requires a certain willingness on the part of those involved. Mediation can often be thwarted by the attitude and actions of one of the parties. In addition the Government failed to fund and train sufficient mediators to provide a nationwide service.

The most serious flaw shown by the pilot schemes is that it is a mistake to think that legislation can control human emotions at such a traumatic time. The information meetings were badly thought out, and whilst objective information is desirable, the compulsory nature of the meetings antagonised and humiliated some participants. The nature of these meetings was also not properly thought through, and it is unrealistic to think that parties really do spend the period for reflection and consideration doing these two things.

The complex statutory provisions, far from reducing conflict, actually increased the potential for an obstructive party to delay the divorce and obstruct resolution of issues regarding the children and finances. Whilst the current law is far from ideal, and although the Family Law Act 1996 had many laudable aims, the practical experience of the pilot schemes has led to the conclusion that the law would be 'jumping from the frying pan into the fire'. Consequently, the Government has abandoned plans to implement the far reaching provisions of the Family Law Act 1996 relating to divorce, and decided to stick with 'the devil we know', the Matrimonial Causes Act 1973.

In conclusion, therefore, it does appear that the present system and procedures for obtaining divorce fail the parties, their children and society generally. Whilst no reform seems perfect, a move towards no-fault divorce in the Family Law Act 1996 with an emphasis on conciliation would go some way to ensuring that failed marriages end with the minimum of animosity and that future relationships between family members are not irrevocably soured. However, a completely no-fault scheme may leave those who have been grievously upset by the behaviour of their spouses feeling badly treated. Whatever reform is made, there will always be those who feel let down at the ending of their relationship.

CHAPTER 3

FINANCIAL PROVISION AND CHILD SUPPORT

INTRODUCTION

The following two chapters consider financial provision. Chapter 4 looks at financial relief on divorce. This chapter looks at financial relief during the marriage and at child maintenance.

FINANCIAL RELIEF DURING MARRIAGE

It is common to encounter examination questions which require candidates to outline the financial options if the parties are not prepared, or able, to divorce. It is crucial to remember when the examiner tells you that a party is not intending to divorce, that this is done to help guide you. Do *not* consider the extensive possibilities under *ss 23* and *24* of the *Matrimonial Causes Act (MCA) 1973*. Instead, financial provision for spouses may be sought from the Magistrates' Court under the Domestic Proceedings and Magistrates' Courts Act DP (MCA) 1978, or from the County Court under the provisions in *MCA 1973 s 27*.

You must explain the relative advantages and disadvantages of the various jurisdictions. Applications to the Magistrates' Court are generally quicker and cheaper, but their powers are more limited. The County Court, on the other hand, has more extensive powers, and its orders are not automatically affected by cohabitation of the parties. This makes it suitable for those married to financially irresponsible spouses who they may want to force into providing more regular financial support, without necessarily separating.

Section 2 of the *DP (MC) A 1978* allows for periodic payments and lump sum orders to be made for a spouse. These orders are only available if one of the grounds in s 1 can be established. These are: failure to provide reasonable maintenance (a) for the applicant; (b) for any child of the family; (c) behaviour which the applicant cannot reasonably be expected to live with; and (d) desertion. If the Family Law Act 1996 had been introduced, the grounds for financial provision orders in *s 1* would have been amended. It would no longer have been possible for an applicant to rely on ground (c), that the respondent has behaved in a way that the applicant cannot reasonably be expected to live with the respondent, or ground (d) that the respondent has deserted the applicant. These grounds are essentially fault-based, and it was considered that these grounds were incompatible with the move towards no-fault divorce. Many couples use the Magistrates' Courts to obtain financial support, and it may sour future divorce discussions if there have been allegations of fault at an earlier stage. Section 7 was also amended to delete reference to the words 'neither party having deserted the other'. This meant that in all cases the court would have been able to regularise the financial provision where the couple had been living apart for three months or more. In making such an order, the court will consider the factors in s 3, which mirror those in *MCA s 25*. Any order will terminate if the parties cohabit for more than six months: *s 25(1)*. In the event, however, the Government has not brought into force that section of the 1996 Act which would have made these changes possible.

Section 6 of the DP (MC) A 1978 can be used by the court to formalise agreements reached by the parties, to make what is in effect a consent order. Section 7 of the DP (MC) A allows the court to make an order based on the fact that there has been some form of financial provision in the past. The s 7 order cannot exceed the average amount of previous payments, so is only useful to regularise an existing situation. Both ss 6 and 7 orders are affected by cohabitation.

The County Court's powers to make secured and unsecured periodic payments and unlimited lump sum orders can only be exercised on proof that there has been a failure to provide reasonable maintenance: *MCA s 27*. Reference is made to the criteria in s 25, and this is not affected by cohabitation, although this can provide grounds for variation.

MAINTENANCE FOR CHILDREN

Provision for children depends upon whether the parent is the natural biological parent of the child or if the parent has merely treated the child as a child of the family. Financial responsibility towards children that are not biological offspring is incurred under the *DP (MC) A 1978* and MCA 1973. *Sections 2, 6* and 7 of the *DP (MC) A* allow orders to be made in respect of children of the family. A s 2 order is governed by additional criteria in *s 3(3)* which include the financial resources and needs of the child, and the manner in which it was expected to be educated. Section 3(4) further provides that in the case of a non-biological child of the family regard must be paid to whether the respondent assumed responsibility for the child, on what basis and for how long; whether the respondent knew that this was not his child; and the liability of others to maintain the child must also be considered. This is mirrored in the county court under s 27. Another option for claiming child maintenance is the Children Act 1989. Under this Act, maintenance can be claimed from step-parents as well as the child's birth parents. Furthermore, this Act can be used by children of unmarried as well as married parents. The Children Act 1989 is also quite broad in terms of the maintenance available, as well as periodic payments and lump sums, property settlements are also available provided that they are for the benefit of the child (*A v A (A minor: Financial Provision) (1994)*).

Financial responsibility for natural children is no longer governed by the provisions of the DP (MC) A 1978 and MCA 1973. Whilst the court can still embody consent orders in relation to such children, there are now the Child Support Acts 1991 and 1995. This applies to all disputed child maintenance, and the Child Support Agency can take over agreed cases where the caring parent receives State benefits. You need to be able to explain the concepts of the caring parent and the absent parent and qualifying children. The statutory formula for calculating the maintenance requirement and assessable income must be understood, but most examinations would not require you to have any detailed knowledge of the financial limits and allowances, or of the minute detail of the Act. The *Child Support Act 1991* was amended following much criticism of its provisions in the *Child Support Act 1995*. However, there has been continued dissatisfaction over the efficiency and fairness of the scheme and in the Child Support, Pensions and Social Security Act 2000 wide ranging reforms have been introduced. In particular the calculation of payments has been simplified and rather than it being based on a formula there is now a set amount that is payable depending on the number of children – 15 per cent for one qualifying child, 20 per cent for two qualifying children and 25 per cent for three qualifying children.

Question 12

Hilary and William were married in 1996, and William has two children, Charles and Henry, from his previous marriage to Victoria, who died giving birth to Henry. William has sent his two sons to expensive boarding schools, and their fees are paid in part by a school fees plan that William subscribed to when the boys were born, and partly from William's income, which is substantial and currently in the region of £60,000 per annum.

Hilary and William's marriage encountered difficulties and they separated in 2002. Both are opposed to divorce for religious reasons, and yet they are reconciled to living apart. At the time of separating, William used all of his capital, including an inheritance, to pay £100,000 towards a luxury flat for Hilary. The balance of the price, some £25,000, was raised by mortgage, for which Hilary was responsible. William remained in the former matrimonial home, which was valued at £300,000. The outstanding mortgage was £20,000. The two boys use this as their home when they are not at school, although they have remained on good terms with Hilary, who they visit occasionally.

Hilary earns £10,000 in her part-time job in a florist's shop. She wants more financial security, as she has recently been diagnosed as having multiple sclerosis, and will not be able to increase her earnings. She has no savings to fall back on, and at 50 she does not want to face an uncertain financial future.

William is unwilling to consider providing Hilary with any financial support, feeling that he has been more than generous in the past.

Advise Hilary on her prospects of obtaining financial support from William if there is no divorce.

Answer plan

This question is limited to the availability of financial provision for spouses where the parties are not seeking divorce. The wide powers in ss 23 and 24 MCA 1973 are not available and students should consider the powers in the DP (MC) A 1978 in the magistrates' court, and the county court in s 27 MCA 1983. Ensure that some mention is made of the respective advantages and disadvantages of these two possibilities.

Examine s 2 powers:

- available only on proof of one of s 1 grounds;
- consider failure to provide reasonable maintenance and how this is assessed;
- no relevance in behaviour or desertion;
- look at s 3 factors and how they apply to this couple – effect of cohabitation.

Not appropriate for s 7 order, but possibility of s 6 order.

Also consider county court's power under s 27 MCA – failure to provide reasonable maintenance.

Answer

Hilary and William will not divorce, and therefore Hilary's entitlement to financial provision could be determined either by the Magistrates' Court under the DP (MC) A 1978 or by the County Court under the MCA 1973. The provisions of these Acts apply to spouses, and it is necessary to consider the basis of provision in each.

Hilary could make an application to the Magistrates' Court under the DP (MC) A 1978. There are three possible orders that could be sought, namely a s 2, 6 or 7 order. Application to the Magistrates' Court is usually quicker and cheaper than that to the county court, although the powers of the Magistrates are more limited.

An application for a s 2 order can only be made if the applicant can satisfy one of the s 1 grounds. The first possibility is that the respondent has failed to provide reasonable maintenance for the applicant (*s 1(a)*), and/or a child of the family (*s 1(b)*). Whether William has failed to provide reasonable maintenance for Hilary would be determined by the court by examining the level of financial provision that it would order, and comparing that with the level of provision provided by William. If the level of provision provided by William falls short of that which the court would order, then the s 1 ground will be established. There is no need to show that William was deliberately depriving Hilary of support; he may well feel he has been generous enough in the past, but if circumstances require greater provision, then this will be ordered.

The court will pay regard to the factors in *DP (MC) A s 3(1)*, which are similar to those in *MCA 1973 s 25*, and look at all the circumstances of the case. First, consideration is given to the welfare of any children of the family, and here it would seem that both Charles and Henry are children of the family. This concept is described in *MCA s 52* to mean a child who has been treated by both parties as a 'child of their family'. Although Charles and Henry are William's children from his first marriage, they have had their home with William and Hilary during the first years of the marriage and seem to have been treated by Hilary as if they were children of the family. She has remained on good terms with them, and they often stay with her during holidays from school. It is in the interests of both boys that William and Hilary are financially settled with suitable accommodation.

The court will then look at the income, earning capacity and financial resources of the parties (*s 3(2)(a)*). This has been a relatively wealthy family; William has a valuable home with little mortgage outstanding, and has been able to earn a significant income. Nothing is known of William's age and it is assumed that he will continue to work for some time, and is not yet approaching retirement age. Hilary does not earn as much as William, earning £10,000 per annum, but it does look as if her earning capacity will reduce as her illness develops. She also has a home with a relatively modest mortgage. The courts try to encourage spousal self-sufficiency but it would seem that the prospects of Hilary continuing to be self-sufficient look unlikely. By examining the financial obligations and responsibilities of the parties, it can be seen that they both have mortgages to pay, and William is paying school fees in respect of his two sons. Even when the school fees end, there is the possibility that the boys will need financial assistance if they go to university. However, it is obvious that William is in a far stronger financial position than Hilary, and it seems likely that he may have to make some kind of provision for her.

Looking at the standard of living enjoyed by the family, it would seem that they have enjoyed a comfortable existence. The court would be keen to ensure that any drop in standard is equally borne, but since William is wealthy, he might well be expected to help improve Hilary's lifestyle, especially given her relationship with the two boys and their visits to her, as in *Calderbank v Calderbank (1975)*.

Looking at the age of the parties and the duration of the marriage, it can be seen that Hilary is now 50, and would possibly find it difficult to greatly increase her earning capacity. The marriage took place in 1996 but the couple separated after six years. This is not such a short marriage that William could avoid financial obligation to Hilary, especially given her continuing role as mother substitute to his children. There is no indication of William's age, and this could affect his ability to pay if he were close to retirement age.

Hilary's disability would be another relevant factor (s 3(2)(e)), as it affects considerably her ability to provide for her future. It will also mean that her expenses may increase as her multiple sclerosis worsens, and, as in *B v B (1982)*, this may well justify imposing a maintenance burden on William.

Section 3(2)(f) requires an examination of the parties' contributions to the welfare of the family, and again both appear to have made significant contributions. William has worked and provided a high level of financial security for the family, and also provided the capital for Hilary's present home, but Hilary has provided care for the two boys and William, and has continued a relationship with the sons after the ending of cohabitation. There is no conduct that would be taken into account under s 3(1)(g), as this seems to be a tragic drifting apart rather than gross and obvious misconduct by one party: *Wachtel v Wachtel (1973)*.

It seems likely, given the onset of Hilary's multiple sclerosis and the uncertainty it creates for her in the future, that the court would find that William's provision of no financial support to be a failure to provide reasonable maintenance. It may well be that the court awards an extensive sum initially by way of periodical payments, but this can be varied as Hilary's illness worsens. The Magistrates can also award lump sums up to a maximum of £1,000 per application (DP (MC) A s 2), and this may be appropriate here, to help Hilary defray any expenses or debts she has incurred. A s 2 order will end if the parties cohabit for more than six months: *DP (MC) A 1978 s 25(1)*.

This is not an appropriate situation for a s 7 order, since there have been no payments by William to Hilary during their separation. If William and Hilary can reach agreement on a reasonable level of financial support, then this can be embodied as a court order under s 6. Again, this order would terminate if Hilary cohabited for more than six months: *DP (MC) A 1978 s 25(1)*.

Hilary could also make an application to the County Court under *MCA 1973 s 27*. The basis for provision is that William has failed to provide reasonable maintenance for Hilary, and this would be determined in much the same way as in the magistrates' court, by reference this time to the provisions in *MCA s 25*. The County Court's powers are somewhat wider than those of the magistrates' court, in that either secured or unsecured periodical payments may be sought. If William is wealthy enough, and has assets that can provide security for his payments, then this would be advantageous to Hilary, as she would still receive provision in the event of William's death. There is also the possibility of seeking a large lump sum if William is very wealthy. Cohabitation by the parties does not automatically affect a County Court award, although it may give grounds for variation, *MCA 1973 s 31*.

Question 13

Philip and Rosy married six years ago, and have two children, Holly and Molly, aged four and two respectively. After the birth of the children, Rosy suffered from severe post-natal depression and, much to Philip's concern, she began to neglect the children. He frequently came home to find the children locked in the house, and Rosy nowhere to be seen. Matters came to a head three months ago, when the couple had a heated argument, during which Philip slapped Rosy once after she made unfounded allegations that he had abused the children. Rosy stormed out of the house and since then has not visited Philip or the children. Philip has sent Rosy money on occasions, but he has found it very difficult to meet the bills and pay for child care from his modest income. Philip has now received a letter from Rosy threatening to take him to court unless he sends her £100 each week. Philip says he cannot afford to pay anything like this sum, as he earns £120 per week, out of which he must pay child care costs of £60 as well as other household bills.

Advise Philip, indicating what impact the *Child Support, Pensions and Social Security Act 2000* will have.

Answer plan

Another question concerning financial provision for spouses who are not divorcing. Rosy is not seeking provision for the children, as they are in Philip's care, so it is only necessary to consider the level of provision for her as a spouse under the DP (MC) A 1978 and MCA 1973. Ensure that some mention is made of the advantages of each method.

- examine the s 2 DP (MC) A 1978 powers:
  - proof of one of s 1 grounds,
  - failure to provide reasonable maintenance and how it is assessed,
  - the s 3 factors as they apply to the facts of the case.
- consider the s 7 power and how it would operate;
- mention s 6 power to embody any agreement into court order;
- outline the s 27 MCA 1973 option in the county court;
- briefly mention Philip's option of seeking maintenance under the Child Support Act 1991;
- consider the effect of cohabitation;
- consider the impact of the *Child Support, Pensions and Social Security Act 2000*.

Answer

The courts have wide powers to order ancillary relief if the parties divorce, but it seems in the instant case that the issue of financial provision must be resolved without recourse to such powers. If, in the future, Philip and Rosy are unable to reconcile, then financial provision can be reorganised on divorce.

In the meantime, there is the possibility that Rosy could seek financial provision from Philip by applying to either the magistrates' court or the county court. Since Philip is caring for the children, she will be seeking maintenance for herself only.

An application may be made to the Magistrates' Court under the DP (MC) A 1978, and this is a somewhat cheaper and quicker process than an application to the County Court under the Matrimonial Causes Act 1973. Only spouses may use the Magistrates' Court, and Rosy may seek relief under s 2, or possibly s 6 or 7. If she applies for an order under s 2 for periodical payments and/or a lump sum, then Rosy must establish one of the grounds in s 1. Section 1 provides jurisdiction for the court to make a s 2 order if the respondent has failed to provide reasonable maintenance for the applicant or a child of the family or has behaved in such a way that the applicant cannot reasonably be expected to live with him or has deserted the applicant.

The most likely ground is that the respondent has failed to provide reasonable maintenance. The behaviour ground may be difficult to establish for Rosy, as it mirrors the test for behaviour in MCA 1973 s 1(2)(b). The only behaviour by Philip was when he struck Rosy after her accusations of child abuse. This is an isolated act of violence, and whilst violence should not be condoned, Rosy's behaviour had been extremely provocative. There is also no substance to an allegation of desertion.

Consequently, the court will consider whether the level of maintenance provided by Philip was reasonable in the circumstances of the case. First, the court will consider what level of maintenance it would be minded to award, given the factors in *DP (MC) A 1978 s 3*. This will be compared with the level of maintenance paid by Philip, and if Philip is paying less than the court would have awarded, the s 1 ground will be established. It is immaterial whether Philip was deliberately depriving Rosy of support, or whether he was innocently believing she was managing.

The level of maintenance is determined by the facts in *DP (MC) A 1978 s 3(1)*, which are broadly similar to those contained in MCA 1973 s 25. All the circumstances of the case will be examined, giving first consideration to the welfare of the two children of the family, Holly and Molly. These children are staying with their father, who is struggling to care for them and pay for child care whilst he works. This means that whilst Philip may have financial resources in terms of his income of £120 per week, he has considerable financial obligations of child care and housing as well as feeding and clothing the children. It is not clear, on the facts, whether Rosy is earning any money; if she does have income it would seem that she only has herself to support on it. Even if she has no income, the court is required to consider any earning capacity she has or can reasonably be expected to acquire. Whilst she may not have worked whilst the children were so small, now that she no longer cares for them, she should be able to seek work.

Usually, the court will not take into account the availability of State benefits as a resource for the applicant. However, this family does not appear to have sufficient resources for Philip to be able to support the children himself and still send money to Rosy. The net-effect method (*Stockford v Stockford (1981)*) whereby the court looks at what each party has, rather than the one-third rule, would be appropriate here, but it is unlikely that the court would want to make any order that would take Philip below subsistence level (*Barnes v Barnes (1972)*).

The court will also look at the other factors in s 3, namely the standard of living enjoyed by the family, the age of the parties and the duration of the marriage. Any drop in the standard of living should be equally borne if possible: *Scott v Scott (1978)*. Physical and mental disability also requires consideration and here Rosy is suffering from severe post-natal depression. This may affect her ability to support herself.

In terms of contributions made by the parties, initially both contributed, one by working, the other by looking after the home and children. However, as Rosy has deteriorated in health, so Philip's contribution to the welfare of the family has increased, with him ultimately bearing responsibility for child care. This further contribution must be taken into account, thereby, possibly, reducing his obligation to maintain Rosy. Conduct will also be taken into account if it would be inequitable to disregard it. Philip has been violent towards Rosy on one occasion; however, the violence was not extreme, nor was it repeated (*Bateman v Bateman (1979)*), nor did it affect Rosy's earning capacity (*Jones v Jones (1975)*).

Indeed the violence was provoked by Rosy's unfounded suggestion of abuse, and by her chronic neglect of the children. It may be that this could amount to conduct on her part, but if it is involuntary and caused by mental illness, as in *J (HD) v J (AM) (1980)*, then it may not result in an immediate ending of Philip's obligations to Rosy.

In conclusion, it would seem that there are very few resources in this family, and if Rosy is well enough to work, it is unlikely she would receive much, if anything, by way of financial support from Philip. However, if she is too ill to work, it may be pointless making anything more than a nominal order, because to do otherwise would reduce Philip and the children to below subsistence level. Instead, Rosy would need to claim State benefits. Given the unavailability of resources, it would not be possible to order Philip to pay any lump sum to Rosy either.

An application could be made by Rosy under *DP (MC) A 1978 s 7*, if the parties have been separated for a continuous period exceeding three months, with neither in desertion. The reference to neither party being in desertion would have disappeared if the appropriate section of the *Family Law Act 1996* had been brought into force. Rosy would need to show that Philip has been making payments to her, and this is so, even though the payments have been made irregularly and infrequently. However, the court only has power to make a periodical payment order that does not exceed the aggregate value of payments made by Philip over the previous three months: *s 7(3)(2)*. If the court considers that this is insufficient for Rosy's reasonable maintenance needs, it can treat the application under s 7 as an application for a s 2 order: *s 7(4)*. Given the relatively small sums Philip has paid to Rosy, it is unlikely that a s 7 order would be sought or ordered.

If Philip and Rosy could come to some reasonable arrangement about financial provision, then this arrangement can be formalised by court order under *DP (MC) A 1978 s 6*. Again, the court would need to be satisfied that the level of maintenance was fair, and, given the circumstances, a s 6 order does not seem likely.

Rosy could also make an application to the County Court for financial provision. The County Court has powers to make secured or unsecured periodical payments for the applicant and/or a child of the family, and lump sum orders of unlimited amounts. The basis for financial provision in *MCA s 27* is that the respondent has failed to provide reasonable maintenance for the applicant and/or a child of the family. This would be determined in much the same way as in the Magistrates' Courts, with reference being made to the factors in s 25. Again, the County Court is unlikely to make any order that would reduce Philip to below subsistence level.

If Rosy were in employment there is the possibility that Philip could seek financial assistance in the upkeep of the children under the *Child Support Act 1991*. Rosy would be an 'non-resident' within the meaning of the Act, and both Holly and Molly would be 'qualifying children'. Philip is a 'person with care' and therefore a maintenance requirement would be established. That maintenance requirement would then need to be discharged in part by Rosy and in part by Philip's income.

The *Child Support, Pensions and Social Security Act 2000* has replaced the complex Child Support Act formula with a percentage method of assessment. Rosy would be termed a non-resident parent (Sched 3 para 11), and she would pay 20 per cent of her net income for the support of her two children. Philip's income would be ignored, and there are no allowances for Rosy's housing costs, etc. However, this figure may be adjusted downwards if Rosy acquires a second family, or if the children spend time living with her.

If Rosy moves back to live with Philip, then any s 2 or s 6 order that had been made would terminate after six months cohabitation: *s 25(1)* and *(2) DP (MC) A*. A *s 7* order would terminate on resumption of cohabitation: *DP (MC) A 1978 s 25(3)*.

A County Court order is not affected automatically by a resumption of cohabitation, although this would be a change in circumstances that would entitle the respondent to apply for variation or discharge of the order: MCA 1973 s 31.

In conclusion, it would seem that whilst Rosy may apply to the courts for financial provision, the precarious financial position the family are in may make it unlikely that she will receive any, or any substantial, financial provision from Philip.

Question 14

Rebecca and Sam married three years ago after cohabiting for two years previously. Rebecca has a daughter from a previous relationship, and this daughter, Tilly, is now eight. Rebecca and Sam's relationship has encountered problems, mainly over his insistence that she remains at home as a full-time wife and mother. Rebecca feels increasingly isolated, especially now that Tilly, an exceptionally intelligent child, is at school. Sam has threatened to withdraw all financial support from Rebecca and Tilly if Rebecca insists on finding herself a part-time job.

This situation concerns Rebecca, who does not want to divorce but wishes to be advised of her position and possible options if Sam were to withdraw support.

Advise Rebecca.

Answer plan

The question requires an examination of financial provision for spouses and for children of the family, who are not the natural children of the payer. Both the DP (MC) A 1978 and MCA 1973 must be considered. The Child Support Act 1991 does not apply here but, since Tilly is a child of the family, she is covered by the DP (MC) A 1978 and MCA 1973.

Explain s 2 orders:

- the need to satisfy the s 1 grounds;
- failure to provide reasonable maintenance;
- how this is assessed;
- factors in s 3;
- additional factors for child of family;
- effect of cohabitation.

Not appropriate for ss 6 and 7.

Explain s 27 MCA 1973 as it applies to spouses and children of family.

Answer

Rebecca is married to Sam, and, as a spouse, is entitled to a reasonable level of financial support. If Sam withdraws that, then she may apply to the Magistrates' Court under the DP (MC) A 1978, or to the County Court under the MCA 1973, to obtain financial provision for herself.

Tilly is not Sam's natural child, and consequently the provisions of the Child Support Act 1991 do not apply. This Act only applies to qualifying children, that is, children under 16, or under 19 if receiving full-time education, who are also the natural children of the parties. Biological parenthood is the basis of liability, and therefore liability to maintain Tilly by Sam falls outside of this Act. There is the possibility of seeking maintenance under the Child Support Act from Tilly's natural father, but on the facts, it is unclear whether he is identifiable, alive and traceable.

Consequently, financial support from Sam for Tilly can be sought under the DP (MC) A 1978 or the MCA 1973 as Tilly is a 'child of the family'. This concept is defined in *s 52 MCA* to include a child who has been treated by both parties as a child of their family. Tilly has been with Sam and Rebecca for five years, and it seems likely that she is a child of the family.

Applications to the Magistrates' Courts are generally quicker and cheaper than those made to the County Court, although the County Court's powers are somewhat wider. In the instant case, Tilly and Rebecca's financial support has not yet been withdrawn, and there is no indication that at present there are any grounds for applying. However, if Sam were to withdraw support then Rebecca may apply to either court.

An application to the Magistrates' Court may be made for an order under s 2 of the *DP (MC) A 1978*. Under *s 2*, the Magistrates' Court has power to order unsecured periodical payments for the applicant and child of the family in addition to lump sums up to a maximum of £1,000 per application. The applicant must, satisfy however, one of the grounds in *s 1* of the *Act*: namely, that the respondent has failed to provide reasonable maintenance; or the respondent has behaved in such a way that the applicant cannot reasonably be expected to live with him; or that the respondent has deserted the applicant. These last two grounds would have disappeared had the relevant sections of the Family Law Act 1996 come into force.

An application under s 2 may be made even if the parties are still living together (*DP (MC) A 1978 s 25*), but it will cease to have effect if they cohabit for more than six months. This is important, since it means that Rebecca can seek financial support without having to leave Sam.

The first possibility is that the respondent has failed to provide reasonable maintenance for the applicant. Clearly, if Sam provides no money for Rebecca, since she has no way of immediately supporting herself, and then there will be no reasonable maintenance. The court looks at the level of maintenance it would usually order to the applicant and compares it with that being provided by the respondent. If, as in this case, the respondent is providing less than the court would order, the ground is established. It is no defence for Sam to argue that he did not realise this, or that he had good reason for not paying Rebecca. Once this ground is satisfied, the court has the power under *s 2(1)* to make an order for periodical payments for both Rebecca and Tilly.

If Sam were to continue to provide for Rebecca, but stop paying for Tilly, it would be necessary to show that one of the other s 1 grounds exists. In determining whether reasonable maintenance is being provided or contributed to, the court will again have regard to what it would normally order.

It would not be possible to argue that Sam was in desertion, and the behaviour point would also be difficult to establish. It might be argued that Sam's overbearing and dictatorial treatment of the family would suffice, but the application is most easily established by arguing a failure to provide reasonable maintenance.

In determining what level to award, the court will take into account the factors in *DP (MC) A 1978 s 3(1)*, which are based on the factors in MCA 1973 s 25.

Looking initially at the income, earning capacity and financial resources of the parties, it seems that Sam works and earns an income. Rebecca has not worked during the relationship at Sam's insistence; therefore, she will be in need of financial support initially. However, the court will have regard to her earning capacity and whether she can reasonably be expected to work to support herself. Rebecca's qualifications or occupation before she met Sam are unknown, and although she is willing to work, it may not be easy for her to obtain employment immediately such that it enables her to support herself and care for Tilly. The court will encourage spouses to become self-sufficient and it can place a limit on the time that the financial support will continue for: *DP (MC) A 1978 s 4*. However, given the uncertainties of Rebecca's position, it is more realistic to make an unlimited order, indicating to Rebecca that she should seek employment, and then Sam can apply for variation of the order if she does this, or if she should have achieved self-sufficiency: *DP (MC) A 1978 s 20(1)*.

The financial needs and obligations of the parties must be considered (*s 3(1)(b)*), and clearly both Rebecca and Sam need housing and Tilly must be cared for. The standard of living enjoyed by the parties prior to the conduct alleged as the ground for the application should be considered to ensure that any drop in standards does not fall inequitably on one party. There is nothing exceptional about the age of the parties, but the marriage has been relatively short. The marriage followed a period of cohabitation, and there has been a child for whom Sam has assumed responsibility. Although cohabitation before marriage is usually irrelevant (*Campbell v Campbell (1977)*), in *Day v Day (1988)*, on similar facts to this, the court did accept that cohabitation could in certain cases be a factor to take into account as part of the circumstances of the case. Sam and Rebecca have had a long-term relationship during which he has assumed responsibility for Tilly, and has prevented Rebecca from working. It would not be right for him to be able to argue that as it was a relatively short marriage, he should avoid financial obligation towards Rebecca.

There is no disability to take into account (DP (MC) A s 3(1)(e)), and both parties appear to have contributed to the marriage, Sam by working and Rebecca by being a wife and mother. Conduct under DP (MC) A s 3(1)(g) is only taken into account if it would be inequitable to disregard it. Rebecca has done nothing that would amount to conduct sufficient to deny her financial support.

In determining the level of financial support, regard must be had to the family resources. If this is an average, middle-income family, then the one-third guideline in *Wachtel v Wachtel (1973)* is a useful guide. However, this may not be appropriate if the family is poor, in which event the net-effect method of *Stockford v Stockford (1981)* where the availability of State benefits is considered may be used. If Rebecca and Sam were an exceptionally high-income, wealthy family, then the court would be inclined to award financial provision based on Rebecca's reasonable needs: *Preston v Preston (1982)*.

When the court looks at making an award in respect of Tilly, they will take into account not only the parties' resources and obligations, but also those of the child: *DP (MC) A 1978 s 3(3)*. Tilly is not disabled in any way; in fact she is particularly intelligent. If this affects the way she was being educated, or the way the parties intended to educate her, possibly sending her to a private school, for example, then this is a factor affecting the level of maintenance awarded. The standard of living of the family is examined, and the court would obviously be concerned to ensure that Tilly does not suffer enormous disruption by the removal of financial support by her stepfather, Sam.

The amount payable in respect of Tilly will further be affected by the fact that she is not Sam's natural child. *Section 3(4) of the DP (MC) A* requires consideration of certain factors when the child of the family is not the child of the respondent. First, it is necessary to examine whether Sam ever assumed responsibility for Tilly. On the facts, it seems as if he did since they have lived together for five years, and he has financially supported her. Then it is necessary to consider the basis and extent of the assumption of responsibility. Sam appears to have acted as a father figure during this time, and he did so realising that Tilly was not his child. Finally, the liability of any other person to maintain the child should be considered, and it may be that Sam's liability will be reduced if Tilly's father can be traced and made to pay under the Child Support Act 1991.

It is not appropriate to consider *ss* 6 or 7 of the *DP (MC) A 1978* here, and so the other possible action for Rebecca is to apply to the County Court under MCA 1973 s 27. It would seem that if Sam refuses financial support, he would have failed to provide reasonable maintenance for Rebecca, the applicant, and Tilly, the child of the family. The factors to be taken into account in assessing the measure of support are those in MCA 1973 s 25, and operate in the same way as those discussed earlier in reference to *DP (MC) A 1978 s 3*. In addition, since Tilly is a child of the family, but not Sam's natural child, the additional factors in *s 25(4)* will need to be considered. These provisions reflect those in *DP (MC) A 1978 s 3(4)* and have been discussed above.

The County Court can order secured or unsecured periodical payments, and there is no upper limit on the amount of a lump sum order. The order can be sought even though the parties are still living together, and, unlike the Magistrates' Court order, the order is not terminated by continued cohabitation, although there is always the possibility of variation.

Thus, it can be seen that if Sam were to withdraw financial support, Rebecca could pursue her remedy in either the County Court or the Magistrates' Court, and she does not need to seek a divorce in order to do so.

Question 15

Abigail and Ben have been married for eight years. They have no children, and both of them have worked throughout the marriage. Abigail has had a successful career as a solicitor, but recently lost her job when the firm she worked with closed their local office. However, she was offered a job in an office with an associated firm of solicitors, some 250 miles away, and as the job situation was bleak, Abigail accepted the position. She rented a small flat near her new job, and returned home to Ben each weekend. However, her visits became more infrequent, and she hardly ever returns home.

When Abigail and Ben married, Ben was a school teacher with a passion for composing music. With Abigail's encouragement, he gave up his job and has concentrated on composing. However, not many pieces attracted the music companies' approval, and his earnings have averaged £6,000 per annum. Abigail's earnings are in the region of £30,000 per annum, but she only sends money to Ben occasionally. Ben does not want to get a divorce, but needs money to cover the mortgage and other bills.

Advise Ben as to any remedy he may pursue in the Magistrates' Court or County Court.

Answer plan

Again, a question on financial support of spouses within a marriage, but from the somewhat unusual standpoint of the husband seeking the support. The powers of the magistrates' court under the DP (MC) A 1978 and the county court under s 27 MCA 1973 must be examined, with mention being made of the relative advantages of each.

Consider s 2 application:

- proof of a s 1 ground necessary;
- failure to provide reasonable maintenance more applicable than behaviour or desertion;
- how this is assessed;
- look at s 3 factors.

Examine possibility of s 6 or 7 orders. Describe the s 27 MCA 1973 powers of the county court.

Answer

The parties in the instant case do not wish to divorce, and therefore the wide powers available for ancillary relief applications are inapplicable. Ben is experiencing financial difficulty in maintaining his lifestyle and the former matrimonial home in the absence of regular financial support from Abigail.

In order to remedy this situation, Ben must either seek a court order requiring Abigail to provide him with financial assistance, or negotiate some kind of separation or maintenance agreement with Abigail. The present case is somewhat unusual in that the wife is in the dominant financial position, but the courts treat applications by husbands and wives on property and financial matters on the 'basis of complete equality': *Calderbank v Calderbank (1975)*.

Therefore it is possible for Ben to apply either to the Magistrates' Court under the DP (MC) A 1978 or to the county court under the MCA 1973.

Most applications are made to the Magistrates' Court since it is a quicker and cheaper process. Often spouses who rely on legal aid will only receive legal aid for proceedings in the Magistrates' Court. The DP (MC) A only provides financial relief for spouses, and this may be available by virtue of *s* 2, 6 or 7 of the Act.

In order to apply under *s* 2, the applicant, Ben, must establish one of the grounds in s 1, namely that the respondent has failed to provide reasonable maintenance for the applicant, or failed to provide or make proper contribution to the maintenance of a child of the family, or has behaved in such a way that the applicant cannot reasonably be expected to live with them, or has deserted the applicant. (These last two grounds would have been abolished had the appropriate provisions of the Family Law Act 1996 come into force.) It is certainly arguable that, on the facts, Abigail has failed to make reasonable provision for Ben.

Whether Abigail has been making reasonable provision for Ben will be determined by the Magistrates' Court. They will first consider what level of maintenance they would have ordered and this is compared with what Abigail is in fact paying. If, as seems likely in this case, Abigail is paying less than the court would have ordered, the ground of failure to maintain will be established. There is no need to show that Abigail was deliberately depriving Ben of support; she may genuinely have thought he was managing, yet still find the s 1 ground established.

There are no children of the family and behaviour does not seem an issue. Desertion is a complex concept, and although there is no requirement for a specific time it could be difficult to establish that Abigail is in desertion. Whilst there is physical separation, it would seem that the job situation would give just cause for the initial separation, and so, consequently, Ben would be best advised to use the failure to maintain ground. Section 2 gives the court the power to make periodical payment orders, and to award lump sums up to a maximum of £1,000 per application. The lump sum can be awarded to cover debts or expenses already incurred by the applicant, so if Ben has incurred such expenditure he could seek a lump sum. The periodical payments will be unsecured, and in determining Ben's entitlement, the court will have regard to the factors in s 3(1) of the Act. These factors are similar to those contained in MCA 1973 s 25, and the court will look at all the circumstances of the case.

First consideration is given to the welfare of any children of the family, but there is none in the present case. The court will then look at the income, earning capacity and financial resources of the parties: *DP (MC) A s 3(2)(a)*. Abigail's income is considerably greater than Ben's, but he may be earning at a lower level than his earning capacity. Consideration must be given to whether Ben can reasonably be expected to take steps to increase his earning. Ben is a qualified teacher, who would normally earn in excess of £6,000 per annum. His composing was undertaken with Abigail's encouragement, and so it is likely that the court would agree that he needs financial assistance for the immediate future. However, the policy of encouraging spousal self-sufficiency would mean that Ben would not be able to expect support to continue indefinitely.

By examining the needs and obligations of the parties, *DP (MC) A s 3(2)(b)*, it is obvious that Ben's resources will not stretch to maintaining himself and the mortgage on the matrimonial home, whereas Abigail's needs can easily be met by her resources. It seems likely therefore that Abigail will be ordered to pay some kind of periodical payment to Ben. The court will try, where possible, to have regard to the standard of living enjoyed by the couple previously, and ensure that any drop in standard does not fall inequitably on one party: *Scott v Scott (1978)*.

At present, Ben seems to be struggling to live frugally, whilst Abigail's income is enabling her to enjoy a much higher standard of living.

The age of the parties is unknown, but there is no indication that they are particularly old, and the marriage has lasted eight years, so cannot be regarded as short. There are no known disabilities (*DP (MC) A s 3(2)(e)*), and so the only other relevant factors are the parties' contributions (*s 3(2)(f)*), and conduct (*s 3(2)(g)*). Each party seems to have contributed in his/her own way to the marriage; each has worked and there is no evidence of any conduct that it would be inequitable to disregard. This seems to be a case where the couple have unfortunately drifted apart, without any blame to be attached.

Consequently, it seems apparent that a periodical payment order would be made, and since Abigail and Ben are neither very rich nor very poor, the one-third guideline in *Wachtel v Wachtel (1973)* would seem to be appropriate. The joint income of Abigail and Ben is £36,000 per annum, one third of which is £12,000. Since Ben already earns £6,000, the balance of £6,000 should be paid by Abigail by way of periodical payments of £500 per month.

The court could also award Ben a lump sum up to a maximum of £1,000, and since Abigail has been away for some time, it is likely that he could have accumulated debts and a lump sum payment would enable him to pay off the debts. However, the order ends if the parties cohabit for more than six months.

It is also possible to make an application under *DP (MC) A s 7* where the parties have been separated for a continuous period of more than three months, with neither being in desertion. (The reference to neither being in desertion would have been removed once the appropriate parts of the Family Law Act 1996 were in force.) This would seem to be the case here and so if Ben can show that Abigail has been making payments to him, albeit sporadically and differing sums, he can apply for an order placing those payments on a permanent and compulsory basis. However, he must specify to the court the total or aggregate amount of these payments in the three months prior to the application. The court is then limited to making a periodical payment order that does not exceed the aggregate amount. This may not help Ben, as it seems that Abigail's contributions over the past three months have been inadequate for his needs, and so the court will not make an order if it does not provide reasonable maintenance, and will treat the application as if it had been made under s 2: *s 7(4)*. Section 7 also does not provide for lump sums, so would be inappropriate where Ben needs help to repay debts, etc.

If Ben and Abigail can agree a level of financial provision, then such an agreement can be embodied in a court order by virtue of *DP (MC) A 1978 s 6*. The court would still need to be satisfied that the level of provision is adequate and fair, and can refuse the order if the parties refuse to agree to amendments required by the court: *DP (MC) A 1978 s 6(5)*.

If a periodical payment order is made, it can be payable weekly or monthly, and Maintenance Enforcement Act 1991 s 2 enables the Magistrates to specify how the payments should be made, for example standing orders or attachment of earnings orders. The order would end on the death of either party or if they cohabit for more than six months: *DP (MC) A 1978 s 25(1)*.

The other possibility available to Ben is to make an application to the County Court under MCA 1973 s 27. The ground for applying is that Abigail has failed to provide reasonable maintenance for Ben. This is established in the same way as the Magistrates' Court would, and reference is made to the factors in s 25 MCA 1973 in determining the level of maintenance. These factors mirror those already discussed in relation to *DP (MC) A s 3*. Although application to the County Court is more costly, its powers are somewhat wider than those of the Magistrates' Court are in that it can order both secured and unsecured periodical payments, and lump sums of unlimited amounts.

Question 16

The *Child Support Acts 1991* and *1995* – laudable objectives, laughable results.

Discuss with reference to the objectives of the Act and the criticisms they have provoked.

Anwer plan

- explain why Child Support Act (CSA) 1991 was introduced and its objectives:
  - cost saving,
  - encouraging responsibility,
  - replace fragmented system.
- what is covered by CSA?
- problems with old system;
- explain how CSA works;
- problems with the working of the Act;
- the reforms in the *Child Support, Pensions and Social Security Act 2000*.

Answer

The Child Support Act 1991 was enacted in order to meet objections raised by many, including the then Prime Minister, Mrs Thatcher, to the State being forced to provide maintenance for children through the welfare and social security systems. The perception was that many parents, most commonly fathers were avoiding their financial responsibility towards their children and that the existing system for determining and enforcing child maintenance was inadequate. Faced with an everincreasing social security budget, the Government instructed a somewhat hurried consultative and legislative process culminating, after much controversy, in the *CSA 1991*.

The Act replaces to a great extent the existing framework for determination of child maintenance by the courts, although there are still some areas of child maintenance within the jurisdiction of the court. These include maintenance for stepchildren, disabled children, the older child (who does not come within the definition of 'child' in *s* 55) and not in full-time education, and those children of exceptionally wealthy parents for whom the courts have a power to 'top up' the CSA award. Technically, the CSA replaces the powers of the court to award periodical payments; lump sum and property transfer orders, though rare, may still be made.

It was felt that the existing framework provided a fragmented jurisdiction, which was applied with enormous inconsistencies and which took little or no account of the taxpayer and State's interests in awarding financial provision for children. The Matrimonial Causes Act 1973 and *Domestic Proceedings and Magistrates' Courts Act 1978* provided maintenance for children of the family. The criteria for making such awards were very similar, although the powers of the courts varied in the type of order that could be made. Neither placed great emphasis on the public interest, and it became increasingly common in the 1980s for the courts to take into account the safety net of welfare benefits in determining disputes. The Children Act 1989 provided a mechanism by which an unmarried parent could claim maintenance for a child, and if a parent, married or otherwise, was in receipt of State benefits, the Secretary of State could apply to the Family Proceedings Court for an order requiring a liable person to provide maintenance for those on income support: Social Security Administration Act 1992.

The Government White Paper 'Children Come First' Cmnd 1264 (1990) found disturbing evidence of widespread variation in the level of child maintenance ordered, and a very low success rate in DSS recovery cases. Given the scale of the problem, which involved over three-quarters of a million single parent families receiving income support, urgent action was recommended. The existing system was inefficient in its enforcement of maintenance awards, with many cases involving arrears, and a radical reform was proposed.

First, the court's role would be taken over by a new organisation called the Child Support Agency. It would employ a large number of people to assess child maintenance by reference to a statutory formula, and then ensure that parents paid the due amount. The haphazard judicial discretion was replaced by a rigid administrative formula, necessitating the use of computers, and unfortunately resulting in a larger than acceptable number of errors in assessment. The Child Support Agency has attracted a good deal of adverse publicity in the media, and its first Head, Ros Hepplethwaite, resigned after a particularly stormy introductory period. In 1997, the Agency appointed its third head, with criticism still being made about its performance. The Agency is seen as bureaucratic and inefficient, and has been criticised for its insensitive handling of cases, resulting, it is argued, in suicides. Its initial policy of targeting fathers who were already paying maintenance as a soft target seemed to contradict the philosophy behind the Act, which was to make errant parents pay.

This philosophy stemmed from concern that parenthood was something lightly undertaken and easily discarded. Only about one-third of single parents received maintenance according to the White Paper, and this dropped to about one-quarter of those on income support. This gave the appearance of parental responsibility in a financial sense being a sham in many cases, and, given the enormous burden on the taxpayer of the Social Security bill, it was felt that steps needed to be taken to relieve the burden on the State. Parents were to be made to take financial responsibility for their children, regardless of whether they married the other parent. However, reports of the CSA confirm fears that the wrong fathers may have been targeted. There has been little success in ensuring that fathers who had previously avoided responsibility pay up; rather it is fathers who have always paid their child maintenance who have been the first to receive demands for higher payments.

The previous law had resulted in widely differing orders being made in respect of men with apparently the same financial resources. The amounts ordered were unrealistically low, given the cost of bringing up children, and were often closer to income support subsistence levels rather than the more realistic figures given in relation to fostering children. Frequently, in calculating financial matters on divorce, the maintenance for the children was an afterthought, and the CSA aims to alter this. The provisions of the Act do mean that anyone advising a divorcing couple will need to ensure that the provisions of the Act are complied with and that, where possible, a level of maintenance at least on a par with that in the Act is agreed.

The Act adopts a strict statutory formula to calculate the maintenance requirement for the caring parent and children in their care. This maintenance requirement is met by the absent parent from his assessable income, although in some cases the caring parent may also be required to contribute. The very certainty that the statutory formula sets out to create has been the subject of much vehement criticism. No account was taken of any generous financial settlement that may have been made in the past by way of a clean break. This has resulted in many absent parents being hit by demands for increased maintenance when they had rebuilt their lives on the understanding that they had met their previous obligations. The government agreed that this could operate unfairly and so the CSA 1995 does give a discretion to take this matter into account if there would be unfairness by way of an application for a 'departure discretion'. However, it does not alter the fact that parties cannot avoid responsibility for their children.

The formula also failed to take into account the travel costs and costs involved in maintaining contact with the child concerned. Contact is generally considered to be in the best interests of the child, yet the costs of this, which can be considerable if the parents live a distance away, did not feature in any calculation. This too was amended after considerable criticism. Neither was account taken of financial commitments such as HP, loans, etc that the absent parent may have incurred prior to the Act coming into force. The CSA 1995 amends this to allow this to be taken into account by way of a departure discretion. Any additional burden of maintenance can create intolerable pressure on families who are barely coping already.

Conversely, the formula seems to have worked well for some self-employed parents who, with the benefit of some creative accounting, have been able to minimise their disposable and assessable income, thereby reducing their maintenance obligations.

Although many single parent organisations have welcomed the idea that absent parents should contribute, they have expressed concern at the somewhat punitive measures that can be taken against women who do not name the father of their child, thereby running the risk that their benefit entitlement will be reduced. This invasion of civil liberties causes concern, given that some men may have been violent or may demand to see the child if made to pay, which might not, depending on the parent involved, be in the child's interests.

The child's welfare is not a paramount, nor even a first, consideration in determining the level of child support. That hardly accords with the stated philosophy of 'putting children first'. For many parents receiving benefit, there is no financial gain if the absent parent is made to pay; this merely results in a £1 for £1 deduction in benefit. Ultimately, the child will be no better off, and it may well suffer from parental antagonism. A possible reform could implement a scheme whereby there was a financial benefit to the family. At present, there will only be a benefit if the level of maintenance paid is sufficient to remove them from the benefit system entirely.

The maintenance requirement may also serve to increase contests over contact. Many men may demand contact with their children rather than pay maintenance for nothing. There is also a financial incentive, for an absent parent who cares for the child for at least two-sevenths of the time may have his maintenance liability reduced accordingly. This may result in more disputes over contact.

The Act has provoked extreme criticism and many support groups have been set up giving advice on how to thwart the Child Support Agency. One way of doing this is to deny paternity of the child in question. Paternity then needs to be established before liability can be enforced. This can cause delay and has been used by a number of men to avoid liability.

The *Child Support, Pensions and Social Security Act 2000* is an attempt to address the problems of the Child Support Acts 1991 and 1995. First, the complex statutory formula of the CSA based on allowances and deductions has been abolished. Instead the non-resident parent will pay 15 per cent of his net income to the caring parent if there is one child, rising to 20 per cent for two, and 25 per cent for three or more. There is no upper limit on this, which could result in a very wealthy payer having to hand over enormous sums of money to the caring parent. At the lower end of the scale, those with earnings of £100 or less will only pay £5, and those earning between £100 and £200 pay a reduced percentage.

This amount will be reduced if the non resident parent has a second family, that is, is living in a household where there are other children or step children. This is to prevent the second family suffering hardship, by reducing the payer's net income by 15 per cent if one child, 20 per cent if two and 25 per cent if three or more, before any assessment for the first family can be made.

The income of the caring parent is ignored under the new Act, but the amount payable can be reduced pro rata if the non resident parent has the child for at least 52 nights per year. It will be possible to seek a variation of the amount payable if the nonresident parent incurs travel expenses in order to maintain contact, and variation is also possible to take into account debts incurred in relation to the child before the parties separated.

The Act also attempts to tackle the negative image of the CSA, by introducing longer working hours, making it more accessible and user friendly. Telephone discussions and face to face talks will be used as well as simpler letters.

The main problem of payers avoiding responsibility will be tackled by stricter penalties, including the introduction of powers to confiscate driving licences, which has proved very effective in other jurisdictions such as Texas.

Whilst these reforms may go some way to addressing the deficiencies of the Child Support legislation, it remains to be seen whether they will succeed in 'putting children first'.

CHAPTER 4

FINANCIAL PROVISION ON DIVORCE

▌INTRODUCTION

When a couple divorce, there are often very complex financial implications. The court has wide powers to order maintenance pending suit (MCA 1973 s 22), although it is usually quicker and cheaper to go to the Magistrates' Court under the DPMCA 1978 until the ancillary relief can be sorted. The long-term financial solutions are provided by the powers in *ss 23* and *24* of the *MCA 1973*, which are exercised in accordance with the principles in *MCA 1973 s 25*.

Section 23 allows the making of secured or unsecured periodic payments and lump sum orders, whereas s 24 permits various orders in relation to transfer, settlement and variation of settlements of property. The factors in s 25 allow the court to take into account all the circumstances of the case, and, as each family is different, subtle varieties of the facts can lead to very different conclusions.

In the autumn of 2000 the House of Lords gave judgment in *White v White*. This was an important re-evaluation of s 25 and how it should operate. In that case the couple had been married for over 30 years, had four children and built up a successful farming business. Their assets were considerable. Their Lordships were critical of the trend that had grown up in high value cases to limit the wife's award to her reasonable needs, especially where the marriage was a long one. The factors in s 25 did not have an order of precedence, and there was no authority for limiting a wife to a sum for her reasonable needs if that ignored the fact that there were substantial assets from which she could be awarded more. Section 25 required that the parties be treated fairly, without discrimination between husband and wife, wage earner and home care provider. Although the House of Lords made it quite clear that they were not creating a presumption of equal division, it was stated that the judge should use the factors in s 25 to form a tentative view of the level of provision called for and then check that against 'the yardstick of equality'. The judge should then give reasons for departing from equality of division if good reasons made this appropriate.

In *White* the House of Lords disagreed with the trial judge's limiting of the award for the wife to her reasonable needs and upheld the Court of Appeal decision that she should acquire 40 per cent of the joint assets in recognition of her needs, the resources available and her contribution alongside her husband. The reason for not giving equal division was cited as the contribution given by the husband's father to the business, although one judge thought that this was questionable justification for a 20 per cent difference.

The House of Lords also deplored the costs involved in bringing the case – over £500,000. It stated that in s 25 cases there was no need to come to court with incredibly detailed accounts of who owned what share of the business, as the court's discretion rendered detailed knowledge of individual property entitlements unnecessary.

One of the main questions raised by *White* was whether it introduced a presumption in favour of equality and if so to what extent. *White* was followed by *Cowan v Cowan (2001)*, in which the court decided that the husband deserved a greater share of the marital assets because of the extraordinary contribution that he had made towards the couple's finances. This was followed by *Lambert v Lambert (2002)* in which the court decided that the wife's contribution as a homemaker and mother deserved equal recognition to the husband's contribution as a breadwinner. Finally, in *Macfarlane v Macfarlane, Parlour v Parlour (2004)*, the Court of Appeal decided that equal division could apply to capital as well as income.

Another issue where there has been recent judicial development is that of pre-nuptial agreements. Whilst these are not binding, courts may take them into account as far as it seems reasonable and fair to do so (*M v M (pre-nuptial agreement)(2002), K v K (Ancillary relief: pre-nuptial agreement) (2003)*).

First consideration is given to the welfare of the children of the family, and you should bear in mind the provisions designed to ensure that the court considers whether to impose a clean break between the parties. Ensure that all of the factors that are relevant to the case are explored in turn. These include the following:

- the income, earning capacity and financial resources of the parties – this is a realistic assessment of what the parties have and what they can reasonably be expected to acquire in the future;
- the financial needs and obligations of the parties – bearing in mind housing needs, children's costs, and so on;
- the standard of living enjoyed by the family, trying to ensure that any resulting drop in standards because of the divorce is borne equally;
- the age of the parties and duration of the marriage – the usual argument here is that greater provision is needed for an elderly spouse who has been disadvantaged after a long marriage, whereas a young childless spouse when

the marriage has been short should quickly adjust. However, it may still be possible for a short marriage to lead to considerable financial relief – *Miller v Miller (2006)*. Whilst traditionally courts have ignored pre-marital cohabitation, recent decisions seem to be taking a more liberal approach (*GW v RW (2003)*);

- any physical or mental disability – looking at the effect this has on the spouses' needs and ability to provide for themselves;
- any contributions made or likely to be made in the future to the welfare of the family – this includes financial and other contributions such as care and housekeeping;
- any conduct, if it would be inequitable to disregard it – does not make the mistake of dragging in any misbehaviour. It will be exceptional for conduct to be taken into account;
- any loss of benefit in the future, such as lost pension rights, which often need to be compensated for.

The new *MCA 1973 s 21* defines financial provision orders and property adjustment orders. The Act introduces the concept of interim financial provision and lump sum orders for a party to a marriage or child of the family, new *MCA 1973 s 22(4)*. Whilst maintenance pending suit has always been a feature of the existing law, and is replaced by the concept of an interim financial provision order, the power to make an interim lump sum is an innovation. This could help alleviate financial pressures on a party during what might be a lengthy period before a divorce order can be made, and can also help them finance their legal costs, or re-house themselves. The courts will be careful in making such orders to avoid prejudicing the ability of the court to make final orders.

Where a lump sum is ordered it has always been possible to order it to be paid in instalments, but any order for interest to be paid had to be made at the time of the original lump sum order.

With property adjustment orders, if possible the court should try under the new provisions to make all the property orders on one occasion, new *s 23A*. There is also an amendment to the clean break provisions in *s 25A*, which will enable the court to order a clean break and that a party shall not be entitled to apply for financial provision at any time of the court's own motion: *s 25A(3)*.

Orders will not usually take effect until the making of the divorce order, although there is a power to backdate periodical payments orders. The order in relation to spouses will end on the death of the payer (if unsecured), or the payee or on the remarriage of the payee. The Act did not provide for the ending of an order on cohabitation by the payee with another. Orders for children can be for such term as the court sees fit (*new s 29(1A)*) but will usually be until the child reaches 17, unless they are in education or training or special rules apply.

Section 25(2)(a) has been amended by the *Pensions Act 1995 s 166*, to allow the court to take into account any benefit under a pension scheme that a party has or is likely to have and there is no need for this to be in the foreseeable future, and part (h) is amended to allow consideration of the loss of pension scheme benefits.

The Pensions Act 1995 also allows for earmarking of pension scheme funds, so that when the pension becomes payable the receiving party can receive income from the pension fund of the yielding party and a lump sum. This represents an improvement on the old position, but still has disadvantages in that it forces the receiving party to wait for payment and may be defeated by the early death of the yielding party. A more far-reaching reform is the concept of pension splitting, introduced in *s 16* of the *Family Law Act 1996*, amending MCA 1973 s 25. The pension adjustment order will enable the court to order the immediate division of a pension fund thus facilitating a clean break and avoiding the need for the receiving party to wait. The complex statutory provisions governing this are contained in the *Welfare Reform and Pensions Act 1999*, which came into force on 1 December 2000.

▌FINANCIAL RELIEF FOR CIVIL PARTNERS

Section 72 and *schedule 5* of the *Civil Partnerships Act 2004* provide for civil partnerships to receive financial relief on the dissolution of the civil partnership.

Question 17

Angela, aged 25, has four children: Bobby, aged 8; Cindy, aged 6; Darren, aged 4; and Elzine, aged 2. Bobby and Cindy are children from her relationship with Frank, whom she never married. Darren and Elzine were born during her marriage to Greg. Greg does not think Elzine is his daughter, as her colouring is totally different from either his or Angela's. Greg has petitioned for divorce on the basis of Angela's adultery, and Angela does not intend to defend this divorce. However, she is concerned about the financial consequences of this for herself and her children. She is living, at present, in the former matrimonial home, a council flat, and Greg is quite happy for her to remain there.

Advise Angela.

Answer plan

A question primarily concerned with financial provision on divorce for children and the spouse.

Explain the powers under ss 23 and 24 and the factors in s 25 of the Matrimonial Causes Act 1973 and their applicability to spouses and children of the family. Mention the Child Support Act 1991 and its principles as they apply to natural biological children. Before conducting any detailed examination, decide which provisions apply to whom.

Two children, Bobby and Cindy, are natural children of Frank who has Child Support Act liability and children of the family for Greg who could have MCA liability. One child, Darren, is Greg's natural child and therefore the Child Support Act 1991 applies.

Elzine is of questionable parentage and the presumption of legitimacy should be considered. If she is Greg's natural child, then Child Support Act liability will follow; if not, there will be MCA liability if she is a child of the family.

Angela will receive provision as a spouse under the provisions of the MCA 1973.

In relation to children of the family, look at the factors that relate to the financial needs and obligations of the parties and children. Examine the special provisions in s 25(3) for children of the family. Further attention must be paid to s 25(4) and the way in which Greg assumed responsibility for the children.

For the natural child or children, the *Child Support Act 1991* must be considered. Explain how the absent and caring parent would apply to each qualifying child. Also detail the statutory formula.

Mention the impact of the *Child Support, Pensions and Social Security Act 2000*. For the spouse, Angela, only Greg has responsibility under the MCA 1973. A general discussion only is possible since no details are known of the financial position of the parties.

Answer

Angela's entitlement to ancillary relief from her husband Greg will be determined by reference to the court's powers in ss 23 and 24 of the MCA 1973 and the guidelines in MCA s 25. However, the issues of financial provision for the children are complex.

There are four children involved here and they need to be considered in turn. Bobby and Cindy are the natural children of Frank, who would be liable to provide maintenance under the Child Support Act 1991. In addition, they may be children of the family of Angela and Greg if they have been treated by Angela and Greg as such: *MCA s 52*. Greg could then incur financial responsibility towards the children under the MCA 1973. There is no Child Support Act liability since they are not his natural children.

Darren is the natural child of Angela and Greg and therefore Greg could incur Child Support Act liability towards Darren. The other possibility is that the Child Support Act can be avoided at present by the making of a consent order.

Elzine was born during the marriage of Greg and Angela and there is a presumption of legitimacy, which may be rebutted on the balance of probabilities: Family Law Reform Act 1969 *s 26*. It will therefore be presumed that Elzine is the natural child of Greg unless this can be rebutted. A confession of adultery does not necessarily establish that the child is not Greg's but it is likely that DNA testing, which can be directed by the court (*Family Law Reform Act 1969 s 20(1)*), would establish Elzine's parentage. It is usually in the child's interests for such testing to be ordered: *S v S (1972)*.

If Elzine is Greg's natural child and this is not impossible even though her colouring may differ, then Greg's liability to maintain will again be under the Child Support Act 1991. If, however, Elzine is not Greg's child, then her natural father, if identifiable and traceable, would have Child Support Act liability. Greg's obligations would be incurred under the MCA 1973, if he had treated her as a child of the family.

It is unclear whether Greg and Angela continued to live together after Elzine's birth. If they separated shortly afterwards because of Greg's suspicions, then he may be able to show that he never treated Elzine as a child of the family. However, if there was a shared family life, when Greg and Angela lived together and acted as Elzine's parents, then Greg, despite his misgivings, will have treated her as a child of the family.

Liability to maintain a child of the family is determined by the provisions of MCA 1973 *s 25(3)*, if the child is not Greg's natural child. Thus Bobby, Cindy and possibly Elzine will be provided for under the MCA. The financial resources and needs of the parties and the children will be considered, together with any disability the child may have. This does not seem to be an issue here, nor is there evidence that the parties were educating children privately, or intended to do so: *s 25(3)(d)*. Thus it will essentially be a question of considering Greg's available resources.

Since the children are not Greg's own children, it is necessary (*s 25(4)*) to consider whether he assumed responsibility for them, and on what basis. The extent of his liability and whether he did so knowing that they were not his children, must be examined, as must the liability of anyone else to maintain the children. From the facts, it is clear that he knew Bobby and Cindy were not his children, but it is unclear what, if any, liability for their maintenance is being borne by their natural father, Frank. If the Child Support Agency can track him down and succeed in obtaining child support from him, then this could reduce Greg's liability. It does seem, however, that Greg has borne some financial responsibility for both children, and so some periodical payments for their benefit will be ordered.

If Elzine is not his natural child, then his liability towards her as a child of the family will be determined as above. Essentially, much will depend on how he behaved after her birth and on the possible liability of her as yet unnamed father.

Angela can also seek financial provision from the natural father of her children under the Child Support Act 1991. If Angela is in receipt of State benefits, she will have no choice; the Agency is automatically involved in benefit cases. A parent receiving benefit is required to provide information identifying the father of her child and authorise the Child Support Agency to pursue him for child support. If Angela fails to do this, her benefit can be reduced by up to 20 per cent. Thus, Frank, Greg and the as yet unnamed father of Elzine could all be pursued by the Agency. If Angela is not in receipt of benefits, Greg could agree a consent order with Angela regarding financial provision for his natural child or children, but would be advised to ensure that the level of maintenance is equivalent to that which would be ordered under the Child Support Act.

The Child Support Agency will impose liability on an absent parent, that is a natural parent not living in the same household as his or her children. The children all have their home with Angela, the caring parent, and since each child is under 16 with one parent absent, they are all qualifying children. Each child's natural father will have his liability assessed by reference to the statutory formula for calculating the maintenance requirement. This formula is applied automatically and without discretion, giving rise to considerable criticism. Frank, who may have played little role until now in his children's lives, will find that he will incur financial liability.

Under the *Child Support, Pensions and Social Security Act 2000*, Frank would be termed a non-resident parent and he would pay 20 per cent of his net income for the support of his two children. Angela's income would be ignored and there are no allowances for Frank's housing costs and so on. However, this figure may be adjusted downwards, if Frank acquires a second family, or if the children spend time living with him.

This calculation would also be made in respect of the other natural fathers of Angela's children. However, only Greg, the man she married, could incur any direct financial obligations to Angela herself.

This obligation could possibly be by way of periodical payments, either secured or unsecured, lump sum order *(s 23)*, or property transfer, or variations under *s 24*. The factors in *MCA s 25* must be considered, including the welfare of any children of the family as a first consideration *(s 25(1))*.

Here there are a number of children of the family and their welfare requires them to be adequately housed. There does not seem to be any controversy over what should happen to the former matrimonial home, as Greg is happy for Angela to remain there with the children. The court has power to order the transfer of council house tenancies and although the local authority has no right to prevent this, they are entitled to be present and to voice their opinion, as in *Lee v Lee (1984)*.

In relation to financial provision, the court must consider the desirability of a clean break between the parties *(s 25A (1))*, but is under no obligation to impose one *(Clutton v Clutton (1991))*. Clearly, it is difficult to have a clean break if there are young children *(Suter v Suter and Jones (1987))*, or if the wife has been out to work for some time. However, the court may consider that whilst Angela may need immediate support, it could be desirable to limit maintenance for a fixed period: *s 25A (2) Parlour v Parlour (2004)*. This could give Angela time to adjust without undue hardship, but it might not be appropriate if her future is too uncertain, as in *Suter v Suter and Jones (1987)*. Only if the future is sufficiently predictable should limited maintenance be imposed: *Barrett v Barrett (1988)*.

It seems likely that if maintenance is awarded by way of periodical payments, they will not be limited but will terminate on Angela's death or remarriage *(MCA s 28)* or if Greg successfully applies to vary or terminate his obligations *(MCA s 31)*.

The amount of maintenance will be determined by reference to the financial resources, income and earning capacity of the parties. It is not clear how much Greg earns, if at all. If Greg is in receipt of State benefits himself, he will not usually be ordered to pay substantial sums to Angela, although an order may still nevertheless be made *(Freeman v Swatridge (1984))*; usually, however, it is a nominal order *(Berry v Berry (1986))*. If Greg does have earnings, it is likely that he will have to pay something to Angela. She is not earning at present, and with young children it may be difficult for her to realise or acquire earning capacity. Nevertheless, she should be advised that the court will not countenance a 'meal ticket for life' and, since she seems to be young, she will need to take steps towards self-sufficiency in the future. The level of periodical payments may be influenced by the one-third guideline in *Wachtel v Wachtel (1973)* for middle-income families, but if this family is somewhat poorer, the net-effect method in *Stockford v Stockford (1982)* may be more appropriate. No order will usually be made that would take Greg below subsistence level *(Barnes v Barnes (1972))*, and to that extent the court will take into account the safety net of welfare benefits available to Angela.

The drop in standard of living (s 25(2)(c)) should be equally borne (*Preston v Preston (1982)*), but the fact that this seems to be a relatively short marriage is offset by the fact that two more children were born, and that there were two other children for whom Greg assumed responsibility. In those circumstances, Angela would find it impossible to adjust immediately to her changed circumstances. The parties are not particularly old, nor are they disabled, and they both appear to have contributed to the marriage and welfare of the family: s 25(2)(f). The only other factor that may have a relevance is conduct under s 25(2)(g). This is not routinely a consideration (*Wachtel v Wachtel*), and should only be used if it would be inequitable to disregard it. Generally speaking, adultery is not conduct (*Duxbury v Duxbury (1987)*), and it does not appear that there are any additional factors that make Angela's behaviour repugnant and indefensible.

Consequently, it seems likely that some financial provision will be awarded to Angela. The exact amount depends upon Greg's resources and will be affected by his obligations to maintain the various children of the family. In addition, Angela may seek child support from the natural fathers of her children.

Question 18

Caroline, aged 30 met David, aged 35, at a school nativity play some eight years ago. Both Caroline and David had recently divorced their respective partners and both were looking after their children from their marriages. Caroline's children were Emma and Freddie, aged 6 and 3, and David's son, George, was also 6. After a whirlwind romance, David and Caroline married, and for a while they were blissfully happy. Caroline had worked as a legal secretary prior to marrying David but with her child care expenses, she had not been well off. David was a wealthy businessman and he had been keen for Caroline to stay at home, looking after the children and hosting various social events for his clients. Caroline also helped David in his business during busy times. A year ago, Caroline discovered that David had been having an affair with her sister, Harriet. This so infuriated Caroline that she cut up all of David's clothes with the garden shears, including his expensive suits. She also threw acid over his recently restored antique Rolls-Royce, causing £10,000 of damage. Caroline is divorcing David on the basis of his adultery but seeks financial provision for herself and the children. George, David's son by his first marriage, will live with his father but it has been agreed that he will spend every second weekend with Caroline, Emma and Freddie.

The matrimonial home is currently worth £300,000 and there is no mortgage. David's business has a considerable turnover, and last year his drawings were in excess of £100,000. Caroline used to receive £25,000 per annum from the company but David stopped this when she discovered about his affair. Caroline has remained in the matrimonial home but is keen to buy herself another house, free from painful memories of David.

Advise Caroline as to what financial provision, if any, she is entitled to on her divorce from David.

Answer plan

This question requires a detailed analysis of the MCA 1973 s 25 factors as they affect entitlement to financial provision or spouses. There is no Child Support Act 1991 liability as the children involved are not the biological offspring of the payer. Instead, the MCA 1973 provisions for children of the family must be detailed.

First, consideration must be paid to the welfare of the children and the clean break provisions should be outlined. Then the relevant factors of s 25 (2) should be examined as they apply to the parties:

- income and resources; S25(a)
- needs and obligations; S25(b)
- standard of living; S25(c)
- age and duration of marriage; S25(d)
- no physical or mental disability; S25(e)
- contributions; S25(f)
- conduct; S25(g)
- loss of benefit. S25(h) → Pensions

Consider the overall package, the home, and financial provision. Then outline the special provisions in ss 25(3) and 25(4) MCA 1973 as they relate to children of the family.

Answer

On divorce, the court has wide powers to order financial provision under MCA 1973 s 23 by way of periodical payments and/or lump sum orders as well as property orders under s 24. These powers will be exercised by reference to the principles in MCA s 25 in order to achieve a just and equitable financial solution.

In the instant case, Caroline, as a spouse, would be entitled to seek financial provision from David, for herself. She can also seek financial provision for her two children, Emma and Freddie. Since Emma and Freddie are not David's natural children, there can be no application under the Child Support Act 1991. Instead provision for the children will be under the MCA 1973, as they are children of the family. The concept of 'child of the family' is defined in *MCA 1973 s 52* to include a child treated by the parties as a child of the family. Caroline and David treated all three children as children of the family.

In determining financial solutions, the court will first have regard to the welfare of children of the family whilst they are under 18. George and Emma are presently 14 and Freddie is 11, consequently their welfare will need to be borne in mind whilst reaching a solution to Caroline and David's financial problem. All the children need suitable homes, and in a wealthy family such as theirs, there should be no problem ensuring that both Caroline and David have homes in which their children can live and visit.

The court is then required by virtue of s 25A(1) to consider whether it may be possible to achieve a clean break between the parties, either immediately or as soon as possible after the divorce. This should not be taken to mean that a clean break will be imposed routinely; the duty is for the court to consider, not necessarily impose, a clean break (*Clutton v Clutton (1991)*). A clean break may be difficult where there are children, but it is not impossible (*Suter v Suter and Jones (1987)*) and it is often easier to achieve if there is substantial wealth (*Duxbury v Duxbury (1987)*). Even if no immediate clean break is ordered, the court is required to consider whether it would be appropriate to limit maintenance to a particular period to enable adjustment (s 25A(2), *Parlour v Parlour (2004)*).

Bearing this in mind, the court will first examine the parties' income, earning capacity and financial resources, including what each can reasonably be expected to acquire. In the present case, David is a wealthy businessman with considerable income; there is a valuable matrimonial home and the business itself represents a capital asset for David. It is likely that David is earning to the limit of his earning capacity and therefore care will need to be taken to ensure that David's true worth in terms of savings, investments and assets, such as his antique car, are properly taken into account. As far as Caroline is concerned, she, at present, has no income. Throughout the marriage she was encouraged by David to remain at home, and she has only worked by contributing to the business. In the light of the acrimonious nature of the divorce, this income-generating avenue is not open to her and so the court will need to consider what earning capacity she has. Prior to the marriage, she worked as a legal secretary, but after eight years, technological developments may mean she was outdated and would need retraining. The children are all of school age and old enough for her to work and since she is in her late 30s, she should not expect to be maintained by her husband indefinitely. Therefore, whilst initially Caroline has no income, the likelihood is that she would be expected to retrain and begin to bear more of the burden of supporting herself.

The needs and obligations of the parties will need to be considered: *s 25(2)(b)*. The basic needs of both parties is to provide homes and support their lifestyles and those of the children. There is no mortgage on the matrimonial home, nor does there appear to be any debts. Although David has formed a relationship with Harriet, it is unclear whether that will continue. If David was cohabiting with Harriet or even having children with her, then the needs of that second family would need to be taken into account: *Barnes v Barnes (1972)*. In the present case, it does seem that David will need to provide some assistance to his wife and the children given that she does not have the ability to be immediately self-sufficient.

Since this is a relatively wealthy family, it should be possible to avoid a drastic reduction in the standard of living (*Foley v Foley (1981)*) and the court will have regard to the standard of living enjoyed by the parties (*s 23(2)(c)*). The age of the parties and duration of marriage must also be considered under *s 25(1)(d)* but since both parties are approaching early middle age, this should not be an influence. There is no disability to be considered under *s 25(2)(e)* and so the consideration of contributions (*s 25(2)(f)*), and conduct (*s 25(2)(g)*) must be made.

David has obviously worked hard to provide the family with the comfortable lifestyle they have enjoyed. However, Caroline has contributed in terms of being a wife and mother (*Wachtel v Wachtel (1973)*) and there are also her contributions to the running of the business (*O'Donnell v O'Donnell (1975)*). This should be reflected in the level of financial relief awarded (*White v White (2000)*).

Conduct should only be taken into account if it would be inequitable to disregard it: *s 25(2)(g)*. Generally conduct should not be a consideration (*Wachtel v Wachtel (1973)*) but, in the present case, Caroline's conduct has resulted in a dissipation of the family assets, when she deliberately destroyed or damaged David's clothes and car: *Martin v Martin (1976)* establishes that deliberate dissipation can be taken into account if excessive. However, Caroline's behaviour was a response to discovering David's affair with her sister. Mere adultery is not usually conduct (*Duxbury v Duxbury (1987)*) but the fact that it is with Caroline's sister might possibly be equated with cases like *Bailey v Tolliday (1983)* or *Dixon v Dixon (1974)*. However, in those cases the adultery was with a parent-in-law or daughter-in-law, which might be more repugnant than with a sister-in-law. It is possible that David and Caroline's bad behaviour could cancel each other out

(*Leadbeater v Leadbeater (1985)*) with no financial consequences on the level of maintenance.

Last, the court will consider whether any benefit will be lost on divorce: s 25(2)(h). This usually involves benefits such as pension rights but could include the loss of a share in the business if one had been promised by David: *Trippas v Trippas (1973)*. *The Pensions Act 1995 s 166* alters the s 25 factors to ensure that any pension entitlement that David might have acquired is considered as an asset of his and that any loss of pension rights by Caroline is also considered, even though this might not be for some considerable time. The court has the power under the Act to earmark some or all of the pension assets, so that when the pension matures and becomes payable to David, it is possible to order that some of the income and/or the lump sum are paid to Caroline. Obviously, this is a deferred benefit to her, which she may or may not live to realise. A preferable option may be the *Welfare Reform and Pensions Act 1999*, which allows the court to make an order splitting a pension fund and ordering part of the fund to be made available for the other party to the marriage.

It would seem, therefore, that this case will require some kind of redistribution of the family assets, as well as some financial provision at least initially by David. A lump sum may be ordered if David has the means to pay (*Davis v Davis (1967)*) but it should not be ordered if he would only be able to raise it by selling shares in his company (*Smith v Smith (1983)*). Here, however, there is the asset of the matrimonial home which could be sold, and the proceeds used to rehouse the parties. It would seem appropriate to give Caroline a greater share than David, to take into account both her need for housing and her contributions to the business and loss of any share in it: *Trippas v Trippas (1973)*. This would not be unjust to David, who could still use his capital as a deposit on a new home and raise the remainder on mortgage from his income.

Caroline will also need some financial provision, which is no longer limited to her reasonable needs (*White v White (2000)*). Therefore, periodical payments will be ordered, unless David is able to settle a large lump sum, obviating the need for periodical payments and achieving a clean break: *Duxbury v Duxbury (1987)*.

David will also need to provide some kind of maintenance for Emma and Freddie. The court will take into account the financial resources and obligations of the parties and then examine what the needs of the children are: s 25(3). This takes into account how the children were being or expected to be, educated and so David's liability may be greater if the children were at fee-paying schools: *O'Donnell v O'Donnell (1976)*. Since Emma and Freddie are not David's natural children, the court will further consider whether David assumed responsibility for their maintenance, to what extent and on what basis, and whether he knew that this was not his child. On the facts, it seems clear that David did assume responsibility for Emma and Freddie, knowing that they were not his children. However, *s 29(4)* requires the court to consider the liability of anyone else to maintain the child. Therefore, David's liability may be reduced if their natural father is alive and can be traced. However, it seems likely that some order will be made.

Any order made for Caroline will terminate on her death or remarriage: *s 28(1)*. It will also terminate on David's death unless secured. If the court does not make a limited term periodical payment order then David can apply to vary or extinguish his obligation to Caroline under s 31 if circumstances change.

The order in respect of the children will end when they reach 17 years of age (MCA s 29), unless they are in full-time education and their needs require an extended order.

Question 19

Edward and Fiona met whilst at university 15-years-ago. They lived together for a while, but then married after the birth of their child, George, now aged 12. Subsequently, two daughters were born, Isobel, aged 6 and Jessica, aged 2. Unfortunately, Jessica was born severely disabled and requires constant care and attention. The strain on the couple has been enormous, and there have been several rows. Fiona, in desperation, had a brief affair with Jessica's physiotherapist, Kevin, but felt so guilty about it that she confessed to Edward and begged forgiveness. Edward reacted violently at the news and seriously injured Fiona, leaving her also severely disabled.

Fiona had worked as a teacher throughout the marriage, taking maternity leave when she had the children. Since Jessica's birth, she had found it increasingly difficult to work and care for Jessica, but since Edward attacked her she has been unable to work.

Fiona is divorcing Edward, citing his behaviour, and it seems, that Edward will not contest the petition. However, it is proving difficult to get agreement about the financial aspects of divorce. The former matrimonial home is valued at £25,000 with an outstanding mortgage of £20,000. Edward earns £140,000 per year as a manager of a small supermarket and the couple have no other assets, save for a small car, valued at £2,000 that Edward uses to go to work, and £3,000 in a building society account. Advise Fiona on her prospects of obtaining ancillary relief for herself and the children.

Answer plan

Details required of the parties under ss 23 and 24 of the MCA 1973 and what orders will be made in the light of the MCA s 25 factors for the spouse. Further discussion is required in respect of the Child Support Act 1991 provisions for the support of the payer's biological children and the possibility of this being bypassed by a consent order.

It is probably safest to consider the Child Support Act liability first. Explain the concepts of the qualifying child, and the absent and caring parent.

Then consider the MCA provisions for spouses:

- first consider the concept of children;
- then look at clean break provisions;
- income and resources of parties;
- needs and obligations;
- standard of living;
- age and duration of marriage;
- disability is relevant here;
- contribution;
- conduct;
- loss of benefit.

Consider basis for support (possible one-third guideline); also what should happen to the home (possible Mesher order).

Answer

If Edward and Fiona divorce, then the court has wide powers to achieve a just and reasonable financial settlement. Section 23 of the MCA 1973 permits awards of secured or unsecured periodical payments as well as lump sum orders; whereas s 24 permits property orders, including sale, transfer and settlement of property. These powers are exercised with reference to the guiding principles in MCA s 25, and allow for provision for spouses.

As far as provision for children is concerned, it is necessary to examine whether the children involved are the natural children of the parties. If so, their provision will be ordered by reference to the *Child Support Act 1991*. This Act will always apply where the caring parent is in receipt of State welfare benefits and it will apply in other cases at present where the parents are unable to agree the level of financial provision. The court has no jurisdiction to make orders for natural children of the parties under the MCA 1973 in a disputed case. However, the parties can bypass the provisions of the Child Support Act by way of an agreed consent order. Both possibilities will be examined since all three children are the natural children of Edward and Fiona.

If provision is ordered under the Child Support Act 1991, it will be made by reference to the statutory formula for child support. Fiona is the caring parent, as the children have their home with her, and she usually provides their everyday care. Edward is the non-resident parent, as he does not live in the same household as the children, and the children have their home with Fiona, a parent with care. All three children are qualifying children in that they are under the age of 16, and one of their parents is absent.

Once these preliminaries are established, it will be necessary to calculate the maintenance requirement by reference to the statutory formula.

The *Child Support, Pensions and Social Security Act 2000* has altered the basis of child support and Edward will be ordered to pay a percentage of his net income to Fiona 25 per cent, as there are three children. In addition, because Jessica is disabled, a court will also be able to award maintenance.

It is very important for Edward to consider the level of maintenance that could be awarded under the Child Support Act. Even if he were to agree a consent order with Fiona, the Child Support Agency could become involved if Fiona resorted to State benefits, and, in the future, once the transitional period is over, the Child Support Agency will control even existing consent orders; therefore, it is sensible to ensure that the level of provision for children is at least that which the Agency would order.

Once provision for the children is determined, it will then be possible to consider the level and nature of provision for the spouses. This is a reversal of the old position, where there was a tendency to deal with provision for children as an afterthought.

First consideration will be the welfare of any children of the family under the age of 18. The three children here will need secure accommodation with their mother, and it is important to ensure that, whatever financial arrangements are reached, the children have a roof over their heads: *Harman v Glencross (1986)*.

The court must then bear in mind the desirability of a clean break and the policy of encouraging spouses' self-sufficiency: *MCA 1973 ss 25A (1)* and *25A (2)*. However, it is clear on these facts that, because of Fiona's disability which was inflicted by Edward, a clean break is unlikely. The obligation is for the court to consider, not necessarily impose, a clean break (*Clutton v Clutton (1991)*) and, consequently, in a case such as this where the presence of the children and other factors make a clean break unsatisfactory, it will not be imposed (*Suter v Suter and Jones (1987)*).

First, the court will examine the income, earning capacity and other resources of the parties: s 25(2)(a). Edward earns an average income of £18,000 per annum, and there is no evidence that he could reasonably be expected to earn more. He is not deliberately under-earning: *Hardy v Hardy (1981)*. There are few assets here; only the house which is in joint names, one car and modest savings. Fiona, on the other hand, has no financial resources beyond these assets. She has no income, and her earning capacity as a teacher has been destroyed by her disability. Although the facts disclose that she was having difficulty coping with the demands of Jessica, she did have income and now she can earn nothing. It is unclear what would happen if she were to receive compensation for her injuries, for example from the Criminal Injuries Compensation Scheme, or from an insurance policy. Traditionally, damages for pain and suffering were not included as a spouse's assets (*Daubney v Daubney (1976)*), and this case is similar to that of *Jones v Jones (1975)* where the husband could not include damages as part of his wife's assets when he himself had been responsible for inflicting the injury. However, this policy has been criticised in *Wagstaff v Wagstaff (1992)* and it is possible that if Fiona were receiving substantial income from an insurance policy, for example, that it might be taken into account.

From the facts, it seems obvious that whilst Edward's means are reasonable, Fiona has no means of supporting herself. There is a safety net of State benefits, but generally the courts are unwilling to take this into account, as it enables a husband to avoid his obligation to his wife by having the State maintain her: *Barnes v Barnes (1972)*. The courts try to protect public funds by refusing to take such benefits into account (*Ashley v Blackman (1988)*), unless the husband's means were so limited that any order would take him below subsistence level (*Stockford v Stockford (1981)*). In the present case, Edward's means are such that he would be expected to support his wife without her recourse to State benefits.

It is then necessary to examine the financial needs and obligations of the parties. Edward clearly needs to be able to house himself, and provide accommodation for his children when they visit him: *Calderbank v Calderbank (1975)*. However, Fiona needs to provide the children with a permanent home, and Fiona's disability and Jessica's disability are special considerations that increase her needs: *Smith v Smith (1975)*. Fiona would have difficulty in housing herself and it seems likely that she will need to remain in the former matrimonial house.

The standard of living enjoyed before the breakdown of the marriage is not often maintained on divorce, but the court will be concerned to ensure that the drop in standard is not borne unequally: *Preston v Preston (1982)*. The parties are not particularly old, nor has the marriage been particularly short, s 25(2)(d), but clearly Fiona's disability is a relevant factor under s 25(2)(e): *Jones v Jones (1975)*.

In terms of contributions made by the parties or likely to be made in the future (s 25(2)(f)), both parties have worked to support the family, and Fiona has been a wife and mother. *White v White (2000)* suggests there should be no discrimination between the contribution of the wage earner and the contribution of the home maker. Looking at future contributions, Fiona will have day-to-day care of the children, which will involve her in added responsibility, in that she will have to supervise the children and obtain physical assistance for tasks she and they cannot perform.

The court will also consider conduct if it would be inequitable to disregard it: s 25(2)(g). Usually conduct is irrelevant (*Wachtel v Wachtel (1973)*), and ordinary adultery is irrelevant (*Duxbury v Duxbury (1987)*). However, Edward's extremely violent response is likely to count against him (*Jones v Jones (1975)*) since it has effectively destroyed Fiona's financial prospects.

The facts do not disclose if Fiona will lose any benefit because of the divorce: s 25(2)(h). Consequently, it seems that the facts require some kind of financial provision for Fiona, as well as her being allowed to remain in the matrimonial home. The home in the instant case is jointly owned, but if it were sold there would be inadequate proceeds to rehouse the parties. It is relatively easier for a single person to obtain accommodation than a disabled woman with three children, and so Fiona would be able to remain in the home. It could be argued that whilst it is not usually desirable to deprive a husband of his equity in the home, it may be sensible to do so in instances of extreme bad conduct (*Bryant v Bryant (1976)*) or where there may be problems enforcing maintenance. Here it may be desirable to order Edward to transfer his interest in the home to Fiona, but this may cause difficulty, given the outstanding mortgage. Fiona would then need to receive sufficient financial provision from Edward to enable her to pay the mortgage and must be borne in mind that the Child Support Act will impose additional requirements on Edward by way of child support.

Another option is to allow Fiona to remain in the matrimonial home until her death or remarriage. Since both she and Jessica have disabilities, any shorter period is inappropriate. This is a variation on the Mesher order (*Mesher v Mesher (1980)*), which postpones sale indefinitely, but which will not necessarily deprive Edward of his capital interest in the home. It is also possible for Edward to pay the mortgage, by making an undertaking.

The parties would be well advised to try to reach some kind of agreement and avoid the need for litigation. A party receiving legal representation under the Access to Justice Act 1999 may well find that the statutory charge cuts into the value of any property recovered or retained by the proceedings. This must be borne in mind as expensive litigation could dissipate the parties' assets, as in *Piglowska v Piglowski (1999)*, where lengthy litigation left the couple with virtually no assets once their legal bills were paid.

Question 20

Henry and Wanda married five years ago, after the death of Henry's first wife, Bronwen. Henry and Bronwen had two children, Scott, now aged 14, and Charlene, now aged 12. Henry and Wanda have one child, Jimmy, aged 3. Henry owns the matrimonial home, which is a large four-bedroomed executive house, valued at £250,000 with a mortgage of £10,000 outstanding. When Jimmy was born, Wanda used her entire savings of £12,000 to build an extension to the house, which included a playroom and 'den' for the children. Wanda has no further savings, and has not worked since before Jimmy was born. Henry earns £40,000 per annum. The marriage has encountered difficulties, and both parties agree that a divorce is the best option for them. Scott and Charlene will remain with their father, and Wanda will care for Jimmy. Wanda wishes to obtain periodical payments for herself and Jimmy, and a lump sum to enable her to buy a new home. Wanda is legally aided and has heard horror stories about what can happen if the dispute drags on. Henry is being quite reasonable and his lawyer has indicated to Wanda that he feels a compromise can be negotiated and agreed by way of a consent order.

Advise Wanda on her entitlement to ancillary relief, the effect of the statutory charge, and the consequences of making a consent order.

Answer plan

Explain the provisions of the MCA 1973 as they relate to spouses and children of the family. However, the biological child, Jimmy, would be a qualifying child for the *Child Support Act 1991*, and the statutory formula will apply unless the parties make a consent order:

- explain how a consent order operates and how the parties are often influenced by the s 25 factors;
- detail the Child Support Act provisions and the need for maintenance to be agreed at least at this level;
- give a general discussion of what the parties might agree vis à vis the home and continuing financial provision;
- explain the consequences of the statutory charge and the desirability of reaching agreement.

Answer

If the parties divorce, then the court has wide powers to order ancillary relief in the form of secured or unsecured periodical payments or lump sum orders (MCA 1973 s 23), and property orders under MCA s 24, which will be determined by reference to the factors in MCA s 25. However, the instant case is one of the few relatively amicable 'divorces' and the parties are keen to agree the level of ancillary relief rather than have it imposed on them by the courts. If the parties are able to reach agreement then the various aspects of the agreement are embodied in a consent order. This order is then formally presented to the court which can approve it under *MCA 1973 s 33A*. The order will then be enforceable as any other order, and will mean that any maintenance payments made under it are 'qualifying maintenance payments' for the purposes of the Finance Act 1988, thereby attracting additional tax allowances for the payer and being tax free in the hands of the payee. The parties are often influenced in reaching agreement by the realisation of what a court is likely to order on the s 25 guidelines.

It is necessary to ensure that a consent order embodies all aspects of ancillary relief, as such an order is usually regarded as full and final, and consequently difficult to vary or appeal against. Wanda should therefore ensure that the consent order properly reflects any agreed financial provision for Jimmy, herself and any lump sum that Henry is agreeable to paying. In terms of financial provision for Jimmy, he is the natural child of both Henry and Wanda. Henry, as a non-resident parent, would be liable financially to support Jimmy under the Child Support Act 1991. Jimmy is a qualifying child, that is, aged under 16 who has his home with a parent with care, Wanda. Henry would be liable to pay 15% of his income to support Jimmy. However because Henry has care of Scott and Charlene, their needs will first be taken into account it will reduce the income available to Jimmy by 10%.

The two children of Henry's former marriage, Scott and Charlene, may well qualify as children of the family (MCA 1973 s 52), as they have been treated by both Henry and Wanda as such, even though not Wanda's natural children. Wanda will have no Child Support Act liability towards them as they are not her natural children, but she could potentially have to contribute to their maintenance under the MCA 1973. However, she has no job or obvious resources and it would seem inappropriate for her to have to support them. Therefore the consent order should reflect this.

In terms of periodical payments for Wanda, it is clear that she will initially require them. She has no job, nor any savings and would find it difficult to get work given the young age of her child and the fact that she has not worked for a number of years. Consequently, she will need to look to Henry for such support but as she is relatively young, she cannot expect there to be a meal ticket for life. The one-third guideline may be an appropriate starting point (*Wachtel v Wachtel (1973)*), giving her an entitlement to periodical payments in excess of £16,000 per annum, although this may be reduced somewhat given Henry's financial obligations for his various children. Assuming that substantial sums can be agreed upon, it will then be necessary to agree the period during which these will be paid. As indicated earlier, it is unlikely that Henry will want to continue to support Wanda indefinitely. However, an immediate clean break would be unfair to Wanda; even if the clean break were to be deferred, it would not be possible to predict her future accurately. Therefore, it might be best to agree that the order can be varied or discharged later in relation to periodical payments for Wanda.

Wanda also needs a home for herself and Jimmy and it does not seem unreasonable to suggest that, whilst Henry can remain in the matrimonial home with his two children, he should raise a lump sum to enable Wanda to buy a small home for herself. Although the home is owned absolutely by Henry, Wanda has contributed during the marriage by paying for the extension, looking after the house and children, and it is right that she should have some share of the family assets. It is also in Henry's interest that his son, Jimmy, should be properly and securely housed. In *White v White (2000)* the House of Lords suggested that any financial resolution considered by the judge should be measured against the yardstick of equality and that equal division should only be departed from if there were good reason, which should be explained by the judge. This should enable her to buy a modest home and is within the range of what Henry could borrow by way of mortgage on his home. However, this increase in Henry's borrowing may mean he is less able to make periodical payments at the level suggested earlier, and so Wanda must be prepared to make some sort of compromise here. It should be pointed out to Henry that by paying for the extension, Wanda could acquire an interest in the house by virtue of her contribution, under Matrimonial Proceedings and Property Act 1970 s 37.

Wanda is being assisted by legal representation paid for by the Community Legal Services Fund. and as such needs to be advised as to the consequences of this. The dire warnings she has received refer to the impact of the statutory charge under *s 10(7)* of the *Access to Justice Act 1999*. This means that if a party retains, recovers or obtains property in the dispute, a charge can lie against that property in respect of the costs of the action to the Legal Aid Fund. This means it is essential to keep costs down by not prolonging the dispute unnecessarily and by seeking to have costs paid by the other side where possible. It may be that

Henry will agree to pay the costs of the negotiations, in which case this should be embodied in the consent order.

If, however, there is a shortfall, then the Community Legal Services Board can seek to recover this by way of the statutory charge. If the property involved was the matrimonial home then the effect of the charge can be postponed until the house is sold. However, interest is payable, as in *Hanlon v The Law Society (1981)*, and eventually the sum must be repaid. The charge does not attach, however, to periodical payments and the first £2,500 of a lump sum. However, Wanda will receive a larger lump sum and the charge would attach to this. However, there is a discretion to postpone the charge if the money is to be used to buy a house. Then the charge is registered against the home and interest is payable by Wanda.

Question 21

Peter and Wendy were divorced eight years ago, when they were both aged 36. Peter was ordered to pay periodical payments of £200 per month for Wendy and £100 per month for each of the couple's two children, Michael, then aged 8 and John aged 6. The former matrimonial home was jointly owned, and an order was made permitting Wendy to remain there until John, the youngest child, was 17. At that point, the house was to be sold and the proceeds divided equally between Peter and Wendy.

At the time of the divorce, Wendy worked part-time, earning £4,000 per year, but one year later Peter was made redundant, and Wendy was forced to work full-time to make ends meet. Peter applied to the court for variation of the order, and the court substituted a nominal order for Wendy and reduced the payments for the children to £50 per month each. Peter worked only occasionally for the following five years and did not obtain employment until he met and married Belle, a wealthy widow. Peter now lives with Belle, and earns £25,000 per year in a job Belle got for him with her father's company. Wendy earns £8,000 per year and has now applied to the court for the last order to be varied so as to obtain substantial periodical payments from Peter. Wendy is also reluctant to sell the matrimonial home, which is worth £120,000 with a £20,000 mortgage.

Peter is annoyed at the prospect of having to continue to support Wendy, and seeks advice as to whether he can be free of future obligations to her.

Advise Peter.

Answer plan

In this case, the original orders for ancillary relief on divorce were made some years ago, and advice is sought on variation. Variation is possible under s 31, but the court can also limit the term for future provision or terminate obligations entirely.

* examine exactly what can and cannot be varied. Only periodical payments in the case; examine those in relation to the children and their father's changing circumstances;
* then examine the case in relation to the spouses and their circumstances.

Answer

This question requires an analysis of the powers of the courts to vary orders that have been made for ancillary relief. The original order, made on divorce, provided for periodical payments for Wendy and the children under MCA 1973 s 23, and a settlement of property order, the so called Mesher order, under MCA 1973 s 24.

These orders would have been made after a consideration of the factors in MCA 1973 s 25 and have already been varied once when Peter became redundant. In order to alter arrangements once more, Wendy has made an application for variation under *MCA 1973 s 31*. The court has power under s 31 to vary periodical payments for a spouse or children of the family, and this may involve increasing or reducing the amount payable. The court must also consider under *s 31(7)* whether to impose a fixed term for which the order will be paid, thereby enabling the payee to readjust before terminating the payer's obligations. It is also possible on variation that the court will terminate the order.

The court cannot order that periodical payments are replaced by a lump sum order for a spouse, although this is possible for a child: *s 31(5)*. This means that the court cannot force Peter to pay a lump sum to Wendy in lieu of periodical payments, although he could, if he wished, negotiate this with Wendy, and their agreement could then be conveyed to the court, who would terminate the periodical payment order after the lump sum is paid, as in *Peacock v Peacock (1991)*. (However, if the financial provisions of the Family Law Act 1996 had been in force the court would have had the power to make compensatory orders in relation to a party, if it ordered a clean break on an application to vary the payments to that party). He would be ill-advised to pay a lump sum in lieu of his periodical payments for the children, as there is always the possibility that the Child Support Agency may intervene later. There is no absolute entitlement to have prior financial generosity taken into account. Instead the payer must apply for a departure direction under the reforms introduced by the *Child Support Act 1995*.

There is no power to vary what are seen by the courts as one-off final settlements, such as lump sums *(s 31(2))*, unless to vary the instalments, or property transfer orders. An order for sale of any property can, however, be varied: *ss 24(A)(1)* and *31(2)(f)*. In the instant case, there were no lump sum orders, and the property was dealt with by way of a Mesher order. Therefore, as there is no power to vary this, both Peter and Wendy will have to wait until John reaches 17 for the house to be sold and proceeds divided. There is no way that the court can order the sale to be postponed or for Wendy's share in the proceeds to be increased: *Carson v Carson (1981)*. Nor can the court order the sale to be brought forward. It would seem that the only variation here would be by consent of both parties.

Consequently, the only aspect of the order that can be varied is the periodical payment part. It seems clear that Wendy wishes to increase this, whereas Peter would like to reduce, and hopefully extinguish, his obligation. The periodical payments for children usually do not extend beyond their seventeenth birthday: *MCA 1973 s 29*. Michael is now aged 16 and John aged 14, therefore, the order in relation to Michael will end shortly. If Michael is working and supporting himself, then Peter could ask the court to end the order earlier than Michael's seventeenth birthday. This increase in his son's income and financial resources would satisfy the change in circumstances normally required for variation: s 31(7). However, if Michael has remained in full-time education, it may be that Peter's liability to maintain him will be extended up to 18, or beyond: *s 29(3)*. The amount payable in respect of Michael and John may also be increased. The court will examine any change in circumstances (s 31(7)), taking into account, any change in the MCA 1973 s 25 factors.

Since the last order was made, Peter has obtained a job, and therefore his income and financial resources have increased. In addition, he has remarried Belle who is wealthy in her own right. Although a court will not make a periodical payment order that would have to be paid by a second spouse (*Macey v Macey (1981)*), the second spouse's resources are relevant in that they free up Peter's income to meet the needs of his first family. Thus, it seems likely that the court would take the view that Peter could afford to increase the periodical payments for his sons who, as they have grown older, have increased needs and costs.

Insofar as Peter's obligations to Wendy are concerned, again his income and resources have improved since the last order. In addition, during the period of his redundancy, Wendy has had to make increased contributions to the welfare of the family, by looking after both boys, working full-time and trying to make ends meet in difficult financial circumstances. The court might well feel that, now Peter's prospects have improved, he should do something to mitigate the drop in Wendy's standard of living. Applying the one-third guideline (*Wachtel v Wachtel (1973)*), which is still of use for middle income families such as Wendy and Peter, it seems that Peter and Wendy have a combined income of £33,000, which should result in Wendy receiving one-third of this, that is £11,000, comprised of her own £8,000 earnings and £3,000 by way of periodical payments from Peter.

Peter's main argument would lie in the fact that Wendy is now working full-time and that since the children are older, she can support herself. The court must consider the desirability of limiting periodical payments to a fixed period of time (*s 31(7)*), to enable the payee, Wendy, to adjust without undue hardship. In the circumstances, it would be harsh immediately to terminate Wendy's order and, in *Whiting v Whiting (1988)*, the Court of Appeal said that a wife's order could be her guarantee against ill health or redundancy in the future. Given that she has shouldered responsibility for financially maintaining the family for the five years of Peter's redundancy, it would not be equitable to allow him to terminate her order now that he has improved his financial position. Even the imposition of a fixed term may not occur, as the courts have shown a marked reluctance to do this: *Hepburn v Hepburn (1989); Fisher v Fisher (1989)*.

In conclusion, it would seem that there is no prospect of varying the Mesher order, but the periodical payments may well be varied. Peter's chances of terminating his obligations seem to be slim.

Question 22

Robert and Susan were divorced after 15 years of marriage. They had four children, now aged 14, 12, 10 and 8. It was agreed between the parties that the two eldest children, both boys, would live with Robert, and the two youngest children, both girls, would live with Susan. Robert has agreed that Susan can remain in the former matrimonial home, now worth £150,000, with an equity of redemption of £120,000. He is also agreeable to paying £800 per month for the support of the youngest children.

However, Robert is unhappy about having to support Susan, who, he feels, could support herself. Susan is now aged 36, and although she has never worked since the marriage, she has developed her own interior design business over the past two years, during which time she has earned £4,000 for the first year and £8,000 for the second year. Susan is sharing the former matrimonial home with Tony, a freelance photographer, but she says they have no intention of marrying. Robert is somewhat suspicious, as his youngest daughter has spoken excitedly of when she will be 'Mummy's bridesmaid'. Tony does not contribute anything towards the household expenses and Susan has said that he only earns £5,000 per year. Again, Robert is suspicious, as he has often seen Tony's photographs in magazines and newspapers, and Tony also drives an expensive new car.

Robert is 40, and earns £50,000 per year as a surveyor. He has set up home in rented accommodation with Vicky and his two children, as well as her child from a previous relationship. Robert intends to marry Vicky.

Advise Robert on his potential financial responsibilities towards Susan, and how these may be met in the most tax efficient way.

Answer

On divorce, the courts have wide powers to order ancillary relief for the parties to the marriage. This can take the form of secured or unsecured periodical payments, lump sum orders (MCA 1973 s 23), and property orders (MCA 1973 s 24). In deciding what kind of order to make, the court will have regard to all the circumstances of the case and the factors mentioned in MCA s 25. In the instant case, the parties have reached agreement on certain matters, which will be taken into account when advising Robert as to his potential liability.

The children in this case are the natural children of both parties, and, as such, Robert's liability to maintain them will be subject to the provisions of the Child Support Act 1991. The provisions of this Act can be avoided at present by the parties reaching agreement by way of consent order, but Robert would be advised to ensure that the level of maintenance he agrees is broadly that which would be awarded under the Act. In addition, if the Child Support Agency do become involved, for example because Susan is in receipt of State benefits, there is no guarantee that account will be taken of any generous financial provision he may have made to Susan on the divorce.It is possible by virtue of the *Child Support Act 1995* amendments to seek a departure direction requiring any transfer of assets to be taken into account. The making of the direction depends upon whether it would be just and equitable in all the circumstances to reduce the payment. It would seem that the £800 per month is reasonably generous, especially since he is maintaining the two older children without contribution from Susan.

The needs of the children of the family are a first consideration under MCA s 25(1). Whilst this is not an overriding consideration, it will be necessary to ensure that, in the redistribution of family assets following divorce, the interests of the children are well served. Both parties need to be able to house themselves and the children in their care, as well as have suitable accommodation for the other children of the family to visit: *Calderbank v Calderbank (1976)*. It seems that the parties have agreed that Susan should remain in the former matrimonial home, although the basis of that occupation has not been determined.

The court will also consider the desirability of a clean break (s 25A(1)), although it will not strive to impose one in unsuitable cases (*Clutton v Clutton (1991)*). Spousal self-sufficiency is to be encouraged, although this can be difficult with children to care for: *Suter v Suter and Jones (1987)*. In Susan's case, her children are of school age and she could well become self-sufficient in the future. The court can impose a limit to the time for which she would receive support although this should only occur where her future independence can be predicted with a degree of certainty (*Barrett v Barrett (1988)*).

Looking at the income, earning capacity and financial resources that the parties have or can reasonably be expected to acquire, it can be seen that Robert earns a large salary of some £50,000 per year. This seems to be the limit of his earning capacity and is not being artificially depressed. In terms of assets, he has his share in the matrimonial home, but it is unclear whether there are any other substantial assets. The home he shares with Vicky is rented, and there are no apparent savings. Vicky's resources are irrelevant in that the court will not make an order that would need to be paid out of a third party's resources. However, her resources may release more of Robert's income to meet the needs of his first family: *Macey v Macey (1981)*.

The *Pensions Act 1995 s 166* alters the s 25 factors to ensure that any pension entitlement that Robert might have acquired is considered as an asset of his, and that any loss of pension rights by Susan is also considered, even though this might not be for some considerable time. The court has the power under the Act to earmark some or all of the pension assets, so that when the pension matures and becomes payable to Robert, it is possible to order that some of the income and or the lump sum are paid to Susan. Obviously this is a deferred benefit to her, which she may or may not live to realise. More radical provision is also possible using the pension splitting provisions of the *Welfare Reform and Pensions Act 1999*. This will enable an order to be made effecting the immediate division of the pension assets between the parties, although such assets will need to be reinvested in new individual pensions.

In examining Susan's means, it is obvious that she is capable of earning money to help support herself; however, the income generated thus so far has been modest. It may be that she has only been working part-time; if so, she might be expected to work longer hours. She is also cohabiting with Tony, and whilst she claims he makes no contribution, his lifestyle would indicate that he is capable of contributing to household expenses, thus freeing more of her income.

Both parties have housing needs that will need to be considered under s 25(2)(b), as well as costs involved in caring for the children. It seems that

Robert will be taking on additional obligations if he marries for the second time, and these obligations must be recognised: *Barnes v Barnes (1972)*. Fortunately, Robert earns a lot of money and should be able to provide for both families.

The standard of living enjoyed by the parties must be considered, and in very wealthy families it may be possible to avoid any drop in such standards: *Calderbank v Calderbank (1976)*. If there is a drop, it should not be borne inequitably: *Preston v Preston (1982)*. This marriage is not of short duration, nor are the parties particularly old or suffering from any disability: s 25(2)(d) and (e). However, the court will look at the contributions each has made and is likely to make to the welfare of the family: s 25(2)(f). Robert has worked throughout the marriage, and Susan has been a supportive wife and mother (*Wachtel v Wachtel (1973)*), and so both have contributed (*White v White (2000)*). Susan has also made a financial contribution in recent years, and the child care burden will fall on them both in the future.

As far as conduct is concerned, only behaviour that it would be inequitable to disregard will be taken into account: s 25(2)(g). This means that most conduct is irrelevant: *Wachtel v Wachtel (1973)*. The parties seem to have drifted apart, and there is little by way of conduct. However, it may be argued that, by allowing Tony into the matrimonial home without requiring him to contribute to costs, Susan establishes the requirement of conduct, as in *Suter v Suter and Jones (1987)*. This could have the effect of reducing Susan's entitlement.

Susan is cohabiting with Tony and has indicated that she has no intention of remarrying. Remarriage is an important consideration when making a consent order or a court order, and a party who remarries having indicated that they have no plans to do so, may well find the order being set aside: *H v H (1975); Livesey v Jenkins (1985)*. Robert should be alerted by his daughter's comments and should not be too keen to make generous property orders in exchange for reduced financial provision, as periodical payments would terminate on Susan's remarriage: *MCA 1973 s 28(1)*.

The matrimonial home is jointly owned, and Robert has agreed that Susan can remain there. Robert has not behaved in such a repugnant or financially irresponsible way that the court would consider depriving him of his interest: *Bryant v Bryant (1976)*. Nor, given the possibility of Susan remarrying, would it be sensible for him to agree to transfer his interest in return for terminating or reducing his periodical payments. Therefore, it would seem appropriate to allow Susan to remain in the house under a Mesher order, that is until she remarries, dies or the youngest child reaches 17, or, more generously, until she dies or remarries, (*Martin BH v Martin BW (1978)*). If Susan did remarry, the house would be sold and the proceeds of sale divided between her and Robert.

This would still mean that Robert may need to make periodical payments, at least initially, to enable Susan to readjust, become more financially self-sufficient or remarry. Robert is earning £50,000 per annum, but has agreed to provide £9,600 for the children. He is also looking after the other two children, Vicky and her daughter, and renting accommodation whilst Susan remains in the matrimonial home. In these circumstances, the one-third guideline, whereby Susan would be awarded periodical payments to bring her up to one-third of their joint incomes, would seem over-generous. Instead, it may be more appropriate to assess Susan's reasonable needs: *Preston v Preston (1982)* although the House of Lords was cited on this approach in relation to capital (*White v White (2000)*). The one-third rule would result in periodical payments in the region of £9,000 to Susan (£50,000 + £8,000 = £58,000 3 = £17,333, less the £8,000 she earns = £9,333), but it is likely that this would be substantially reduced.

In the past there was a tax allowance in respect of qualifying maintenance payments. However, this has been abolished in the Finance Act 2000 and from 5 April 2000 there is no tax relief in respect of maintenance orders made after 5 March 1988.

Question 23

The clean break – fact or fiction?

Discuss with reference to the concept of a clean break and how the Matrimonial Causes Act 1973 achieves it.

Answer plan

Policy of encouraging spousal self-sufficiency:

- difficulties experienced by spouses;
- explain new s 25 and factors to encourage self-sufficiency;
- duty to consider clean break or to limit payments to period;
- power to end obligations on application to vary.

Answer

The Matrimonial and Family Proceedings Act 1984 amended the Matrimonial Causes Act 1973 in a number of respects designed to encourage greater spousal self-sufficiency on divorce. These reforms were intended to meet, in part, criticisms of the existing system which many viewed as placing an ex-wife like a ball and chain around her husband's leg for the rest of his life! It would be a mistake, however, to assume that these provisions make a clean break a routine result in ancillary relief proceedings. This was never the intention of the legislation and, in an economically uncertain climate; it is an unrealistic expectation in most cases.

The Law Commission issued a discussion paper in 1980 to seek views on the financial consequences of divorce and, as a result, in 1981 they issued a report proposing change. It was felt that the change in the basis of divorce from fault-based divorce to that based on irretrievable breakdown meant that it was no longer appropriate to provide continuing lifelong maintenance for an ex-spouse. There had also been a dramatic increase in the number of divorces over the years, and so many divorced people go on to remarry and incur new financial commitments. There was considerable pressure from so-called second families to be relieved of the financial pressures caused by the first family. Many women also worked or had the opportunity to do so, and the concept of man as a lifelong provider for his ex-wife was the subject of much criticism.

The Law Commission did not, however, feel able to recommend a radical alteration to financial provision on divorce and a complete shift to total spousal self-sufficiency in all cases was ruled out. In many families this would not be possible. Women frequently are disadvantaged in employment matters, as they often give up work, or take less demanding work to fit in with family commitments. Where there are children, it is usually the woman who gives up or adapts her career to look after them, and after a divorce most children continue to live with their mother. The demands of child care, and the difficulty of finding flexible employment provide considerable handicaps to a woman's earning capacity. Many women could only work for school hours or must pay considerable costs of child care, and it is unrealistic to expect her to be able to support herself in such circumstances.

Likewise, a woman who has been married for a considerable time and who has been absent from the workplace would find it difficult to be self-supporting. There is considerable age discrimination and an elderly or middle-aged woman would experience difficulty in acquiring a job or retraining and acquiring relevant skills. Nevertheless, there are spouses who could readjust quickly on the termination of marriage and support themselves, and the lack of continuing support obligations may help reduce animosity. The young, childless wife could arguably adjust without hardship, so could a spouse where the family resources are considerable and can be divided and invested to provide an income. Consequently, it was felt desirable that in appropriate cases self-sufficiency should be encouraged.

The new *Matrimonial Causes Act 1973 s 25* attempts to provide the court with the appropriate powers to achieve this, and there are a number of alterations that affect the concept of clean break and financial support for spouses. The first reform is that the old requirement for the court to seek to place the parties, insofar as it is possible, in the position they would have been in if the marriage had not broken down was abolished. This was an unrealistic expectation and financially it is not possible to maintain two families at the same level as when there had been one family. The reformers argued that this was like trying to achieve the impossible, and there was considerable resentment by the spouses, usually husbands, who had been compelled to strive to maintain the ex-spouse in the style to which they had become accustomed.

Second, in considering the financial resources of the spouses under *s 25(2)(a)*, the court must take into account not only the present resources of the parties but also include 'in the case of earning capacity any increase in that capacity which it would . . . be reasonable to expect a party to the marriage to take steps to acquire'. This provision means that spouses will not be able to rely on the fact that they earn nothing or very little at the time of the divorce. The court will look at the spouses and what kind of job they could reasonably be expected to do and with what possible income. In *Mitchell v Mitchell (1984)* a wife's prospects as a trained secretary were taken into account, but the court must be realistic; jobs are not freely available to all who want them, and it would be wrong to set unrealistic expectations for a spouse's potential earning capacity. There are many who cannot find jobs, or who would find retraining difficult. In addition, a spouse who has the care of young children will be further hampered in choice of suitable jobs.

The desirability of clean break is highlighted in *s 25A(1)* where the court is given a duty to consider whether it would be appropriate to order that the financial obligations of the parties towards the other be terminated as soon as is just and equitable. This is a duty to consider a clean break, not to impose it routinely (*Clutton v Clutton (1991)*), where the Court of Appeal recognised that a clean break is often inappropriate and unfair. It was thought initially that the presence of children would make a clean break impossible (*Suter v Suter and Jones (1987)*), and this has been highlighted by the controversy surrounding the Child Support Act 1991, whereby any arrangements made, including generous clean break provisions, were disregarded in assessing the father's financial liability for his children. Although the *Child Support Act 1995* allows the payer to apply for a departure direction, such payments will not automatically be taken into account; it will depend on whether it would be just and equitable to do so. Consequently, consent orders enacting clean breaks will be more infrequent, and the court will no doubt bear this in mind in considering whether to impose a clean break. The older wife is also in a precarious financial position and is often an unsuitable candidate for a clean break (*Scallon v Scallon (1990)*) unless there is sufficient family wealth to settle some capital to provide an income (*Duxbury v Duxbury (1987)*).

If the court decides to provide maintenance for a spouse, then it is given an additional duty under *s 25A(2)* to consider whether it would be appropriate to award maintenance for a limited period only (*Parlour v Parlour (2004)*). This would then in theory allow the spouse to adjust without undue financial hardship. In practice, however, there are still many women who could not readjust with any degree of certainty because, for example, they are too old (*Morris v Morris (1985)*), or because there are very young children (*Suter v Suter and Jones (1987)*). It is arguably dangerous to make a limited order in respect of a woman with no job, and for whom the future is uncertain. However, a limited order might be advantageous to a man, who could then plan his own future, and possibly a second family, with more certainty. Thus a limited order might be desirable where the woman has reasonable prospects of readjusting, but with the safety net of applying for a variation by way of an extension if her plans do not work out.

The final power that the court has is under *s 25A(3)* which is to completely end all further financial obligations of the spouses to one another, including applications under the Inheritance (Provision for Family and Dependants) Act 1975. This power could be used where it is considered desirable to remove the possibility of a spouse claiming increased provision in the future. It will be exercised rarely, for instance, in cases where a generous financial solution has already been agreed or in special cases, such as *Seaton v Seaton (1986)*, where the severe disability of one spouse and the inability of the other to improve his quality of life led to a termination of obligations.

The Law also encourages a clean break by its introduction of the concept of pension splitting, which will divide up pension assets at the time, rather than earmarking provisions as contained in the *Pensions Act 1995*, which will still link the parties to one another. This has been enacted in the *Welfare Reform and Pensions Act 1999*, but the complex procedures and the financial reality of pension splitting mean this is only worthwhile where the pension holder has built up a sizeable pension fund.

Emotionally, most divorcing couples would prefer a clean break However, the financial uncertainty of the present economic climate has left many spouses in difficult financial positions, with future predictability very unclear. Although the clean break is desirable in that it encourages self-sufficiency and, arguably, reduces animosity, it is not the solution for most divorcing couples. The English system is following that of some American States where spousal support is not awarded.

In most situations the clean break will be an unattainable ideal, rendered even more unlikely by the provisions of the Child Support legislation, which acts as a disincentive for many men.

Question 24

Ursula and Vincent have been married for 32 years. Six years ago Vincent began a relationship with his secretary, Wendy and after six months he moved in with her. Vincent and Wendy now have two children, Yvonne and Zachery, aged 4 and 2. Vincent has decided that he would like to divorce Ursula and marry Wendy. Wendy is opposed to the divorce. She is Roman Catholic and feels that divorce is wrong. She also believes that eventually Vincent will tire of Wendy and return to her.

When Ursula and Vincent got married, she was a primary school teacher and he worked as a photographer. Vincent wanted to set out on his own and the couple rented a small shop. At weekends and during the evenings, Ursula would help him as his assistant and she would drive him to assignments. After two years, Vincent decided to enter some of his photographs in a national competition. He won and suddenly became a very sought after and fashionable photographer. He was able to move to better premises in a more exclusive area and to take on staff. About this time, the couple also had the first of their six children. Ursula decided to leave her job and become a full-time housewife and mother. She was often on her own as Vincent spent a lot of time abroad on fashion shoots. The couple's youngest child, currently aged eight, is autistic.

Over the years, Vincent's career has gone from strength to strength. He not only makes a lot of money from photography itself but he now is in demand as a celebrity himself. In all, his income per annum is £450000. Fifteen years ago, Vincent brought a penthouse flat in London which is now worth £2.5 million. Ursula and the children still live in the family home which has been valued at £3.5 million.

Advise Ursula, on the divorce and the ancillary relief for her.

Question plan

Can Ursula prevent the divorce?

If they do get divorced what sort of financial relief will she be entitled to? The welfare of any children of the family would be the court's first consideration. What contributions have Vincent and Ursula made to the marriage, in particular the answer should consider the impact of cases such as White, Parlour and Lambert. Why is a clean break not appropriate? Note, the question is about financial relief for Ursula, therefore child maintenance does not need to be discussed.

Answer

In order to obtain a divorce, Vincent will have to prove that his marriage to Ursula has broken down irretrievably and that one of the five facts in the Matrimonial Causes Act 1973 s 1 is satisfied. On the facts it seems that Vincent has been living with Wendy for five and half years, and therefore he could use five years separation without consent. However, Ursula may try and prevent the divorce under section 5 of the Matrimonial Causes Act claiming that, as a Roman Catholic, it would cause her grave hardship to be divorced. It is unlikely though that her claim would be successful. Cases such (*Rukat v Rukat (1975)*) suggest that claims under section 5 are rarely successful. It is probable that the court would allow the divorce and therefore the next issue to discuss is financial relief.

The court will use section 25 of the MCA to determine financial relief. According to the section 25(1), the court's main consideration is the welfare of the children. Given that the couple have been married for over 30 years it is likely that some of their children are now adults and would no longer be a consideration for the court, but their youngest child (and possibly some others) are still minors and therefore they would be the court's first consideration. Furthermore, the fact that the youngest child is autistic is likely to be significant. Having a disabled child may make it more difficult for Ursula to obtain work outside the home. In addition, it might be that Ursula could argue that she and her children need the stability of being able to remain in the family home.

The court will look at the couple's contributions to the marriage – *Matrimonial Causes Act 1973 s 25(2)(f)*. Vincent has been the breadwinner. Thanks to his hugely successful photography business he has been able to provide the couple with a very high standard of living. Ursula has been the homemaker and mother. In the leading case of *White* (2000), the House of Lords were clear that there should be no distinction between the two types of contribution. Applied to the facts this would mean that Ursula's contribution could be assessed as being as valuable as that of Vincent. However in *Cowan* (2001) the Court of Appeal allowed the husband a greater share of the couple's wealth because his business acumen and design skills meant that he had make an extraordinary contribution. Applied to the facts, perhaps Vincent could argue that his particular skills should mean that he should be allowed a greater share. On the other hand, Ursula could argue that she showed particular talent as a homemaker during the times when Vincent was absent, and that her contribution also included helping with the business in the early days. In any case, the later case of *Lambert v Lambert* (2002) suggests that contributions should be assessed equally in part because unfair as homemaker difficult to show special contribution. It is also worth noting that Ursula will not be restricted to her reasonable requirements.

The facts state that Vincent now has two children with Wendy. Although these children will not be the court's main consideration under *s 25(1)*, under s 25(2)(b) the court will take account of Vincent's need to maintain these children. Another important factor is the earning capacity of Vincent and Ursula. Thanks to his talent and high profile, Vincent looks to enjoy continued professional success. Ursula, on the other hand, has had her more modest career interrupted, and it is likely that it would prove more difficult for her to find financially rewarding employment that would fit around the demands of caring for a disabled child. The court would also consider the fact that this has been a long marriage.

Having identified relevant factors in MCA 1973 s 25, it is now possible to suggest how a court might deal with ancillary relief in this question. The facts state that Ursula and the children are currently living in the family home. It would be appropriate to transfer this home outright to Ursula. This provides the children with security and it is not unduly harsh on Vincent as he could keep the penthouse.

Under *s 25A of the Matrimonial Causes Act 1973*, the court would also have to consider whether a clean break would be appropriate. In this case, it is unlikely that a clean break would be appropriate because the marriage has lasted a long time and because the couple still have children who need care. As a clean break is not appropriate, it is likely that the court would also award Ursula periodic payments.

Question 25

The Use of Mediation has Enabled Divorcing Couples to Decide on their Financial Relief Fairly and Cheaply – Discuss.

Answer plan

- How is mediation involved in the divorce procedure – Part III of FLA, Access to Justice Act 1999.
- Advantages of Mediation.
- Problems.
- Is it cheaper.

Outline answer

Although, the planned divorce reforms in the Family Law Act 1996 have not been implemented, Part III of that Act, which concerned mediation, has. According to Part III anyone who was obtaining legal aid funding for their divorce would be required to consider whether mediation would be suitable in their case. *Part III of the Family Law Act 1996* is now to be found in the Access to Justice Act 1999.

The Government support mediation because it is seen as a less acrimonious way of resolving financial relief and it is cheaper for the State to fund that legal advice. It is suggested that parties will know their circumstances and requirements better than a lawyer or judge, and therefore any agreement which they reach through mediation is more likely to be effective than one imposed on them by lawyers. Moreover, it might be that individual who has been involved in mediation and has had a say in the settlement is more likely to accept that settlement than someone who feels that the financial relief has been imposed on them.

On the other hand, it is clear that mediation will not always be effective or fair. The Government advice recognises that there are some situations where mediation would not be appropriate because of the risk of one party being intimidated by the other. The obvious example of this is a marriage where there has been domestic violence. In such a case, it is probable that one update could be intimidated and mediation would not be effective. Nevertheless, there are other, less evident, cases where mediation may also not be appropriate. What if during the marriage one spouse has worked, whilst the other has stayed at home, it is possible that the employed spouse may be more confident, or may have developed negotiating skills that will help during mediation.

Another problem, is that whilst courts are bound by the considerations in s 25 of the Matrimonial Causes Act to reach a settlement that is fair and puts the interests of children first, the same is not true of mediating parties. It is possible that a spouse could accept a settlement through mediation that is considerably less than a court would have awarded him or her.

In addition, evidence suggests that even when a spouse does use mediation to decide on their financial relief, they still employ a lawyer. This is perhaps not surprising, as for many individuals going through a divorce their main concern will be to protect their interests rather than to reach what is objectively a fair compromise.

Another problem is that mediation was initially intended to operate within the framework of Part II of the Family Law Act 1996, instead because that provision has not been introduced, mediation has instead been grafted on to the MCA 1973.

CHAPTER 5

PROPERTY DISPUTES

INTRODUCTION

It is necessary for students of family law to be able to use their knowledge of property law principles to resolve disputes between people over ownership of property. If the persons are not divorcing, then the court has no discretionary powers under the Matrimonial Causes Act (MCA) 1973; instead, the dispute must be resolved according to normal property law rules.

Many disputes centre on the home, which is often, in examination questions, owned by one party, yet the other party claims to be entitled to a share. In such a situation, mention should be made of the legal interests and then the case should be examined to see if there is any valid declaration of a trust which would give a beneficial entitlement. Usually, however, there will be none, and it will be necessary to see if there is an implied, resulting or constructive trust.

Essentially, there needs to be evidence of a common intention to share, and detrimental acts by the party seeking an interest. After *Lloyds Bank v Rosset (1991)*, you must examine critically what will amount to evidence of a common intention to share, although a slightly more flexible approach to quantifying the amount of such an interest is suggested in the case of *Midland Bank v Cooke (1995)*. Courts have now decided that when determining the proportion of each parties' share they should look to all the circumstances (*Oxley v Hiscock (2004), Cox v Jones (2004)*).

There is the additional possibility that an interest may be acquired or enlarged by virtue of *Matrimonial Proceedings and Property Act 1970 s 37*.

Some examination questions may also require you to consider equitable estoppel and contractual licences. Many questions require students to consider what protection, if any, the law gives to a party who has a beneficial entitlement. The Land Registration Act 1925 and the concept of overriding interest in *s 70(1)(g)* should be considered, as well as the provisions in *s 14* of the Trusts of Land and Appointment of Trustees Act 1996 for ordering a sale when there is a dispute.

Section 1 of the Married Women's Property Act 1964, concerning things bought and savings made from housekeeping allowances, provides that such property belongs to both parties equally. There is also the Law Reform (Miscellaneous Provisions) Act 1970, which deals with engagement rings.

Question 26

The marriage between Michael and Sarah has encountered difficulties, and the couple have decided to part amicably. They are both keen to go their separate ways with no financial responsibilities towards each other, and so they propose to divide their assets according to their beneficial entitlements in property law. They do not want the court to impose an arrangement under the MCA 1973.

Advise Michael and Sarah on their beneficial entitlement to the following:

(a) On their engagement, Michael gave Sarah an antique diamond ring, worth £5,000 that belonged to his grandmother,

(b) £20,000 invested in a building society savings account, which is held in joint names,

(c) Shares to the value of £6,000 registered in Michael's name, but paid for with a cheque drawn on the couple's joint bank account,

(d) The matrimonial home, registered in Sarah's name. The initial deposit of £20,000 was paid by Sarah with money from an inheritance, but the mortgage instalments have been met from the joint bank account. Michael spent every weekend for a whole year renovating the property and carrying out all the interior design. The house was purchased for £100,000 five years ago, and is now worth £150,000. The outstanding mortgage is £20,000.

Answer plan

It is clear that the couple do not want an MCA 1973 solution to their problems, and so normal property law rules apply.

- the engagement ring: look at *Law Reform (Miscellaneous Provisions) Act 1970 s 3* – likely that she will keep it;

- the money invested in a joint account: arguably used as a common fund – presumption that jointly owned;

- the shares bought from the account: conflict between presumption that jointly owned and argument that each individual can buy for himself;

- the matrimonial home is registered in Sarah's name only – she has legal entitlements. Examine if beneficial entitlement by way of implied, resulting or constructive trust, and consider Matrimonial Proceedings and Property Act 1970 s 37.

Answer

(a) The position of engagement rings is often determined by reference to s 3 of the Law Reform (Miscellaneous Provisions) Act 1970. This section provides that the gift of an engagement ring should be assumed to be an absolute gift but the presumption may be rebutted by proving that the ring was given on the implied condition that it should be returned if the marriage did not take place for any reason. In the instant case Michael and Sarah have gone on to marry. However, the presumption that a man has given a woman a gift in such a situation would be very strong. The diamond ring, however, is quite valuable and has been a family heirloom; so in order for it to belong to Michael rather than Sarah it would be necessary for Michael to show that the presumption of advancement has been rebutted by a contrary intention. This contrary intention needs to be that he only intended the ring to be a conditional gift upon the marriage subsisting. It is easier to show in the case of a valuable family heirloom but nonetheless, the presumption that this is a gift appears to be quite strong and on balance it would seem that Sarah is entitled to keep the ring.

(b) Money invested in a joint savings account may cause difficulty in that it will often depend on the intention of the parties and their respective contributions as to who is entitled and in what proportion. In the instant case, the parties have contributed to the savings account but little is known as to what arrangements they made for withdrawing from the savings account. Where money is invested in a joint account there is an argument that the money should be regarded as jointly owned. In *Jones v Maynard (1951)* both husband and wife contributed to the account just as Michael and Sarah have done. In that case, as in the present, both paid in their various earnings and funds and, although the husband paid in more than the wife, it did seem that they viewed the account as a common savings account. The argument would be that this is a joint account and that they are therefore both equally entitled since they viewed it as a common pool. There is no evidence that they merely intended the shares to reflect their contributions.

(c) The shares purchased for £6,000 which are registered in Michael's name only were purchased with a cheque drawn on the couple's joint account. If the case of *Jones v Maynard* (1951) were to be followed then the shares would be jointly owned since the investments could be regarded as joint investments and merely a continuance of their arrangements for the joint account. However, there is an argument that if both were entitled to draw on the account to purchase whatever they wished to by way of investments or chattels, then each separate investment or chattel should be regarded as belonging to the person who made the investment or purchase of the chattel as in *Re Bishop (Deceased) (1965)*. If that were the case then the shares would be owned by Michael absolutely since they are registered and purchased in his name. If, however, they could regard it as an extension of the joint account then the shares would be jointly owned.

(d) The former matrimonial home is registered in Sarah's name only. This declaration of legal title in the conveyance would conclusively establish that Sarah is the sole legal owner unless it can be established that there is fraud or mistake (*Goodman v Gallant (1986)*). There is no evidence that there has been any separate declaration of a beneficial entitlement in favour of Michael and an interest under a trust must be created and evidenced in writing. However, it is possible that Michael may have an interest in the home by way of some resulting implied or constructive trust. The initial deposit of £20,000 was paid by Sarah and the mortgage instalments have been met from the joint account. Michael has renovated the property and carried out interior design. It is necessary to examine to what extent, if any, Michael has acquired or enlarged his interest in the home. To acquire an interest under a resulting, implied or constructive trust it will be necessary to show that there is a common intention between the parties that, although Sarah has the legal entitlement, Michael has a beneficial interest in the home. It will also be necessary to show that Michael, as the owner of the beneficial interest, has acted to his detriment based on this common intention. Michael has not made any direct contribution towards the deposit; however, it is arguable that he has made contributions towards the mortgage instalments. The couple have had a joint bank account which they have regarded as a common pool and both have paid into the account their salaries and both have made various drawings on the account. This would seem to provide evidence of a direct contribution as required in *Lloyds Bank v Rosset (1991)*, which would thereby establish an interest on behalf of Michael. His contributions do appear to be substantial in terms of meeting the mortgage requirements and it seems that the £80,000 mortgage that was initially required has reduced to some £20,000 outstanding now. Therefore, if one could argue that there is a joint contribution to the mortgage instalments then Michael will acquire some kind of interest in the home. There is the further possibility that this interest may have been enlarged by his efforts each weekend, renovating and designing the interior of the home.

According to *Lloyds Bank v Rosset* (1991) the only way that this contribution would suffice would be if it were to be substantial in money or money's worth to the improvement of the property. In *Lloyds Bank* itself the wife's decorating and supervision of workmen was insufficient to give rise to an interest. In Michael's case, much would depend upon the extent of the renovations that he carried out. The interior design really would be superfluous. However, the renovation and the amount of impact that is made on the transformation of the property would determine whether this would give or enlarge any interest in the home. Following *Lloyds Bank v Rosset* (1991), caution must be exercised in trying to give an interest under this head. The cases of *Cooke v Head (1972)* and *Eves v Eves (1975)* illustrate just how substantial the work must be in order to qualify under this head. However, there is the possibility that if Michael does not acquire an interest under a trust by virtue of this work he may nevertheless enlarge his interest in the home by reference to *s 37* of the *Matrimonial Proceedings and Property Act 1970*. This section provides that where a husband or wife contributes in money or money's worth to the improvement of property in which, or in the proceeds of sale of which, either or both of them have the beneficial interest, the person who contributes shall, if the contribution is of a substantial nature and subject to any agreement to the contrary, be treated as having acquired by virtue of his contribution a share or an enlarged share. The extent of such a share is the extent that the court considers just and equitable.

Here it could be argued that Michael has contributed to the improvement of the property. His work can be measured in money or money's worth; he has spent every weekend for a substantial period of time; and it does seem to be the sort of work that would normally be paid for if done by someone else. The question is, then, whether the work is of a substantial nature. Ordinary everyday do-it-yourself and common repairs to property should not suffice to enlarge Michael's interest. However, if the work has been substantial and has improved the house then he ought to be entitled to enlarge his share. The enlarged share must not be negatived by any agreement by the spouses and the court has a discretion in deciding to what extent Michael's share will be increased.

In conclusion, therefore, the house is now valued at £150,000 with a mortgage outstanding of £20,000; this leaves equity of £130,000 in the house. The initial deposit of £20,000 by Sarah represents one-fifth of the original value of the home; the remaining four-fifths was contributed to by both parties in paying the mortgage and since their intention appears to have been that they should require a joint interest by so doing, the mortgage contributions will be split two-fifths to Michael, two-fifths to Sarah. This would give Michael a two-fifths share in the equity and Sarah three-fifths share in the equity. However, some adjustment may need to be made for the improvement effected by Michael's renovations and on balance it would seem that the couple would more or less be jointly entitled to any proceeds of sale.

In *Midland Bank v Cooke (1995)* it was stressed that it is important to establish an interest under a constructive trust by reference to the strict rules in *Gissing v Gissing (1971)* and *Lloyds Bank v Rosset (1991)*. However, once the common intention to share can be shown by reference to those rules, as it can in this case, then, in quantifying the shares of the parties, the court can take into account the whole history of the relationship, including behaviour and contributions that would not suffice in themselves to create the interest in the first place. Thus, whilst Michael's renovations would not suffice as evidence of a common intention giving rise to a constructive trust, they can be referred to so as to determine the size of the shares the parties intended. This arguably reinforces the argument that the parties should have more or less equal shares here.

Question 27

Arthur and Guinevere married 16 years ago, and they have three children, aged 12, 10 and 8. The matrimonial home, Camelot, was bought when they married, with a deposit of £3,000 provided by Arthur's parents as a wedding present, and the remaining £27,000 paid by mortgage. The house was registered in Arthur's name only. Guinevere worked briefly before the children were born, and has worked as a teacher since the youngest child started school. The mortgage instalments were paid from a joint bank account into which both Arthur and Guinevere paid their salaries. Two years ago, Guinevere used £3,000 she won in a competition to re-decorate and re-carpet the house.

The mortgage on the house was virtually paid off when Arthur decided to go into business on his own. He borrowed £50,000 from the Westland Bank and secured the loan on the home, without Guinevere's knowledge. The business failed; Arthur defaulted on the mortgage, and has left Guinevere.

The Westland Bank is seeking to evict Guinevere from Camelot, and she does not wish to leave.

Advise Guinevere on:

(a) her property rights, if any, in Camelot,

(b) whether the bank will be successful in evicting her.

Answer plan

(a) Examination of property entitlement will be under normal rules of property law, not MCA 1973.

- She has no legal entitlement, so must examine beneficial entitlement. Was there a common intention to share any detrimental acts by Guinevere? Look at deposit, contributions to mortgage from bank account, and the use of the competition prize.

- Also consider s 37 Matrimonial Proceedings and Property Act 1970.

(b) The way of protecting her interest would be by relying on s 70(1)(g) Land Registration Act 1925, to claim an overriding interest that binds the bank. However, it would then be necessary to consider the provisions of s 14 Trusts of Land and Appointment of Trustees Act 1996 whereby the bank could apply to sell the property.

Answer

Guinevere is seeking advice on her property rights, if any, in Camelot, the matrimonial home. Normally, on the breakdown of a marriage, a spouse would be better served by seeking a financial settlement under the wide powers of the Matrimonial Causes Act 1973. However, in the instant case, these powers could only resolve the financial situation between Arthur and Guinevere on divorce. Guinevere's most immediate problem concerns her possible eviction by the bank who are her husband's creditors. Her best chance of avoiding or postponing this is if she can show that she has an entitlement in property law to the home, or part of it. This may then possibly be enforceable against the bank.

Any such interest must be determined according to strict rules of property law (*Pettitt v Pettitt (1970)*), with no room for the court to order what seems fair in the circumstances. On the facts, it is clear that Guinevere has no legal interest in the property which is registered in Arthur's name only. The original conveyance will be conclusive unless it can be shown that there was fraud or mistake: *Goodman v Gallant (1986)*. Consequently, there is no legal or beneficial entitlement evidenced in the conveyance. There does not appear to be any subsequent declaration of trust either, since that must be writing (Law of Property Act 1925 s 53(1)(b); Law of Property (Miscellaneous Provisions) Act 1989 s 2). Therefore, any beneficial entitlement on Guinevere's part must be by way of implied, resulting or constructive trust, which does not need to comply with formalities.

Although technically there are legal differences between these three different kinds of trust, the courts frequently make no attempt to distinguish (*Gissing v Gissing (1971)*), since the basic requirements of the trusts are the same. Such trusts require evidence of a common intention to share an interest in the property, together with detrimental acts by the party seeking the beneficial interest. The technical distinctions between the trusts arise in how such a common intention is established, or deemed to exist, by the courts.

Often a common intention is established by pointing to a direct contribution made by a party towards the acquisition of the home. This may be the provision of a deposit or part of a deposit, or by paying some of the mortgage. Such a contribution would tend to show an intention to share, unless it could be argued to be a loan, *Sekhon v Alissa (1989)*. The amount of the share is usually in proportion to the parties' respective contributions (*Cowcher v Cowcher (1972)*), unless the contrary intention can be shown. In the present case, the initial deposit came from Arthur's parents as a wedding present to the couple. Wedding presents do not always belong to the couple jointly; it depends on the intention of the donor (*Kilner v Kilner (1939)*). Arthur's parents could arguably be said to be providing a gift for them both to share. In *McHardy & Sons v Warren (1994)* the Court of Appeal held, in a case such as Arthur's

119

and Guinevere's, that where the husband's parents had provided a deposit as a wedding gift, there was a common intention to give the wife a beneficial interest. Somewhat surprisingly, the Court of Appeal held that this gave her a half-share with her husband, not just in the proportion of the home that the deposit represented, but in the whole home! This case would benefit Guinevere enormously, but has been subject to criticism since it would enable the wife to defeat a creditor's claim.

In addition to the deposit, it seems that the mortgage instalments have been paid from a joint bank account, into which both parties paid their salaries. Although there was a period during which Guinevere did not work, it can be argued that by their behaviour the parties have provided evidence of a joint enterprise. They both placed all their income into this account for their joint use and benefit, and neither has reserved any individual interest (*Chapman v Chapman (1969)*). This would reinforce the argument that they have equal joint interests.

Guinevere has made the further investment of her £3,000 competition prize to redecorate the house and buy new carpets. This would be an indirect contribution, and likely, following *Lloyds Bank v Rosset (1991)*, to be inadequate since it is not substantial. Minor redecoration and the buying of household goods does not acquire or enlarge an interest at common law: *Pettitt v Pettitt (1970)*. Neither will her contribution as wife and mother assist her: *Burns v Burns (1984)*.

The only other way in which Guinevere may increase her interest is by way of *Matrimonial Proceedings and Property Act 1970 s 37*. This is available to spouses only and she must show that she has made a substantial contribution in money or money's worth to the improvement of the home. On the facts, although £3,000 is a lot of money, it will not have added much, if anything, to the value of the property, since it was used to pay for things that improve the quality of life for the occupier, rather than increase the value of the property. Only if the property had been very run down or possibly derelict would she succeed.

It therefore seems likely that Guinevere would be able to establish a beneficial interest in the property, possibly in equal share with Arthur. Applying the principle in *Midland Bank v Cooke (1995)* the whole of the history of the relationship and the parties conduct and contributions can be looked at to determine the size of shares intended. Thus, once Guinevere establishes an interest under a trust according to the strict rules in *Gissing v Gissing (1971)* and *Lloyds Bank v Rosset (1991)*, she could argue that there was an intention that they should have equal shares. However, she should be advised that the courts will scrutinise carefully any such claim which would have the effect of depriving a third party creditor of his rights: *Midland Bank v Dobson (1986)*.

(b) It seems, as above, that Guinevere has a beneficial interest in the home. However, the Westland Bank have made a mortgage advance to Arthur which they now wish to recover. It therefore depends on whether the bank are bound by Guinevere's interest. In the case of registered land, the bank take free of interests that are not registered, unless the interest is an overriding interest: *LRA 1925 s 70*. Guinevere's interest may be overriding because of her occupation of the home

(*LRA s 70(1)(g)*), and will bind the bank unless they made enquiry which did not disclose her interest (*Williams & Glyn's Bank v Boland (1981)*). She and the children were clearly in occupation, which does not necessarily need to be continuous or exclusive: *Kingsnorth Finance v Tizard (1986)*. Any bank lending to a man should make enquiries of the existence of a spouse and be alerted to the possibility of her having an interest.

Thus, it would seem that the bank are bound by her interest. It is then necessary to see if the bank could force a sale of the property. The bank have a charge on the property, but have not, as yet, declared Arthur bankrupt. The appropriate provision is *s 14* of the *Trusts of Land and Appointment of Trustees Act 1996* and the court will make such order as it feels is just and reasonable in the circumstances of the case. The court will look at the interests of the creditors, and the conduct of the spouse, Guinevere, in contributing to the situation. In the present case, the Bank have behaved somewhat rashly by granting a mortgage to Arthur without seeking Guinevere's consent and Guinevere has not contributed to the bankruptcy situation. She clearly needs a roof over her head and those of the children, and does not appear to have any substantial resources that would enable her to rehouse herself. The children are still young and need a stable home and this is a genuine case of Guinevere having a real interest, not just a sham arrangement to defeat creditors. In the present case, Guinevere should be able to resist the order for sale, at least whilst the children are still young. However, the courts do not lightly entertain s 14 applications that will leave genuine creditors without recourse. Therefore, it is still possible that a court, depending on the value of the home, might order a sale, since Guinevere's half share might be sufficient for her to rehouse herself.

In *Mortgage Corp v Shaire (2000)* the judge thought that s 14 had altered the law in favour of the family vis à vis the creditor. It was stated that a distinction could be drawn between orders for sale in favour of a creditor in bankruptcy situations, where the creditor was likely to succeed, and orders for sale in favour of a bank or building society which has a charge over the property, and is protected in the long term, where the family might have a greater chance. This greater flexibility may be necessary to enable the courts to comply with the **Human Rights Act 1998**. *Article 8* of the European Convention confers the right to respect for family and private life, and by automatically ordering a sale of the home against the wishes of a blameless spouse there may be a violation.

Question 28

Eric and Elsie were married 40 years ago, and lived in a house purchased by Eric with a deposit of £300, the remaining mortgage of £3,000 being paid by Eric over the following 25 years. The house is now valued at £90,000 and is registered in Eric's sole name. Elsie worked for the first eight years of the marriage, using her earnings to pay all the household expenses, which Eric could not otherwise have afforded. She did not work while the two children of the marriage were small, but has worked for the past 20 years. Elsie's earnings have been used by the couple for household expenses, to install central heating, and recently to add a conservatory to the back of the house.

Eric has just died, leaving all his property to Freda, his secret mistress. Advise Elsie on what her beneficial entitlement is, if any, to the matrimonial home, and how, if at all, her position may be improved.

Answer plan

The question involves a discussion of Elsie's property law entitlement to a share in the home. She will again need to rely on trust principles and/or Matrimonial Proceedings and Property Act 1970 s 37.

Section 14 of the Trusts of Land and Appointment of Trustees Act 1996 must be considered in case Freda applies for a sale.

Further attention should be paid to the Inheritance (Provision for Family and Dependants Act) 1975 as it applies to applications by a spouse of the deceased.

Answer

In the present case, since Eric has died, Elsie's entitlement in the matrimonial home will need to be determined by reference to the ordinary rules of property law. There is no power for the court to order what it considers just and equitable under the *Matrimonial Causes Act 1973*. Instead, Elsie's entitlement to the home or a share of it *vis à vis* her husband's mistress, Freda, will be determined strictly according to the property law entitlement of both women: *Pettitt v Pettitt (1970)*. The legal interest in the property was registered in Eric's name only, and consequently would pass on his death according to his will. The original conveyance in Eric's name would be conclusive as to legal entitlement in the absence of fraud (*Goodman v Gallant (1986)*), and this would pass to Freda if Eric's will is valid. There is no documentary evidence of legal or beneficial entitlement for Elsie, either in the original conveyance or in any subsequent written document: *LPA 1925 s 53(1)(b); LP (MP) A 1989 s 2*.

Consequently, Elsie will only be entitled to the property if she can establish an interest under an implied, resulting or constructive trust, since no formal requirements are necessary in such cases.

The basic requirements of these trusts are the same (*Gissing v Gissing (1971)*), and the courts tend to ignore the technical distinctions between them. There must be a common intention to share an interest in the property, and the party seeking the beneficial interest, Elsie, must show she acted to her detriment.

The usual method of sharing a common intention is to point to a direct contribution to the purchase and acquisition of the property. In the present case, Elsie did not pay the deposit, nor did she pay any mortgage instalments. However, for the first eight years of the marriage, her earnings paid for household expenses, thereby enabling Eric to pay the mortgage, which he otherwise could not have afforded. This is arguably sufficient to show a common intention (*Hazell v Hazell (1972)*), since, without her contribution, there was no way that Eric could have bought the house. However, Elsie only contributed for eight years initially, and then for the last 20 years of the marriage she paid household expenses. For the last 20 years, however, it appears that Eric could manage financially without her paying household expenses. Following *Lloyds Bank v Rosset (1991)*, it is unlikely that the mere payment of household expenses amounts to a sufficiently substantial indirect contribution by Elsie. These could easily be discharged without a common intention that she should acquire or enlarge her share by so doing. There is no evidence of any express agreement by Eric and Elsie that her contributions would acquire her an interest (*Eves v Eves (1975)*), and so, consequently, the second period of contribution will be disregarded.

Elsie may also argue that she has contributed by installing central heating and a conservatory. *Lloyds Bank v Rosset* (1991) requires that such contributions should be substantial. In *Re Nicolson (Decd) (1974)*, the installation of central heating was felt to be substantial, and a conservatory may make a substantial contribution to the improvement of the property. Thus, it should be possible to evidence the common intention to share by reference to Elsie's first eight years' contributions, the central heating and conservatory.

Clearly these show that Elsie acted to her detriment, and so she should have a beneficial entitlement to a share in the home. In assessing the size of the share, *Midland Bank v Cooke (1995)* suggests that the whole history of the relationship can be examined to determine what size share the parties intended. This may mean that other aspects of Elsie's behaviour which were insufficient to create an interest may, nevertheless, be referred to at this second stage to give her a larger share of the home, possibly as much as one-half.

There is the further possibility of relying on *Matrimonial Proceedings and Property Act 1970 s 37* to argue that the central heating and conservatory amount to a substantial contribution in money or money's worth to the improvement of the home. This would enlarge her original interest from her eight years' contributions.

123

Once Elsie establishes an interest in the home, this will bind Freda. Elsie is in actual occupation of the home and by virtue of *LRA 1925 s 70(1)(g)* she has an overriding interest which would bind any subsequent purchaser. There will be no possibility of Freda arguing she was unaware of Elsie's existence, and since Freda is not a bona fide purchaser she will inherit the property subject to Elsie's interest.

Technically, they would both have interests under a trust for sale, and Freda might apply to the court for an order for sale under *s 14* of the *Trusts of Land and Appointment of Trustees Act 1996*. The court can make such order as it sees fit in the circumstances of the case. An examination of Elsie's interests and the purpose of the trust, which had been to provide a home for Elsie and Eric, will be made, and the court will need to consider whether to order a sale and divide the proceeds between the two women.

If Elsie considers that her share under property law is inadequate, she may consider an application to the court under the *Inheritance (Provision for Family and Dependents) Act 1975*.

The wife of the deceased may apply and must show that her husband's will failed to provide reasonable financial provision for her. This is an objective determination, and does not depend upon what her husband Eric wished or thought reasonable. *Section 1(2)(a)* provides that the court must consider whether the financial provision made is reasonable in the circumstances, whether or not the provision is required for the spouse's maintenance. In the present case, no provision has been made for Elsie and even though she may be working, and capable of supporting herself, it seems likely that no reasonable provision has been made.

The general view of the provisions of the Act is that they are designed to ensure that the spouse of the deceased is in a similar position on death as she would have been on divorce: *Re Besterman (Decd) (1984)*.

Section 3(1) provides for a number of factors to be considered, including the resources of the applicant and other beneficiaries, the size and nature of the estate, and any other relevant matter, including the conduct of the applicant. Little is known of Freda's position and financial dependence on Eric, but Elsie appears to have been a devoted and supportive wife for 40 years, and entitled to some provision from Eric's estate. For a spouse, the length and age of the spouse and their contribution to the welfare of the family must also be examined: *s 3(2)*. Elsie has for many years worked, looked after the home and children, and this would ensure she receives the provision she deserves. This would mean that she could obtain an order giving her a larger share in the home, or even allowing her to remain there until her death (*Harrington v Gill (1983)*). Little is known about whether Eric had any other financial assets that could be used to provide periodical payments for Elsie, but at least she can use the Act to ensure that her position is improved.

Question 29

Victoria and James met 15 years ago and began to cohabit. They have four children, aged 2, 4, 6 and 8. Shortly after they met, James bought a plot of land for £5,000 and registered the property in his name only. Victoria and James then set about building the home of their dreams, living in a caravan on the land. James continued to work, using his salary to buy raw materials, and he and Victoria would work on the building of their home each evening and weekends, with Victoria doing what she could during the day. The house took them five years to complete, and they moved in just in time for the birth of their first child. Victoria has never worked, but used a small legacy of £5,000 to buy curtains and soft furnishings for the home and to decorate the nursery.

James has now told Victoria that he feels trapped and wants to leave her and the children to sail around the world on his own. He wants to sell the house and use the proceeds to finance his trip.

Advise Victoria on her property rights, if any, in the house.

Answer plan

Again, this couple will not be using the wide powers the court has on divorce. Instead entitlement must be determined by reference to strict property law rules:

- Legal and beneficial entitlement must be examined;
- is there any evidence of an implied, resulting or constructive trust?
- mention s 37;
- consider what protection, if any, is provided by LRA 1925 s 70(1)(g);
- possible application for sale under s 14 of the Trusts of Land and Appointment of Trustees Act 1996.

Answer

Victoria is seeking advice as to her property rights, if any, in the home she shared with James. The couple have never married, and so the court lacks the wide powers available to it under the Matrimonial Causes Act 1973 to make fair and just resolution of financial matters. The law, therefore, treats cohabitees in an entirely different way when their relationship ends, and consequently Victoria's entitlement must be determined according to the strict rules of property law.

Victoria will need to apply to the court for a declaration of her entitlement in the house, and may need to take steps to protect any interest in case James mortgages the property or otherwise deals with it.

The starting point for any discussion of property law rights is to examine the conveyance to see whether it contains any declaration as to legal or beneficial entitlement: any such declaration is conclusive in the absence of fraud or mistake (*Goodman v Gallant (1986)*). The property in the present case is registered with James as the sole legal owner, and there is no declaration of any beneficial interest for Victoria in the conveyance.

The facts do not disclose that there has been any subsequent express declaration of trust in Victoria's favour. Equitable interests must be vested and evidenced in writing: *Law of Property (Miscellaneous Provisions) Act 1989 s 2; Law of Property Act 1925 s 53(1)(b)*. There is no such declaration, and therefore any interest that Victoria may have must be by way of implied, resulting or constructive trust, which do not require the usual formalities.

To establish such a trust, it is necessary to show that whilst one party is the legal owner, there was a common intention that they should both have a share in the property, and in addition that the party claiming the beneficial entitlement acted to their detriment because of this common intention.

This is easiest to establish where a party can show that he/she has made direct contributions to the acquisition of the home, either by paying part of a deposit, or by paying the mortgage. Then, in the absence of evidence to the contrary, it is presumed that they intended to share the property in proportion to their contributions: *Cowcher v Cowcher (1972)*. Victoria did not, however, pay the deposit; this was paid by James in buying the plot of land. Neither did Victoria pay any mortgage instalments or buy any raw materials. All the materials were paid for by James, and Victoria did not have any paid employment.

If there is no evidence of direct contribution, then Victoria will need to establish a common intention in another way. It may be that there is clear evidence of a common intention, for example, a conversation, a letter, some kind of assurance from James that this would be their house, for example, *Eves v Eves (1975)*. If not, then Victoria will need to prove a common intention by reference to her indirect contributions. It is harder to establish common intention in this way: *Lloyds Bank v Rosset (1991)*. Victoria has not made any financial contribution to the maintenance of the family which has thereby enabled James to pay the mortgage, as in *Grant v Edwards (1986)*. However, by her efforts she has physically helped him to build their house, and transform a building site into a family home.

The courts have been very strict in insisting that the efforts and contribution to the improvement of the property must be substantial: *Pettitt v Pettitt (1970)*. Consequently, the use of Victoria's legacy to buy curtains and furnishings and to redecorate the nursery is not sufficient: *Gissing v Gissing (1971)*. The amount involved, £5,000, is quite a lot of money, but this is the sort of sum that is easily spent on furnishing living accommodation, without thereby acquiring an interest (*Lloyds Bank v Rosset (1991)*). However, Victoria's physical efforts contributed substantially, as she has helped James at weekends and evenings, and worked by herself on the property during the day. Together they have transformed the house (as in *Cooke v Head (1972); Eves v Eves (1975)*), where the women cohabitees acquired interests.

It seems right that Victoria's substantial efforts can be taken as evidence of a common intention to share the property. It is unlikely that she would make such a superhuman effort for no reward, nor that James would expect her to. Her contributions as a mother and a lover do not acquire any interest (*Burns v Burns (1984)*), but her contributions to the building evidence a common intention as well as actions to her detriment. The extent of Victoria's share will need to be determined by the courts, and it would seem that she has made as much, if not more, physical contributions than can be equated as money's worth than James. He, however, did make the original purchase of the land and buy the materials. Applying the principle in *Midland Bank v Cooke (1995)* the whole of the history of the relationship and the parties conduct and contributions can be looked at to determine the size of shares intended. Thus, once Victoria establishes an interest under a trust according to the strict rules in *Gissing v Gissing (1971)* and *Lloyds Bank v Rosset (1991)*, she could argue that there was an intention that they should have equal shares. Victoria could also use *Matrimonial Property and Proceedings Act s 37* to argue that she has acquired or enlarged an interest because of her substantial contributions in money or money's worth.

If Victoria does have an interest in the home, then she must consider how this can be protected should James try to sell or mortgage the property. Since Victoria is in occupation of the home, which does not necessarily have to be continuous or exclusive (*Kingsnorth Finance v Tizard (1986)*), she has an overriding interest (*Land Registration Act 1925 s 70(1)(g)*). This means that even if her interest is unregistered, she will be protected against sale or mortgage to a third party, unless their enquiries could not disclose her interest: *Williams & Glyn's Bank v Boland (1981)*. The only time she may find her interest overreached is if James sells or mortgages to a third party and the proceeds are paid to James and another trustee for sale that he has appointed: *City of London Building Society v Flegg (1987)*.

It is probably wisest for Victoria to register her interest in order to be protected, and if she becomes a co-trustee then she can refuse her consent to any sale. This would force James to apply to the court under *s 14* of the *Trusts of Land and Appointment of Trustees Act 1996* for an order for sale of the house. In determining the application, the court can make such order as it sees fit. This is not a power to alter the actual property rights of the parties, but to determine whether the sale should be permitted to proceed or be postponed. In the case of a matrimonial or family home, the court will look at the purpose for which the house was provided: *Re Evers Trust (1980)*. In the present case, the house was built as a family home, and, since the children of the family are so young, it is still needed as a home and sale will not be ordered.

If, however, Victoria is not a co-trustee then she cannot block the sale as of right, and so she will need to ask the court for an injunction prohibiting sale: *Waller v Waller (1967)*. This would then enable a second trustee to be appointed who could safeguard her interests.

Thus it can be seen that Victoria is likely to have acquired an interest in the home, but she needs to be vigilant in order to protect herself against James' possible future moves.

CHAPTER 6

DOMESTIC VIOLENCE AND OCCUPATION OF THE HOME

▌INTRODUCTION

When a relationship deteriorates, it will often be necessary to examine what protection from personal violence is available. There is the further, and often related, issue of who should occupy the former home.

These areas of law have, in the past, been criticised as a 'hotchpotch of enactments' *per* Lord Scarman in *Richards v Richards (1984)*, and have undergone reform and rationalisation in the Family Law Act 1996. *Part IV* of the Act dealing with these matters came into force in the Autumn of 1997.

The Family Law Act 1996 renames the rights of occupation that used to exist under the Matrimonial Homes Act as matrimonial home rights, and these rights are defined in s 30(2) in much the same way as before. A court order under s 33 of the Act will be needed before a spouse can be excluded from the dwelling house. The significant change introduced is that these rights exist, not only in relation to dwelling houses that are the joint homes of the parties, but are extended to cover dwelling houses that the parties intended to be their joint homes, even though they may never have lived there together.

The Family Law Act replaces the various orders available under the different jurisdictions with a single occupation order, but divides applicants into two categories. The entitled applicant applies under s 33, and the non-entitled applicant may apply under s 35, 36, 37 or 38, depending on whether the respondent is entitled or not, and whether the applicant is a spouse or cohabitant. Students should be aware that the Domestic Violence Crime and Victims Act 2004 has removed *section 41* of the *Family Law Act 1996*.

Non-molestation orders are reformed and dealt with in s 42, which depends on the concepts of 'associated person' and 'relevant child' to determine the availability of such orders. The definition of 'associated person' has been widened by the *Domestic Violence Crime and Victims Act 2004*. The ability of the courts to attach powers of arrest has also been rationalised and improved, and can be found in *s 47* of the *Family Law Act 1996*.

The Act attracted considerable criticism, much of it ill-informed during its passage through Parliament, but its simplification of the law and principles to be applied in cases concerning domestic violence and occupation of the home, has been welcomed by practitioners (and, probably, students of Family Law!).

This is an area where the *Human Rights Act 1998* implications will need to be monitored. Occupation orders interfere with a person's occupation of his home, and regard must be had to *Art 1* of the ECHR relating to peaceful enjoyment of possessions. *Art 8* relating to respect for private and family life, and *Art 6* of the ECHR relating to a fair trial.

Question 30

The sooner the range, scope and effect of these powers are rationalised into a coherent and comprehensive body of statute law, the better.
Per Lord Scarman in *Richards v Richards (1984) 1 AC 174*.

Do you consider that the Family Law Act 1996 provisions relating to domestic violence and occupation of the home address Lord Scarman's concerns and will result in improved protection for the vulnerable and those at risk?

Answer plan

- Look at fragmented jurisdiction in the past;
- highlight the confusing anomalies;
- the different treatment of spouses and cohabitants;
- the exclusion of others at risk;
- the Law Commission proposals;
- the Family Law Act – matrimonial home rights;
  - associated persons and relevant child,
  - non-molestation orders,
  - occupation orders.

Answer

The criticisms made by Lord Scarman were directed at law that had developed on a piecemeal basis, and consisted of a variety of enactments and inherent powers that varied from court to court. The 'hotchpotch of enactments' consisted of the

Matrimonial Homes Act 1983, the Domestic Violence and Matrimonial Proceedings Act 1976 and the *Domestic Proceedings and Magistrates' Courts Act 1978.* All these statutes contained various methods of seeking occupation of a home, and some gave a measure of protection from personal violence. However, the procedures varied from court to court, the principles to be applied also varied, and some measures were available only to spouses whereas others were available to cohabitants. Little wonder that this confusing and anomalous situation led the Law Commission in its report in 1992 on *Domestic Violence and Occupation of the Family Home* to recommend abolition of this variety of enactments and their replacement with a single, comprehensive, statutory formula that would apply to all courts. This would obviate the need to gamble on which court was likely to give the most favourable response, and would encourage a uniform and consistent approach by the courts to the issues of violence and occupation of the home. The Law Commission included a draft bill, and it is this bill which has provided the basis for the Family Law Act 1996 provisions on domestic violence, which came into force in October 1997.

The previous law provided a number of options for spouses, and more limited avenues for cohabitants, but left others at risk to depend upon the inherent jurisdiction of the court. With the increasing incidence of cohabitation as a long-term way of life for many couples, that position could not be justified, and for those who were not in the standard heterosexual relationships, the Law offered little in the way of protection from domestic violence. The Law Commission proposed a radical shake-up in the categories of applicant who would be able to use the new legislation, and the proposals have been accepted.

As well as spouses and those who are living together as husband and wife, applications can be made by ex-spouses and ex-cohabitants. This recognises that, on the breakdown of such relationships, problems may occur and the threat of violence can continue long after a relationship has ended. Similarly, those who have been parties to an agreement to marry are qualified to make applications. These qualifications are recognised in the *Family Law Act* by the concept of 'associated persons', to be found in *s 62*. However, the concept of associated person is wider than the above categories, and includes those who live or have lived in the same household, provided this is not a landlord/tenant or employer/employee relationship. It also includes close relatives of a person or his/her spouse, whether by blood, marriage or adoption. This list includes mother, stepmother, grandmother, daughter, granddaughter, aunt, sister, niece, father, stepfather, grandfather, son, grandson, uncle, brother and nephew. This recognises that such relationships can frequently give rise to issues of domestic violence and occupation of family homes Those who are parents of the same child, or who have or had parental responsibility for the same child are also associated persons, as are those who are parties to the same family proceedings, since these situations can often lead to tension and conflict.

The Law Commission also proposed extending the categories to include those who have had a sexual relationship with each other. Many such relationships turn sour and expose a party to the threat of violence or molestation. This would have been a controversial extension of the law and could have caused difficulty in practice if the sexual nature of the relationship was disputed, or would have been embarrassing. The Act does not contain such a provision, and so, only those with a sexual relationship and who have lived together were initially associated persons more recently the DVCVA 2004 has extended the definition to include couples who have had an intimate relationship but have not actually lived together.

The Act follows the Law Commission recommendations and does not limit relief to heterosexual cohabitants. Provided the couple lived together, it does not matter whether their relationship was homosexual, heterosexual or not sexual at all. This led to considerable criticism in some sections of the press, as indicating an undermining of marriage and an encouragement of cohabitation and homosexuality. The Government responded by pointing out that the Act does seek to promote marriage, and does, in some respects, give more favourable treatment to those who are married. However, there are those who argue that the Act did not go far enough, and that the concept of associated persons is an unnecessary limitation on those who can seek assistance.

It may be that those persons falling outside the categories recognised in the *Family Law Act 1996* can be given some protection by the Protection from Harassment Act 1997, or by the seeking of an injunction under the inherent powers of the court.

The Act also introduces the concept of 'relevant child' in s 62(2). This is a child who is living with a party to proceedings or might reasonably be expected to live with a party, any child in relation to which an application under an adoption order or *Children Act 1989* is in question in the proceedings, and any other child whose interests the court considers relevant.

Under the old law, applicants seeking personal protection faced different criteria in different courts. In the Magistrates' Court it was necessary to show actual violence or the threat of it before an order could be made, whereas in the county court relief was available to prevent molestation. This meant that spouses who had been the victims of harassment and pestering that stopped short of violence could get no assistance in the Magistrates' Court, yet their lives could still be made extremely unpleasant by such behaviour. The Law Commission recommended that the County Court approach be adopted in all courts, so that there would be no need to wait until the situation had escalated into violence before assistance could be sought.

The Act prefers the Law Commission approach, and provides for non-molestation orders in s 42. Such orders are available to protect an applicant who is an associated person and/or any relevant child. The application may be made in conjunction with other family proceedings or may be made on its own, that is, freestanding, or it is possible for the court to make an order without an application being made if it is hearing other family proceedings and considers the order should be made. This power for the court to make an order of its own accord is an advance on the old law, and is to be welcomed in that it gives the court the power to respond to damaging situations that arise as other proceedings unfold.

The court will consider all the circumstances of the case in determining whether to make an order, including the need to ensure the safety, well being and health of the applicant and relevant child (s 42(5)). Thus, there is a change in emphasis away from the old law that concentrated on the nature of the respondent's violent conduct to the new consideration of the effect on the applicant and child. The term molestation is not defined in the Act but would include conduct other than violence. Consequently, harassment and pestering, violence and threats would all be restrained by the order, which can be made for a limited time or until further order (s 42(7)). Molestation was defined in *C v C (Non-Molestation Order) (1998)* as deliberate conduct involving a high degree of harassment, and did not cover an ex-wife giving embarrassing information about her ex-husband to the newspapers.

It is possible for the court to accept an undertaking from respondents instead of making an occupation order or non-molestation order (s 46), but no power of arrest can be attached to an undertaking (s 46(2)). This means that a court cannot accept an undertaking from a respondent if it would otherwise have had the grounds for attaching a power of arrest to the non-molestation or occupation order. By virtue of s 47, if the court makes a non-molestation order and the respondent has used or threatened violence against the applicant or child, then a power of arrest must be attached, unless the court is satisfied that in all the circumstances the applicant and child will be adequately protected without one. This makes it much more likely that a power of arrest will be attached than under the old law, and gives a greater measure of protection to applicants.

The Law Commission recommended that non-molestation orders should be capable of lasting for indefinite periods of time, and the Act provides that such an order may be made for a specific period or until further order (s 42(7)).

Under the old law, a victim of domestic violence was often placed in the difficult position of having to instigate proceedings against a former loved one about whom there might still be mixed feelings. In addition, there was the extra fear that the commencement of proceedings might provoke further violence. In many cases, the police would be involved in attending incidents of violence, but, with the victim often unwilling to pursue a criminal complaint, little effective protection could be given. The Law Commission made the radical proposal of allowing the police to apply for civil protection on behalf of the victim of domestic violence. This could well encourage victims to seek police help, and stop them feeling responsible for commencing actions against the respondent. In *s 60* provision is made for rules of court to be drawn up allowing certain prescribed persons or representatives to act and bring proceedings for the protection of victims of domestic violence.

In cases involving occupation of the home, the old law varied in the principles to be applied in determining applications and the powers available. The Family Law Act 1996 renames the rights of occupation in the *Matrimonial Homes Act 1983* and calls them 'matrimonial home rights'. Such rights are still only given to spouses, and matrimonial home rights are defined in s 30(2) as the right not to be evicted or excluded from the home unless by court order, and the right if not in occupation to enter and occupy with a court order. They exist in relation to dwelling houses that are, or have been, or were intended to be the joint home of the parties. The Act takes up the Law Commission recommendation that such rights should exist in relation to a house that, whilst never actually the home of the parties, had been intended by them to be so. Matrimonial home rights exist if one spouse has an entitlement to occupy the dwelling house by virtue of a beneficial estate, contract or other enactment, and the other spouse has no such entitlement, or has an equitable right only.

Such rights are important in relation to occupation of the home because they will almost inevitably mean that an applicant for an occupation order, who is a spouse, qualifies as an entitled applicant within s 33. The Act draws a distinction between entitled applicants and non-entitled applicants for occupation orders, but simplifies the old law by creating a single occupation order. However, the criteria to be applied in deciding whether to make the order, whilst contained in one Act, vary according to the nature of the applicant and respondent. There is concern that time may be wasted with argument as to the exact nature of the applicant's status, before the appropriate criteria can be selected.

The Law Commission thought it appropriate to retain some distinction between those seeking occupation of a home in respect of which they had some rights, and those seeking to occupy a home in respect of which they had no such rights. Those who have an interest have traditionally always stood a better chance of achieving occupation than those who do not, and this will certainly continue under the Act. Applicants with a beneficial entitlement, or a contractual entitlement, or entitlement to occupy by virtue of any enactment, or matrimonial home rights, will be deemed 'entitled applicants' (s 33(1)). The court can make an order in respect of a dwelling house that is, or was, or was intended to be the home of the applicant and a person with whom the applicant is associated. This concept of associated person is widely defined in s 62 and does not limit the making of occupation orders to married couples or those who are cohabiting heterosexuals.

The order can contain a number of provisions (s 33(3)), including requiring the respondent to allow the applicant to enter and remain in the house or part of it, and restricting or terminating the respondent's right to occupy the house or part of it, and excluding the respondent from the area where the home is situated.

The factors in s 33(6) govern whether an order will be made and the type of regulatory order that will be granted. These factors require the court to consider all the circumstances of the case, including the housing needs and resources of the parties, the likely effect of any order or non-exercise of powers by the court on the health, safety or well being of the parties and any relevant child and the conduct of the parties in relation to each other and otherwise.

In some cases the court has a choice of whether or not to make an occupation order, whereas in other cases, the 'significant harm' cases, the court is compelled to make an order. Under s 33(7), if it appears that the applicant or relevant child is likely to suffer significant harm attributable to the conduct of the respondent if the order is not made, then the court must make an order, unless the respondent or relevant child is likely to suffer equal or greater significant harm if the order is made. This requires the court to, first, consider whether there is the likelihood of significant harm, and, then, balance the harm of making an order with the harm of not making an order. This means that the entitled applicant gets the benefit of a statutory presumption that in cases of risk of significant harm an order should usually be made.

Harm is defined in s 63 to mean ill-treatment or impairment of mental or physical health with the additional criteria of impairment of development for a child. Ill-treatment includes both physical and sexual abuse in relation to a child, and development is widely defined to include physical, emotional, intellectual, social or behavioural development. The concept of 'significant' is likely to mean considerable or important, if guidance in earlier cases on the meaning of such wording in other statutes is followed: *Humberside County Council v B (1993)*.

Entitled applicants can thus seek an order against a wide range of respondents, provided the respondent is an associated person, and there is no maximum period for which an occupation order will be granted. This is to be contrasted with the position of the non-entitled applicant, where orders can last for a six-month initial period, which can then be renewed for an additional six-month period.

The non-entitled applicant can seek an order but only against a spouse, former spouse, cohabitants or former cohabitants. Thus, the category of respondent is more severely limited. If the respondent is entitled to occupy the house, and is a spouse or former spouse, application should be made under *s 35*, whereas if the respondent is entitled, but is a cohabitant or former cohabitant, application should be made under *s 36*.

This would require the court to first consider the making of an occupation rights order, giving the right to occupy the home, and then to make a regulatory order excluding the other party. Under s 35, in making an occupation rights order, the court will take all the circumstances of the case into account including the housing needs and resources of the parties and any relevant child; the financial resources of the parties; the likely effect on the health, safety and well being of the parties and any relevant child of any order or no order being made; the conduct of the parties in relation to each other and otherwise; the length of time that has passed since the parties lived together, the length of time since the marriage was dissolved and the existence of any proceedings between the parties under the Children Act 1989 or in relation to ownership of property.

If the parties were not married but had cohabited, s 36 requires the court to consider the housing needs and resources of the parties; their financial resources; the likely effect on the health, safety and well being of the parties and any relevant child of any order or no order being made; the conduct of the parties in relation to each other and otherwise; the nature of the relationship, specifically that they have not given the same level of commitment as a marriage; the length of time they have lived together as husband and wife; whether there are any children; the time that has passed since they lived together; and the existence of any proceedings between the parties under the Children Act 1989 or in relation to ownership of property (s 36(6)).

Thus, it can be seen that the cohabiting nature of the relationship does not carry the same weight as a marriage would do, and specific regard is had to the length and nature of the cohabiting relationship.

If an occupation order is made, then the court can make a regulatory order excluding the respondent from the home or restricting his occupation. The factors influencing the court in determining whether to make such an order are the housing needs and resources of the parties; their financial resources; the effect of any order or failure to make an order on the health, safety or well being of the parties or relevant child; the conduct of the parties in relation to each other and otherwise; the likelihood of significant harm to the applicant or relevant child if no order is made; and the likelihood of significant harm to the respondent if an order is made. With non-entitled applicants, unlike the position with entitled applicants, there is no compulsion to make an order on the basis of a risk of significant harm. This puts cohabitants at a disadvantage compared to spouses, since spouses will usually be entitled applicants by virtue of their matrimonial home rights.

If the applicant and respondent are both non-entitled to occupy, and this is only likely to be so in the rare cases of squatters and bare licencees, then orders can be sought under s 37 if the parties are spouses or former spouses, and s 38 if they are cohabitants or former cohabitants. The s 37 factors mirror those in s 35, and contain the statutory presumption in favour of making an order for a spouse if there is the risk of significant harm to the spouse or relevant child. *Section 38* contains the same factors as in *s 36* but there is, again, no statutory presumption in favour of an order where there is the risk of significant harm to a non-entitled cohabitant.

In conclusion, the new law goes a long way to answering Lord Scarman's criticisms of the old law. To find the law relating to occupation orders and non-molestation orders in one statute is helpful, but the provisions are nonetheless complex, and will involve categorising applicants before entitlement can be examined according to the correct section of the statute. In addition, there are those who argue that the statute goes too far in offering protection to those beyond the traditional married relationship, whereas there will be those for whom the distinction between those who are married and those who are not cannot be justified.

Question 31

Heidi and Ian, both aged 19, began to live together because Heidi was pregnant. When the baby was born, Ian suspected that he was not the baby's father as its appearance was totally different from his and Heidi's. He said nothing about this at first, and behaved normally towards Heidi and the baby. The couple share a small one-bedroomed flat, and have had numerous arguments. Ian has a short temper and has frequently smashed household objects in his anger at Heidi's burned cooking. One day the couple were out shopping when they met a friend who made a reference, jokingly, to the fact that the baby looked nothing like Ian. Ian exploded with rage and pushed the trolley full of groceries at Heidi, badly bruising her legs. He then pushed the pram over in his haste to leave the supermarket, but the baby was unhurt. Heidi was too scared to go to their home, and has been staying with her mother. Ian, full of remorse, keeps telephoning to speak to Heidi, who will have nothing to do with him. These telephone calls are occurring with increasing frequency, and the last one included a comment by Ian that his family would not stand by and let Heidi make a fool of him.

Heidi wishes to return to her flat with the baby, but does not feel she would be safe there with Ian. Advise Heidi on her possible options.

Advise Heidi, on the assumption that:

(a) she and Ian are married;

(b) she and Ian are not married.

Answer plan

This question requires examination from the standpoint of Heidi and Ian being married, followed by an examination of the position if they are unmarried.

Both situations are now governed by the Family Law Act 1996.

If the couple are married:

- Consider matrimonial home rights under s 30;
- look at excluding Ian by obtaining an occupation order under s 33;
- examine the factors in s 33(6) and s 33(7);
- consider seeking a non-molestation order under s 42.

If the couple are not married:

- No matrimonial home rights;
- exclusion by way of occupation order under s 33 or, more likely, s 36;
- examine the factors in s 36 regarding occupation rights orders and regulatory orders;
- consider non-molestation order under s 42.

Protection from Harrassment ?

Answer

(a) Heidi needs to obtain protection from domestic violence, and occupation of the flat that has functioned as a matrimonial home. If Heidi is married to Ian, she may have matrimonial home rights in relation to the flat, since it has been the matrimonial home (*Family Law Act 1996 s 30(7)*). It is not clear from the facts whether it is only Ian who is entitled to occupy the flat by virtue of a beneficial estate or interest or contract, or whether Heidi is also a tenant. If Ian is the sole tenant, then Heidi, as the non-entitled spouse, is given matrimonial home rights by *s 30*, which are defined in s 30(2) as the right not to be evicted or excluded from the home unless by court order, and the right if not in occupation to enter and occupy with a court order. If they are both joint tenants, then *s 30(9)* gives Heidi the same rights. Heidi can therefore return to the flat, but would rightly be concerned about the safety of this course of action. Consequently, she will need to see whether or not Ian can be excluded, and this will only be possible by way of a court order under *s 33*.

Heidi is an entitled applicant under *s 33* because she is entitled to occupy the home either because she has matrimonial home rights, or because she is a joint tenant. Ian is an entitled respondent, although *s 33* applies to all respondents, whether entitled or not. Consequently, the court can grant an occupation order under s 33 because the dwelling house had been the home of Heidi, the applicant, and Ian, who is a person with whom she is associated. The concept of associated person is defined in *s 62(3)* to include those who are or who have been married.

The occupation order can require Ian to allow Heidi to enter and occupy the flat, and can prohibit Ian or restrict him from exercising his right to occupy the flat, or the area in which it is situated. Since the flat is so small, it is not feasible to expect Heidi to occupy part of the flat, with Ian occupying the rest.

The factors in *s 33(6)* govern whether an order will be made and the type of regulatory order that will be granted. These factors require the court to consider all the circumstances of the case, including the housing needs and resources of the parties; the likely effect of any order or non-exercise of powers by the court on the health, safety or well being of the parties and any relevant child; and the conduct of the parties in relation to each other and otherwise. The baby is a relevant child within *s 62(2)* since it lives with either party, and this is regardless of whether the baby is Ian's child or not.

In some cases, the court has a choice of whether or not to make an occupation order, whereas in other cases, the 'significant harm' cases, the court is compelled to make an order. Under *s 33(7)*, if it appears that the applicant or relevant child is likely to suffer significant harm attributable to the conduct of the respondent if the order is not made, then the court must make an order, unless the respondent or relevant child is likely to suffer equal or greater significant harm if the order is made. This requires the court to first consider whether there is the likelihood of significant harm, and then balance the harm of making an order with the harm of not making an order.

Harm is defined in *s 63* to mean ill-treatment or impairment of mental or physical health, with the additional criteria of impairment of development for a child. Ill-treatment includes both physical and sexual abuse in relation to a child, and development is widely defined to include physical, emotional, intellectual, social or behavioural development. The concept of 'significant' is likely to mean considerable or important, if guidance in earlier cases on the meaning of such wording in other statutes is followed: *Humberside County Council v B (1993)*.

Ian has behaved very badly towards Heidi and the baby. Even though he may be upset and suspicious, this does not justify his explosive and violent temper. Throwing and breaking objects regularly, just because his dinner is burned, is excessive and the incident in the supermarket certainly gives cause for concern about the safety of both Heidi and her baby. The persistent telephone calls and possible threats would all strengthen Heidi's argument that she and the baby run the likely risk of significant harm if no order is made.

Little is known about the living conditions at Heidi's mother's home, but it is not good for the development of the child to be living in cramped conditions. Heidi would seem to have nowhere else to go, yet returning to the flat is not a realistic option whilst Ian remains there. Ian, on the other hand, has behaved in a reprehensible way towards Heidi and the baby, and could well find alternative accommodation. His violence does not appear to be isolated, and the facts seem to indicate the likelihood of significant harm. This would mean that the court must make an order unless Ian would be likely to suffer equal or greater significant harm if the order were made. The consequences of the order for Ian would be that he would need to find alternative living accommodation. There is no evidence to suggest that he would find this impossible, nor is there evidence to suggest that he would suffer any other kind of harm. Consequently, it seems that the court will make an order allowing Heidi to occupy the flat and excluding Ian from the flat. It may be that, given the nature of Ian's behaviour and the threats he has made, the court will go further and exclude him from the general area where the flat is situated.

If an order is made, it can be for a specified period, or until an event takes place, or until a further court order. It remains to be seen whether the new Act will result in courts departing from their previous view that excluding spouses with property interests should only be a short-term measure. In the present case it appears that the flat is rented, and the order may well be of greater duration than if the flat was owned by Ian.

If the court makes an occupation order in respect of the flat, it has power to make ancillary orders under *s 40(1)*, to order either party to pay rent, mortgage, repairs or outgoings on the property. It does not seem appropriate here for an order to be made compensating Ian for the loss of his right to occupy. Whether any order is made depends on all the circumstances of the case, including the financial needs, resources and obligations of the parties *s 40(2)*. On the facts, little is known about the resources of the parties and whether Heidi can pay anything towards the rent, or whether Ian should contribute. Clearly, an order could be made requiring Heidi to take care of the contents of the flat, and, since she has matrimonial home rights, any payment by her in respect of the rent will be treated as if made by Ian; the landlord will be bound to accept her payment (*s 30(3)*).

It would also be sensible for Heidi to apply for a non-molestation order under *s 42*. This order would prohibit the respondent from molesting the applicant if the applicant is an associated person with the respondent and/or any relevant child. As explained earlier, Heidi and Ian are associated persons by virtue of their marriage (*s 62(3)*), and the baby is a relevant child (*s 62(2)*). Such an application can be made with the application for the occupation order, or can be made regardless of whether or not an occupation order is sought (*s 42(2)*). Consequently, if Heidi remains at her mother's home and does not seek an order in relation to the flat, it would nonetheless be advisable to seek the non-molestation order.

The court will consider all the circumstances of the case including the need to ensure the safety, well being and health of the applicant and relevant child (s 42(5)). Thus, there is a change in emphasis from the old law's concentration on the nature of the respondent's violent conduct, to the new consideration of the effect on the applicant and child. The term molestation is not defined in the Act but would include conduct other than violence. Ian's harassment, pestering, violence and threats would all be restrained by the order, which can be made for a limited time or until further order (s 42(7)). It is possible for the court to accept an undertaking from respondents instead of making an occupation order or non-molestation order (*s 46*) and it may be that sometimes, when a respondent is brought to court, he sees the error of his ways and is prepared to give such an undertaking rather than have an order made against him.

However, no power of arrest can be attached to an undertaking (*s 46(2)*), and so a court cannot accept an undertaking from a respondent if it would otherwise have had the grounds for attaching a power of arrest to the non-molestation or occupation order. By virtue of *s 47*, if the court makes such an order and the respondent has used or threatened violence against the applicant or child, then a power of arrest must be attached, unless the court is satisfied that in all the circumstances the applicant and child will be adequately protected without one. This makes it much more likely that a power of arrest will be attached than under the old law, and the facts in the present case seem to indicate that a power of arrest is likely to be attached, given the violence and continuing threats.

It is unlikely that the facts of this case justify the draconian measure of applying for the orders *ex parte*, and it does not seem likely that the *s 45* criteria will be met unless there is the threat of immediate harm to Heidi and the baby. This will mean that Ian will have notice of Heidi's applications, and be able to make his own representations as to why an order should not be made.

(b) If Heidi and Ian are not married, then Heidi cannot have matrimonial home rights in relation to the flat, and she would only be entitled to occupy the flat if she too were a tenant. Even then she would have no right to exclude a joint tenant: *Ainsbury v Millington (1987)* Agaramond. Consequently, Heidi would need to use the provisions of the Family Law Act 1996 to seek an occupation order in relation to the flat, and a non-molestation order in relation to her and the baby. Heidi and Ian are still associated persons by virtue of being persons who are or who have been living together as husband and wife, and the baby is still a relevant child.

To apply for an occupation order, it would be necessary to see if Heidi and Ian are 'entitled' persons. Clearly, Ian as the tenant is an entitled respondent, but it is not clear whether Heidi is an entitled applicant. If she is also the tenant then she would be entitled within *s 33(1)* and the earlier discussion on the occupation order under *s 33* would apply. However, if Heidi is not entitled to occupy the flat by virtue of a beneficial estate, or interest, or contract, or any enactment giving her the right to remain in occupation, then *s 33* will not apply.

Instead, she will only be allowed to apply for an occupation order against a respondent who is or was a spouse or cohabitant. Ian falls into this category, and so the application will be made under s 36 since Ian and Heidi were cohabitants rather than spouses. The order, if granted, will not only allow her to occupy, but will expressly grant her the right to occupy, which she otherwise would not have.

In making an occupation rights order the court will take all the circumstances of the case into account, including the housing needs and resources of the parties and any relevant child; the financial resources of the parties; the likely effect on the health, safety and well being of the parties and relevant child of any order or no order being made; the conduct of the parties in relation to each other and otherwise; the nature of the relationship, specifically that they have not given the same level of commitment as in a marriage; the length of time they have lived together as husband and wife; whether there are any children; the time that has passed since they lived together; and the existence of any proceedings between the parties under the Children Act or in relation to ownership of property.

In the present case Heidi and Ian have cohabited, but as both are still only 19, this will not have been for a particularly lengthy period. They have a child, and Ian has been violent and threatening. Clearly, both Ian and Heidi need a home, and as Heidi is staying in what appears to be unsatisfactory living accommodation with her mother, it seems likely that the court would be prepared to grant her occupation rights in respect of the rented flat.

In addition, the court can make a regulatory order in respect of the flat whereby Ian's occupation right will be restricted or suspended, or he may be required to leave the flat or area in which it is situated. The factors influencing the court in determining whether to make such an order are the housing needs and resources of the parties; their financial resources; the effect of any order or failure to make an order on the health, safety or well being of the parties or relevant child; the conduct of the parties in relation to each other and otherwise; the likelihood of significant harm to the applicant or child if no order is made; and the likelihood of significant harm to the respondent if an order is made.

On the present facts, the needs of Heidi and the baby would seem to take priority, as they will suffer significant harm if Ian is allowed to remain in the flat, whereas Ian will suffer the inconvenience of having to rehouse himself if an order is made. Consequently, an order is likely to be made, but the order is limited to six months duration, and can only be extended once further in the case of cohabitants. Thus, this would provide some interim protection for Heidi and the baby, but would not give a longer period of protection which she might have obtained had she been married.

The same provisions in s 42 regarding non-molestation orders would apply to Heidi as a cohabitant in the same way as it did if Heidi were married to Ian. The two would still be associated persons by virtue of having lived together as husband and wife, and the baby would still be a relevant child. Thus, there is no distinction in relation to protection from molestation between spouses and cohabitants, but it can be seen that a cohabitant can be at a disadvantage when seeking occupation of the home.

Question 32

Julie has been living with Darren for the past year in a house owned by Darren. Julie has just given birth to a baby boy, Billy, and she has a daughter, Gemma, by a previous partner, Rick. Rick was violent to Julie and Gemma and has written several threatening letters to Julie from jail. Rick is due to be released from jail presently.

(a) What, if anything, can Julie do to try to protect herself and her family from Rick?

(b) Julie has been told by her friend that as she is Darren's common law wife, there is no need for her to get married in order to be able to stay in the home. Is this correct?

Answer

(a) In order to determine whether Julie can apply for a non-molestation order under s 42 against Rick, it is necessary to consider whether Julie and Rick are associated persons within the definition in s 62. Persons are associated if they are or have been married, although there is no evidence of such a relationship here. They will also be associated if they are or were cohabitants, that is, lived together in the same household as husband and wife. This may have been the case here, or the couple may merely have lived in the same household, and be associated by virtue of this. Rick and Julie are not relatives, but they are the parents of the same child, and this would suffice to make them associated within Family Law Act 1996 s 62(3)(f).

Gemma is clearly a relevant child within s 62(2) as she is a child living with a party to the proceedings, as is Billy, even though he is not Rick's child. Consequently, Julie can seek a non-molestation order in respect of herself and both of her children. However, Darren cannot be protected by an order applied for by Julie, and would need to make his own application. He could face difficulty in doing this because there is no evidence that he and Rick are associated persons. They have never lived in the same household, and the only other possibility is that they both have or had parental responsibility in relation to the same child. If Julie and Rick were married then Rick would have had parental responsibility for Gemma, but if they were not married then only Julie would have parental responsibility for Gemma. There is no indication that Darren has parental responsibility for Gemma, and so no non-molestation order can be made under the Act in relation to Darren.

Julie can seek a non-molestation order against Rick as a freestanding application; she does not need to be taking any other family proceedings. The court has a discretion whether or not to make the order and will look at all the circumstances of the case including the need to secure the health, safety and well being of the applicant and the two relevant children. There is no requirement that the respondent has to have been violent, the order can be widely drafted to afford protection not just from violence but from pestering and harassment, and can specifically forbid letters and other attempts at communication. Clearly, Rick's violent past and present vindictive campaign would indicate a need for a non-molestation order to be made in order to safeguard Julie and the children.

The order can be for a limited time or until further order, s 42(7). It is possible for the court to accept an undertaking from respondents instead of making an occupation order or non-molestation order (s 46), but no power of arrest can be attached to an undertaking (s 46(2)). Consequently, a court cannot accept an undertaking from a respondent if it would otherwise have had the grounds for attaching a power of arrest to the non-molestation or occupation order. By virtue of s 47, if the court makes a non-molestation order and the respondent has used or threatened violence against the applicant or child, then a power of arrest must be attached unless the court is satisfied that in all the circumstances the applicant and child will be adequately protected without one. This makes it much more likely that a power of arrest will be attached than under the old law, and it seems that the facts in the present case indicate that a power of arrest is likely to be attached, given the past violence perpetrated by Rick and his continuing threats.

Since Rick is still in jail and unable to actually harm Julie or the children until his release, it seems unlikely that an *ex parte* order will be necessary. If, however, Rick's release were imminent, and Julie needed immediate protection, an *ex parte* order could be obtained if, would be just and convenient to do so (s 45). It would be necessary to stress the threat of harm to Julie if the order were not made immediately, although a full hearing would be ordered later, at which point Rick could make representations.

(b) Darren is the sole legal and beneficial owner of the home in which he, Julie and the children live. As such, Julie, as a cohabitant, has no right to remain without Darren's permission unless she obtains a court order. If Julie were to marry Darren she would acquire matrimonial home rights under Family Law Act 1996 s 30. These are defined in s 30(2) as the right not to be evicted or excluded from the home unless by court order, and the right, if not in occupation, to enter and occupy with a court order. These rights exist in relation to any dwelling house that is or was intended to be the joint home of the parties. This means that Darren could not evict her unless he obtained a court order permitting him to do that, and it also means that Julie would be an entitled applicant in any proceedings she might bring to have Darren excluded from the home.

A person with matrimonial home rights can also pay rent or mortgage or other household outgoings, and this has the same effect as if made by the other spouse. This gives a measure of protection, in that she can continue to pay rent or mortgage payments, and if she does so and the mortgagee brings proceedings against her spouse, she can apply to be made a party to those proceedings. There is also protection, in that occupation by a spouse with matrimonial home rights is treated for the purpose of the Rent Acts and Housing Acts as occupation by the other spouse. Matrimonial home rights are also registrable as a notice on the register for registered land and as a Class F land charge for unregistered land, thus giving a measure of protection against subsequent purchasers of the home.

If the relationship between Julie and Darren were to deteriorate then it may be necessary for Julie to seek to occupy the home with the children and to have Darren excluded. If Julie were to marry Darren, then, even though the house is solely owned by him, she would be an entitled applicant by virtue of her matrimonial home rights (s 33(1)). The court would have jurisdiction to make an order in respect of the house since it is, or has been, or was intended to be the home of Julie and Darren, with whom she is associated by virtue of marriage (s 62(3)(a)). The court can enforce Julie's right of occupation and can restrict or suspend Darren's rights and require him to leave the house or part of the house or area in which the house is situated. These regulatory orders are then considered in the light of the circumstances of the case, including the housing needs and resources of the parties; their financial resources; the likely effect of any order or failure to make an order on the health, safety or well being of the parties or relevant child; and the conduct of the parties in relation to each other and otherwise. The court can then exercise its discretion over whether to make an order.

If, however, under s 33(7) it appears that the applicant or relevant child is likely to suffer significant harm attributable to the conduct of the respondent if the order is not made, then the court must make an order, unless the respondent or relevant child is likely to suffer equal or greater significant harm if the order is made. This requires the court to, first, consider whether there is the likelihood of significant harm, and then balance the harm of making an order with the harm of not making an order. In *B v B (1999)*, a woman left her violent husband and his child , taking her baby daughter with her. She applied for an occupation order, and the case was a significant harm case under s 33(7). However, the balance of harm test meant that the husband and his child were permitted to remain in the home, as the husband's child would suffer more harm if the order were made than the wife and six month old baby would if no order were made.

Harm is defined in s 63 to mean ill-treatment or impairment of mental or physical health with the additional criteria of impairment of development for a child. Ill-treatment includes both physical and sexual abuse in relation to a child, and development is widely defined to include physical, emotional, intellectual, social or behavioural development. The concept of 'significant' is likely to mean considerable or important, if guidance in earlier cases on the meaning of such wording in other statutes is followed: *Humberside County Council v B (1993)*. Thus, depending on what Darren does and its effect on Julie and the children, the court may be forced to make an occupation order.

If an order is made, it can be for a specified period, or until an event takes place, or until further court order. It remains to be seemed whether the new Act will result in courts departing from their previous view that excluding spouses with property interests should only be a short-term measure.

If Julie does not marry Darren, and merely continues to live with him, then her status as a so called 'common law wife' does not put her in the same position as an actual spouse. As already indicated, she has no matrimonial home rights, and since she has no other interest or rights in the house she is not an entitled applicant under s 33. She and Darren are, or have been, cohabitants living together as man and wife (s 62(3)(b)). Any application by Julie to occupy the home and have Darren excluded would fall to be determined under Family Law Act 1996 s 36. This would require the court to first consider the making of an occupation rights order, giving Julie the right to occupy the home, and then to make a regulatory order excluding Darren.

In making an occupation rights order the court will take all the circumstances of the case into account including the housing needs and resources of the parties and any relevant child; the financial resources of the parties; the likely effect on the health, safety and well being of the parties and relevant child of any order or no order being made; the conduct of the parties in relation to each other and otherwise; the nature of the relationship, specifically that they have not given the same level of commitment as in a marriage; the length of time they have lived together as husband and wife; whether there are any children; the time that has passed since they lived together; and the existence of any proceedings between the parties under the Children Act or in relation to ownership of property (s 36(6)).

Thus, it can be seen that the cohabiting nature of the relationship does not carry the same weight as a marriage would do, and specific regard is had to the length and nature of the cohabiting relationship.

If an occupation order is made, then the court can make a regulatory order excluding Darren from the home or restricting his occupation. The factors influencing the court in determining whether to make such an order are the housing needs and resources of the parties; their financial resources; the effect of any order or failure to make an order on the health, safety or well being of the parties or relevant child; the conduct of the parties in relation to each other and otherwise; the likelihood of significant harm to the applicant or child if no order is made; and the likelihood of significant harm to the respondent if an order is made. With non-entitled cohabitants, unlike the position with entitled applicants, there is no compulsion to make an order on the basis of a risk of significant harm. This puts cohabitants at a disadvantage over spouses who will usually be entitled applicants by virtue of their matrimonial home rights.

If occupation orders are made for non-entitled cohabitants under s 36, they can only last for an initial period of six months with the possibility of a further six month extension on one occasion only. This contrasts with the position of an entitled applicant who may well be given an order of unlimited duration.

Thus it can be seen that whilst there is little difference in treatment between spouses and cohabitants for non-molestation orders, the spouse gets more favourable treatment in relation to occupation of the home than those who do not marry.

Question 33

Amy married Ben two years ago after her marriage to Charles had ended in divorce. She did not obtain any substantial financial settlement as Charles was a penniless destitute. After their marriage, Amy and Ben lived together in the matrimonial home which Ben had bought in his name 10 years ago. Amy's two children, Diana and Edward, aged eight and six respectively, also lived with the couple.

As time has gone on, Amy has become increasingly bad-tempered with Ben and the children, although she has never actually been violent. She has joined a very extreme religious cult, and since Ben disapproves of it, she has become increasingly critical of his 'heathen influence' on the children. Amy has frequently criticised Ben in front of the children, becoming hysterical if he denies any of her suggestions. On one occasion, Ben slapped Amy whilst she was hysterical. Ben is very fond of the children, who view him as their father, since they have had little or no contact with their real father, Charles, since they were babies.

Five weeks ago, Amy told Ben during the course of a heated argument that she was no longer prepared to allow him to corrupt her children and, against Ben's wishes, she left, taking the children with her. They are all now staying with Amy's parents, Fred and Gertie, in their cramped council flat.

Amy has since confronted Ben, saying that their relationship is over, but that she will never divorce him for religious reasons. She told him to leave the matrimonial home so that she could return with the children, and she is adamant that he cannot remain.

Ben is very unhappy and does not want to leave his home. He still loves Amy and believes that it is the influence of the cult that is causing her to behave like this. Amy has threatened court action, and Ben seeks advice as to what Amy might achieve by this.

Advise Ben on his legal position under the Family Law Act 1996.

Answer plan

- The position under the Family Law Act 1996;
- Amy has matrimonial home rights under s 30;
- she can only exclude Ben by obtaining an occupation order under s 33;
- examine the factors in s 33(6) and s 33(7);
- are there any grounds for seeking a non-molestation order under s 42?

Answer

Part IV of the *Family Law Act 1996* (which Part is now in force) has made wide-ranging changes to the mechanisms by which occupation of the home and issues of domestic violence will be resolved. Whilst many of the principles of the pre-Family Law Act law are retained, many of the problems identified in the law have been addressed, and the simplification of the law into one enactment is a significant improvement.

In the present case, Ben is the legal owner of the dwelling house, and since Amy has no legal or beneficial interest, she is given matrimonial home rights under s 30. These are defined in s 30(2) to mean the right not to be excluded or evicted from the dwelling house by the other spouse except by court order under s 33, and the right to enter and occupy the home with leave from the court, if not in occupation. Amy is not occupying the home at present, but the dwelling house was at one stage the matrimonial home, and so s 30 applies. Therefore, the issue of whether Amy can return and exclude Ben from the home will need to be resolved by the court under its powers in s 33 to make occupation orders.

Amy is an entitled applicant by virtue of her matrimonial home rights in respect of the dwelling house, s 33. Ben would also be an entitled applicant if he were to apply for an occupation order excluding Amy as he has the beneficial estate or interest in the home. The court can have jurisdiction to make a s 33 occupation order if the dwelling house is, has been or was intended to be the home of the applicant and another person with whom the applicant is associated. The concept of associated person is defined in *s 62(3)* to mean those who are or who have been married, or are or have been cohabitants (i.e. living together as husband and wife), or live or have lived in the same household, or are relatives by blood, marriage or, in some cases, adoption of the applicant or their spouse, or they have agreed to marry, or are parents of the same child, or have had parental responsibility for the same child, or are parties to the same family proceedings. Ben and Amy are clearly associated persons on the basis of their marriage. The court can, therefore, make an order regulating the occupation of the home. These orders can allow a person to remain in occupation, or to enter and occupy the home or part of it. It is also possible to prohibit the respondent from exercising his right to occupy, and require him to leave the home, or part of it, or the area in which it is situated.

Whether an order will be made in Amy and Ben's case and the type of any order depends on the application of the factors in s 33(6). These require the court to take into account all the circumstances of the case, including the housing needs and resources of the parties and any relevant child, the financial resources of the parties, the likely effect of any order or non-exercise of powers by the court on the health, safety or well being of the parties and any relevant child, and the conduct of the parties in relation to each other and otherwise. The court can exercise its powers to make or refuse an order in such cases.

However, in some cases the court has no choice, and is compelled to make an order, in the so called 'significant harm cases'. The court is required to make an order under s 33(7) if it appears that the applicant or relevant child is likely to suffer significant harm attributable to the conduct of the respondent if the order is not made, unless the respondent or relevant child is likely to suffer equal or greater significant harm if the order is made. This requires the court to balance the harm done by making the order with that of not making the order to the respective parties and the relevant children.

The concept of relevant child is explained in s 62(2) to include any child living with either party, or who might reasonably be expected to live with them, any child in respect of whom a Children Act 1989 order, or an adoption order, is in question in the proceedings or any other child whose interests the court considers to be relevant. Both Diana and Edward are relevant children since they live with Amy, even though they are not Ben's natural children.

To see whether the court is compelled to make an order or whether it has a choice, it will be necessary to examine the concept of significant harm as it applies to Amy, Ben and the children. Harm is defined in *Family Law Act 1996 s 63* to mean ill-treatment or impairment of mental or physical health for an adult or child and the additional criterion of impairment of development for a child. Ill-treatment is not confined to physical ill-treatment and can include sexual abuse in relation to a child. Development means physical, intellectual, emotional, social or behavioural development. In the present case, it would be necessary to consider whether the impact of an order or lack of one would affect the parties or children in a way that can constitute significant, that is, considerable and important, harm. Ben's isolated act of violence, whilst not to be condoned, is unlikely to be repeated and, therefore, it seems likely that Amy would be unable to show that the risk from not making the order would be the likelihood of significant harm to her or the children. Clearly the living conditions for her and the children are far from desirable, but there is little to suggest that excluding Ben would achieve anything other than to cause him inconvenience and difficulty. Amy cannot demonstrate a threat to her health, and so the court will not be compelled to make an order. Instead it will look at the factors in s 33(6) to see whether or not to make an order.

Both parties need homes, Amy needs adequate accommodation for her and the children, and this need is not really being met by the cramped conditions at her parents. Ben also needs somewhere to live, and if evicted he would not, as a single person, be a priority for local authority housing, although he may have more flexibility if he has income to pay rent in the short-term. If the children were to live with Ben, this would increase his claim to remain in the home, but the presence of the children with Amy strengthens her claim to be able to enter and occupy. There is little evidence of detriment to Amy's health or that of the children if an order were not made, and although Ben has been violent once, his conduct has otherwise been good. Amy, on the other hand has behaved in an extremely provocative manner and has contributed significantly to her own misfortunes. It may be that the court will be reluctant to exclude Ben without evidence that this is really essential. If an order were to be made, it can be for a specified time, or until an event takes place or until a further court order, s 33(10). It remains to be seen whether the court will vary its practice under the old law of viewing exclusion of the spouse with the property interests as a short-term measure.

If an occupation order is made in relation to the dwelling house, either to let Amy occupy, or to exclude Ben or Amy, then the court has power to make ancillary orders under s 40(1) to order either party to pay the rent, mortgage, repairs or other outgoings on the property; or to pay the non-occupying party compensation for the loss of their right to occupy; or to make orders in respect of the furniture. The test as to whether such an order should be made is to consider all the circumstances of the case including the financial needs, resources and obligations of the parties (s 40(2)). There is no evidence regarding these matters in the present case, but if Amy has no resources it will not be possible to order her to make any such payments, although she can be required to take good care of the furniture.

It may also be possible for either Ben or Amy to apply to the court for a non-molestation order (s 42). This prohibits the respondent from molesting a person who is associated with the respondent or who is a relevant child. As explained earlier, Amy and Ben are associated within s 62, and the children are relevant children.

The order can be made on application in any family proceedings or as a freestanding application, or can be made by the court of its own motion if there are family proceedings to which the respondent is already a party and if the court considers it necessary for the benefit of the other party or a relevant child, s 42(2).This means that the application can be made by the parties as an adjunct to the application for an occupation order, or the order can be made regardless of the fact that no application was made if the court considers it necessary. Family proceedings are defined in *s 63*, and include applications under *Part IV* of the *Family Law Act 1996*.

In deciding whether to make an order the court would take into account all the circumstances of the case, including the need to ensure the safety, well being and health of the applicant or relevant child. The term molestation is not defined in the Act, but would include conduct which is not necessarily violent, such as harassment and pestering, as in the old law. Ben has behaved violently on one occasion, but it was the result of prolonged provocation by Amy, and was limited. Amy, on the other hand, has behaved in a way that could be argued to amount to harassment. It would be difficult to justify a non-molestation order being made here, but if one were to be made, it could be made in general terms, or be more specific and prohibit certain behaviour (*s 42(6)*). The order may last for a limited period of time, or until further order (*s 42(7)*).

This is not a case of extreme urgency where it would be just and convenient to grant an *ex parte* order (*s 45(1)*), and so Ben should receive notice of any application that Amy wishes to make, and must be prepared to marshal his arguments as to why an occupation order or non-molestation order should not be made. Since Ben has used or threatened violence against the applicant, Amy, there is the risk that the court could attach a power of arrest to any order it makes (*s 47(3)*). However, the second requirement – that there is a risk of significant harm to the applicant or relevant child if the power of arrest is not immediately attached – is extremely unlikely to be satisfied in Ben's case. It may be that Ben could avoid an order being made by giving an undertaking not to be violent again, under *s 46*, although undertakings are only possible in cases where there are no grounds to attach a power of arrest (*s 46(3)*).

In conclusion, Amy's arguments and claims against Ben seem somewhat flimsy and may not justify the making of an occupation order in her favour. If any order were to be made, given the circumstances, it is likely to be short-term, to avoid the overcrowding until Amy can be re-housed. A non-molestation order does not seem necessary.

CHAPTER 7

PARENTAL RESPONSIBILITY AND DISPUTES ABOUT THE UPBRINGING OF CHILDREN

▌ INTRODUCTION

The Children Act 1989 revolutionised the way in which disputes concerning the upbringing of children should be handled by the courts. It also helped shift the emphasis away from parental rights and towards the concept of parental responsibility. The Act further introduced the statutory non-interventionist policy and recognised the need to avoid delay.

Students will need to understand what having parental responsibility means. In particular, you may have to explain the extent to which one parent with parental responsibility can act without consulting the other parent. They should also be able to explain who has parental responsibility and how it can be gained. They should be aware that the law distinguishes between married and unmarried parents. Whilst both the married father and the married mother automatically have parental responsibility (Children Act 1989 s 2(1)) the unmarried father will only get parental responsibility if he has signed a parental responsibility order with the mother (Children Act 1989 s 4(1) (b)) or if he has been granted it by the court (Children Act 1989 s 4(1) (c)) or following the introduction of the Adoption and Children Act 2002 if has been registered or reregistered as the child's father. In addition, questions could also include non-parents gaining parental responsibility through a residence order under *s 8* of the *Children Act 1989* or in the case of the Local Authority following an emergency protection order (Children Act 1989 s 44(4) (c)) or a care order (Children Act 1989 s 33(3) (a)).

Any answer to a problem question should show an understanding of the philosophy of the Act and an awareness of these basic principles. There are a variety of orders available under s 8 of the Act, namely a residence order, a contact order, a prohibited steps order and a specific issues order. You should be able to explain the circumstances in which each order should be sought, and it is important to realise that these orders are designed to be the usual method of resolving disputes. Wardship should only rarely be sought, and is to be regarded very much as a last resort, giving the High Court a residual jurisdiction.

Some applicants may apply for a s 8 order as of right, whereas others need leave. The criteria for granting leave must be explored, especially those in relation to applications by the child itself. Then the paramount factor of the child's welfare must be explored, in the light of the checklist of factors in s 1(3). A good answer will do more than merely list the factors; it should explore those that are relevant to the situation and attempt to reach a realistic solution.

Disputes involving children, whether between parents or the state, is another area where the *Human Rights Act 1998* will be of importance. The parents and child have Convention rights that need to be recognised. There is the obvious need to consider *Art 8*, the right to respect for a family and private life, *Art 6* the right to a fair trial, *Art 14* prohibition of discrimination. In addition, other Convention rights might be relevant. For example, in *A v UK (Human Rights: Punishment of Child) (1998)*, a man successfully argued in the English court that he was using reasonable physical chastisement when he beat his stepson causing actual bodily harm. The European Court of Human Rights held that the child's right under *Art 3*, 'freedom from inhuman and degrading punishment', had been violated.

This chapter is concerned with disputes over the upbringing of children where the parents are not divorcing. However, much of what is said will also be relevant to determining a dispute about where a child should live on the divorce of its parents. There are an enormous variety of possible problems that may be encountered concerning children, and the following questions are an attempt to provide an insight into some dilemmas faced in such situations.

Question 34

Rupert and Sally married 10 years ago and have three children, William, aged eight, and twins, Polly and Molly, aged five. William has excelled at school and has been offered a scholarship at a private boarding school that specialises in the education of gifted children. Rupert is delighted, as he went to boarding school himself, but Sally is unhappy about William going away to school at such a young age, and is opposed to private education for political reasons. Polly has recently been diagnosed as having a rare form of leukaemia, and her best chance of survival is to receive a bone marrow transplant. The family have all been tested, and Molly is the closest match. The operation to donate bone marrow carries a slight risk to Molly, but the doctors are confident that it could be successful. Rupert is keen that the transplant goes ahead, but Sally has religious objections to such surgery.

Advise Rupert as to what he can do, given that he and Sally disagree on what should be done for the children.

Answer plan

Begin by explaining parental responsibility, and who has it in relation to these children. Also consider what each parent can do to fulfil this responsibility.

Then outline the various s 8 orders available, and whether application may be made as of right or with leave. The general policy of non-intervention and the delay factor should be mentioned.

In relation to children's schooling:

- the welfare principle;
- the s 1(3) checklist and relevant discussion of the factors.

In relation to the medical treatment:

- welfare principle;
- s 1(3) checklist and the difficulty of non-therapeutic medical care.

Answer

Rupert is the father of the three children concerned, and since he is married to their mother, Sally, he has parental responsibility for his children. Sally, as their mother, also has parental responsibility, which is defined in *Children Act 1989 s 3(1)* as 'all the rights, duties, powers and responsibilities and authority which by law a parent of a child has in relation to the child and its property'. This concept emphasises the obligations of both Rupert and Sally to care for and to nurture their child, providing it with a stable and loving background in which it can mature to a responsible adult. Parents do not own children, and it is clear from the Children Act 1989 that the paramount consideration will always be the welfare of the child in issues concerning its upbringing: s 1(1). Thus it is immaterial what the parents want; unless their wishes accord with the child's interests, their wishes will be disregarded in any court order.

In normal everyday situations, both parents exercise parental responsibility, and each can do so independently of the other: *s 2(7)*. The old parental veto that existed before the Children Act 1989 has gone, and consequently either Rupert or Sally, or both, can act to discharge their parental responsibility and make decisions in relation to the child. However, in the present case, it is unlikely that William could be sent away to school, or the twins operated on just on Rupert's instructions.

155

Sally's objections would mean that the school or hospital would be unwilling to act without agreement or a court order.

There is obviously an enormous difference of opinion between Rupert and Sally as to what should happen to their children. There is no evidence that the couple will be divorcing, or taking any other family proceedings, so that both have the option of making an application for one or more of the orders in *Children Act 1989 s 8*. Section 8 provides for residence orders which resolve where and with whom a child should live; contact orders, dealing with contact with individuals; specific issues orders; and prohibited steps orders. It is the last two orders that appear to be most relevant here, as the parties still want the children to remain with them both – whether that desire survives any proceedings is another matter.

A specific issues order is the mechanism whereby a party can raise a particular issue and seek the court's ruling and guidance on the matter. A prohibited steps order prohibits the taking of 'a step which might be taken by a parent in meeting his parental responsibility'. Neither order can be sought if a residence or contract order is more appropriate (*s 9(3)*), but in the instant case the issue of William's schooling and the medical treatment for the twins could be raised by seeking either order. It would seem that if Sally were to apply she would want to prohibit William being sent to school or the transplant from Molly to Polly; whereas Rupert would want to enable these steps to be taken and might seek a specific issue order. Regardless of who makes the application, the principles to be applied by the court are the same.

As parents, both Rupert and Sally can apply as of right for such orders: *Children Act 1989 s 10(4)*. In dealing with such an application, the court must take into account the non-interventionist policy in s 1(5). This requires the court to refrain from making an order unless making an order is better than not making one. This emphasises the commitment of the Act to encouraging agreement and conciliation rather than acrimonious litigation. Unfortunately, Rupert and Sally are too far apart to reach agreement, and as these issues are of enormous importance, it would seem likely that the court's intervention is justified.

Once the court becomes involved in a s 8 application, it must lay down a timetable to ensure that the proceedings proceed as quickly as possible: s 11. Delay is regarded as 'likely to prejudice the welfare of the child' (s 1(2)), and so these proceedings will need to be determined as a matter of urgency given the need for medical treatment in the case of the twins and for William to progress with his education.

In determining the s 8 application, the court must consider the statutory checklist in s 1(3) of the Act. The child's welfare is, as ever, the paramount consideration in matters concerning his upbringing (s 1(1)), and therefore the guiding principle will be to serve the child's best interests, not necessarily those of the parents. The checklist provides a number of factors, including the ascertainable wishes and feelings of the child concerned (in the light of his age and understanding); his physical, emotional and educational needs; the likely effect on him of any change in his circumstances; his age, sex, background and any relevant characteristics; and any harm which he has suffered or is at risk of suffering. This checklist will be applied to the issues concerning each child in turn.

The controversy concerning William's schooling needs to be resolved and the starting point will be to consider William's wishes. The facts do not disclose whether he is keen to go away to school, or whether he would rather remain at home and go to a local school. As a gifted child, it may be that William has a greater understanding and maturity than the average eight year old, and so his wishes would be considered. However, it is unlikely that he will have reached the point whereby his opinion would be decisive. This has generally been accorded to teenagers (*Stewart v Stewart (1973)*), as they are likely to appreciate the long-term consequences of their decisions. In *Marsh v Marsh (1977)* the views of an 8-year-old girl were not decisive, but William is more articulate than most 8-year-olds. If he has been pressurised or 'coerced' by either parent, then his views may be disregarded: *Re S (Infants) (1967)*.

The physical, emotional and educational needs of the child must also be considered. Eight-years-old is very young to go away to school, but many English schoolchildren are sent away to boarding school at that age, or even when younger. Little is known of William's character other than that he is educationally gifted. If he is an independent and confident child, he may be able to make the transition to boarding school very smoothly, but if he is more nervous he may find separation traumatic. More also needs to be known about his schooling; is he so gifted that he cannot benefit from ordinary schooling available locally? The courts place great store on the importance of education (*May v May (1986)*), and this may indicate which proposal is in William's best interests. Certainly his mother's political views are irrelevant as to what kind of education would most benefit this particular child. By being sent away to school, he will lose everyday contact with his sisters, but would still be able to see them during holidays and possibly weekends.

The effect on William of being sent away to school has already been considered and, looking at his age, sex, background and relevant characteristics would require a consideration of the family expectations for William. If he has grown up in a family atmosphere where it was generally accepted that children would go away to school, then it more likely that the court would agree with the boarding school option. If, however, the notion of sending a child away to school was alien to this family, then it may be too traumatic and difficult for William to adjust to. Rupert himself went away to school, but Sally is opposed to the idea, and much would depend on the kind of child William is. For some children, boarding school is a wonderful opportunity and an avenue for excellence; for others it means nothing but misery.

Looking at the issues regarding the medical treatment for the twins, it will be necessary to consider both Molly and Polly separately. Polly is seriously ill and it is part of the obligations of a parent to ensure that their child is properly cared for. Consent to medical treatment is needed, unless in an emergency, and so Polly's transfusion will need to be agreed, or ordered. Clearly, the transfusion is therapeutic in relation to Polly; without it she may die, with it she has a good chance of living. It is not clear whether Sally's objections are to Polly receiving the transplant, or to Molly being the donor, or to both. If there is disagreement over Polly's treatment, then again the court must be satisfied that making an order is better than not making one (s 1(5)) – the non-interventionist policy. Given the opposing views of the parents, it does seem that some intervention by the court will be necessary. The welfare of Polly will be the paramount consideration (s 1(1)), and the court will need to consider whether it is in her best interests to have the treatment proposed in line with the s 1(3) guidelines. The child, at five, is probably too young to realise the implications of her decision, and so, although her wishes might be considered, they would probably not carry much weight. If there was evidence that she had been coerced by either parent, then the views would be disregarded: *Re S (Infants) (1967)*. The physical, emotional and educational needs of the child would also be considered, and it is obvious that Polly is very sick and needs treatment. Whilst the courts might be sympathetic towards a parent whose child had undergone extensive painful treatment for a terminal condition when that parent wanted to choose for the child to die with dignity, the courts will usually order treatment if the child has a good chance of leading a life of some quality afterwards: *Re B (1981)*. Polly does have a good chance with a transplant, and so treatment is likely to be ordered, even though Sally has religious objections. The courts will always put the physical need of the child above the religious or spiritual belief of the parent: *Jane v Jane (1983)*. If nothing is done for Polly she will die, and the court will act to ensure that she receives treatment.

However, in *Re T (A Minor) (1996)*, the court upheld a mother's refusal to subject her child to a liver transplant. Without the transplant the child would die and there was a reasonable chance that with the transplant the child might live. However, the procedure was risky, involved extensive surgery and would have needed the wholehearted commitment of the mother in helping her child through the very painful procedure. The Court of Appeal felt that since the parents clearly loved their child, and were doing what they thought best, it would not be in the child's best interests to order major invasive surgery, which would require major commitment on the part of the mother to a procedure she firmly believed was not in her child's best interests. The court stressed that this was an unusual case, and did not abandon the usual presumption in favour of courses of action that would prolong life. In the present case there are distinguishing features, in that a bone marrow transplant, whilst a major procedure, may not be as extensive as a liver transplant. Also, in *Re T* there was no parent who felt strongly that the procedure should be carried out. If Rupert is close to his daughter and prepared to support her through her treatment then the court will usually order the transplant.

The next issue is whether the transplant should come from Molly. Obviously, the operation is not strictly therapeutic in relation to Molly. She is healthy and does not need medical treatment. However, if no transplant takes place, her twin sister may die. Again, the parents' opposing views mean the court's intervention is justified, and the welfare of the child, Molly, must be the paramount consideration (s 1(1)). She is very young for her wishes to be accorded much weight, but, if it has been explained to her that she can help her sister but that she will need an operation, her attitude could be useful. If she is very unwilling, it will be harder to order the transplant than if she is keen to help her sister. Clearly, there is a slight risk to Molly, as there is in all medical and surgical procedures. But this risk of harm would have to be offset by the possible harm to her if her sister dies. For twins, the trauma of the death of one twin is very great, and it may be that emotionally Molly would benefit from trying to assist Polly. The court has a difficult balancing exercise, but if the statistical chances of complications are less, then the transplant will probably be ordered. It does not place Molly under any continuing disability since the bone marrow deficiency will be made up quickly.

In *Re R (1993)*, the court suggested that applications concerning medical treatment for children should always be made to a High Court judge. Before the Children Act 1989, such applications were usually by way of invoking the inherent jurisdiction of the High Court to make the child a ward of court. In *Re O (A Minor) (Medical Treatment) (1993)*, this use of wardship was approved of, but in *Re R (1993)* the court suggested that a s 8 order was nevertheless the appropriate way to proceed. In *Re CT (1993)* it was stated that wardship was a residual jurisdiction that should only rarely be used when the s 8 orders were inadequate. Thus, it would be appropriate for all the issues regarding William, Polly and Molly to be resolved using *Children Act 1989 s 8*, and not wardship. In *Re T (A Minor) (1996)* wardship was used as the applicant for the order for the transplant was not one of the parents.

Question 35

Samantha, aged 14, lived with her parents, Janet and John, and her younger brother, Martin, aged nine, in the family home. For some time, Samantha has been arguing with John, primarily about her attitude to school and her relationship with her boyfriend, Zak, aged 17. Last month, after yet another argument with her parents, Samantha left home and went to stay with Zak at Zak's mother's home. Zak's mother is rarely at home and has no objection to Samantha staying there, but Janet and John want their daughter to come home.

Samantha has refused to return, and has threatened her parents that she will 'divorce' them, as she has read of similar cases in the newspapers. She also tells them she is going to the family planning clinic to obtain the contraceptive pill.

Advise Janet and John as to whether Samantha can do this.

Answer plan

- The concept of parental responsibility, how it may be exercised and by whom, must be considered;
- the difficulty of conflict between parent and child should be explored;
- the role of s 8 orders and the problem of leave for a child's application is then considered, with an account of the non-interventionist policy and approach to delay;
- first consider the welfare principle and the s 1(3) checklist as it applies to this girl;
- rule out the use of wardship.

Answer

Janet and John are Samantha's parents and as such one or both of them will have parental responsibility for Samantha. Parental responsibility is defined in *Children Act 1989 s 3(1)* as 'all the rights, duties, powers and responsibilities and authority which by law a parent of a child has in relation to the child and its property'. This concept is based on an obligation to nurture and care for a child, and replaces the somewhat possessory concept of parental rights, whereby some parents viewed their children as possessions to be controlled. There is, consequently, no automatic right for Janet and John to insist that their teenage daughter does as they say.

Parental responsibility is borne by the natural mother of the child, and by the father if he was married to the mother at the time of the child's birth or conception: *s 2(1)*. Therefore, Janet definitely has parental responsibility, and John may also have it automatically if he is married to Janet. If not married to Janet, John would only have parental responsibility if he and Janet had entered into a formal agreement, or there had been a court order: Children Act 1989 s 4.

Parental responsibility can be exercised by each party independently (*s 2(7)*), but, in the instant case, there is no conflict between Janet and John as they are both keen for their daughter to return. Parental responsibility lasts until Samantha is 18, or marries, or enters the armed forces. It does not end on the making of any court order, other than adoption, and so it is incorrect to talk of children being able to 'divorce' their parents.

There is clearly a conflict here between the views of Janet and John as to what is best for their daughter, and Samantha's own views. As Samantha is a 14-year-old teenager, she can no longer be physically controlled in the way that a young child can, and parents have to accept that as their child grows older they will do less controlling and more advising: *Gillick v W Norfolk and Wisbech Area Health Authority (1985)*.

However, there is genuine concern on the part of the parents about the suitability of their daughter's living arrangements and her relationship with Zak. This relationship would seem to be sexual, or about to become so, given Samantha's comments about contraception, and it is a criminal offence to have sexual intercourse with a girl under 16, even if she is a willing participant. Janet and John are also concerned about Samantha's education which they have a duty to ensure she receives: the Education Act 1944. They could attempt to remove Samantha from Zak's home, but can only use reasonable force; if excessive force is used then there may be an assault (*R v Smith (1985)*). Ultimately, this might provoke Samantha into seeking assistance from the courts.

There is no automatic right for a child to apply for an order under the Children Act 1989. *Section 10(8)* of the Act specifies that a child will need leave from the court to apply for one of the range of orders in s 8, and leave will only be granted if the court is satisfied that the child has sufficient understanding to make the proposed application. Samantha may wish to apply for a residence order which would determine where she should live, a prohibited steps order to stop her parents removing her from Zak's home, and the issue of contraception could be raised as a specific issues order if still in dispute (*Children Act 1989 s 8*).

The court will look at Samantha's age, maturity and understanding before granting leave. A degree of conflict between teenagers and their parents is inevitable, and the courts have made it clear that the Children Act 1989 is not to be used by any disgruntled teenager (*Re C (A Minor)* (leave to seek *s 8* order) *(1994)*). It should only be used where there is a genuine breakdown in the relationship between parent and child, and where there is such deep disharmony and mistrust that the court's intervention is necessary: *Re AD (A Minor) (1993)*. Such applications are viewed as being serious and sensitive enough to warrant consideration by the High Court, and so Samantha's case, regardless of where it was commenced, would be determined by the High Court.

In *Re C (Residence: Child's Application for Leave) (1995)* the court held that in deciding whether to give leave for a child to make a s 8 application, the child's interests are important, but are not the paramount consideration. The *s 10* principles that apply when other people apply for leave do not apply to children where the consideration is whether the child has sufficient understanding. The court can also take into account the likelihood of the application succeeding. Here, the conflict is between Samantha and her parents, but the court cautioned in *Re C* about the detrimental effect of allowing a child to be a party to proceedings between arguing parents, where the child might hear evidence that could cause upset.

Samantha is 14, and 14-year-old girls would normally have sufficient maturity to realise the long-term consequences of applying to live apart from their parents. The facts disclose that Samantha has not been doing well at school, but there is nothing to suggest that she is of below average intelligence. Her emotional maturity would need to be examined, but she seems to be exercising some degree of responsibility in seeking contraceptives, and it is likely that she is of sufficient maturity and understanding to be given leave to apply for a s 8 order. A 14-year-old's wishes were respected in a case involving education (*Re P (A Minor) (Education: Child's Wishes) (1992)*), and unless Samantha comes across in court as a petulant and stubborn child, it is likely she will be given leave to apply for a s 8 order.

In dealing with applications for s 8 orders, the court is required to take into account a number of important factors. The first of these is the non-interventionist policy (*s 1(5)*), which requires the court to consider whether making an order is better than not making any order. This is in line with the philosophy of the Children Act 1989 which is to encourage consensus, with the court's involvement seen as a last resort. It would seem that Samantha's relationship with her parents has probably deteriorated beyond the point where they are able to reach agreement; they seem to be opposed to each other, and so in a contested s 8 application the court's involvement seems inevitable.

Once the court becomes involved, it must have regard to the fact that 'delay in determining the question is likely to prejudice the welfare of the child': *s 1(2)*. It will therefore be necessary to ensure that the dispute over Samantha's upbringing is resolved as quickly as possible, and to ensure that this happens the court will draw up a timetable for the proceedings: *s 11*.

In a disputed s 8 application, the court must also have regard to the statutory checklist in *s 1(3)*. *Section 1(1)* of the *Children Act 1989* makes the child's welfare the paramount consideration, and therefore this dispute will be resolved in the way in which Samantha's welfare is best served. The checklist in s 1(3) lists a number of factors that should be considered, and these will be examined in turn.

First, the ascertainable wishes and feelings of the child concerned (in the light of her age and understanding) will be examined. As explained earlier, a mature 14-year-old will usually be able to express her wishes sensibly, and will be able to make decisions in her long-term interest: *Stewart v Stewart (1973)*. However, the cases where greatest credence has been given to the wishes of the child have involved a child having to choose between two suitable parents or family members. In the instant case, Samantha is choosing to live away from her parents at Zak's house. It is not clear whether she has a positive relationship with Zak's mother, and it may be argued that it is not in Samantha's long-term interests to effectively live with her 17-year-old boyfriend whilst she is still only 14. If it appears that pressure has been put on her by Zak, then her views may be discounted (*Re S (Infants) (1967)*) if they are not in her long-term interests.

It will then be necessary to examine Samantha's physical, emotional and educational needs. She is still 14-years-old, and has a need for a certain level of care and guidance. Zak's mother does not seem keen to play an active part in Samantha's upbringing, and she has a rather relaxed attitude that might not be in Samantha's best interests. The sexual nature of Samantha's relationship with Zak is something again that the court may be unwilling to condone positively by ordering that she, in effect, lives with him. Janet and John could also argue that they are able to provide a stable and caring home, and that Samantha has just been rebelling against their authority and trying to get her own way. By leaving to live with Zak, Samantha's relationship with her brother might suffer, and the courts take the view that siblings can offer each other support: *C v C (1988)*. There is also genuine concern that Samantha's schooling will suffer if she lives with Zak since Zak's mother does not seem concerned to ensure Samantha goes to school. Education is viewed as important (*May v May (1986)*) and the court will be unlikely to make a residence order if there will be a detrimental effect on Samantha's education.

The court will also look at the likely effect on Samantha of any change in her circumstances. It is considered undesirable to uproot children, since disrupting the status quo is often detrimental to the child's welfare: *J v C (1970)*. However, Samantha has only been at Zak's for one month; it can hardly be said to be disruptive to return her to her parents. It would seem that her parents ought to be able to provide greater stability of care than Zak's mother who does not seem very concerned for Samantha's welfare.

Looking at Samantha's age, sex, background and any characteristics of hers which the court considers relevant, it would seem that 14-year-old girls often have difficulty with their parents, yet are still in need of parental guidance. The next consideration is the harm that Samantha has suffered, or is at risk of suffering. There is no suggestion that Samantha has been harmed or abused by her parents, and this is to be contrasted with the evidence of the under-age intercourse she is having with Zak that a residence order would facilitate and condone.

The capacity of Samantha's parents and of any other relevant person to meet her needs would also be an important factor in determining where Samantha should live. Janet and John have discharged their parental responsibility towards Samantha in the past, and there is no evidence of any undesirable conduct or failings on their part. However, Samantha cannot be allowed to fend for herself; yet the consequences of allowing her to live at Zak's home would appear to be exactly that. Zak's mother is unconcerned about Samantha's welfare, and seems unlikely to make the positive contribution of alternative care in other cases. Zak is only 17, and it seems unlikely that he could promote Samantha's welfare.

Therefore, despite her wishes to live with Zak, the illegal nature of the sexual relationship and the apparent lack of concern for her welfare exhibited by Zak's mother, mean it is extremely unlikely that Samantha would be able to obtain a residence order permitting her to live there.

However, the issue of contraception is likely to be resolved in Samantha's favour. In *Gillick*, the House of Lords recognised that whilst the law prohibited sexual intercourse with girls under 16, many such girls did engage in unlawful intercourse. A girl of sufficient maturity to have a sexual relationship and to seek contraceptive advice and services, ought to be able to protect herself against pregnancy. It would not be in Samantha's best interests to prevent her from using contraception, as this would only lead to an unwanted pregnancy, which is hardly in the interests of the welfare of a girl of 14. This would give a competent child the right to consent to medical treatment against her parents' wishes; however it seems that the Gillick decision has its limitations, and a *Gillick* competent child cannot refuse medical treatment that his or her parents consent to, *Re M (Medical Treatment: Consent) (1999)*.

There is no point trying to use the inherent jurisdiction of the High Court to make Samantha a ward of court. In *Re CT (1993)*, it was stressed that wardship is exceptional and should only be used where the s 8 orders do not adequately cover the problem being experienced in relation to the child. The only possible justification for Samantha being warded would be if her parents wanted to prevent her association with Zak. It would have to be shown that this was an extremely undesirable relationship, which could not be dealt with by making a s 8 order. If Samantha were to become a ward of court, then the court would have responsibility for her welfare and could deal not only with where she lived, but also provide continuous control and supervision to prevent undesirable relationships. Samantha's welfare would be the only consideration, but this is an extreme measure to take.

Question 36

Nina and Rob lived together for five years, during which time their children, Tara, now aged five, and John, now aged two, were born. Nina and Rob's relationship began to deteriorate last year, and they agreed to separate. Nina moved out of the home she shared with Rob, taking the two children to live in a house in the next village. Rob was a frequent visitor to see Nina and the children, and the relationship was amicable until Nina formed a relationship with Brad, a handsome young labourer. Rob was very jealous, and one night, after drinking heavily, he went to Nina's house and stabbed Brad to death. He was tried for murder, but convicted of manslaughter and sentenced to seven years' imprisonment.

Whilst Rob was on remand, Nina allowed Tara to visit her father on three occasions, but John, who was only a baby, did not. Nina wants nothing more to do with Rob, and does not want him to have anything to do with the children. Rob has written to her, demanding his 'parental rights'. She has also received a letter from Rob's mother, asking to see the children.

Advise Nina on whether Rob can apply for a parental responsibility order, Rob's entitlement, if any, to see the children, and on what steps Rob's mother could take to see the children, and how these issues would be resolved.

Answer plan

This question involves an unmarried couple and a dispute over the children of the relationship.

- parental responsibility should be explained, together with who may exercise it and how;
- parental responsibility orders;
- then the role of the s 8 orders should be considered, including the parents' right to apply without leave and the general non-interventionist policy and need to avoid delay;
- then the children's welfare must be considered in the light of the s 1(3) checklist, and contact with the father and grandmother must be explored.

Answer

Rob is the natural father of the two children, Tara and John, but since he did not marry the children's mother, Nina, he may not have parental responsibility for the children. English law has chosen not to give unmarried fathers automatic parental responsibility and whilst the *Adoption and Children Act 2002* has amended s 4 of the Children Act 1989, the unmarried father still does not get automatic parental responsibility. There are currently three ways in which an unmarried father might acquire parental responsibility. The first is if he is registered as the child's father on his birth certificate. Because this was only introduced by the Adoption and

Children Act 2002 it can not apply to Tara as she was born before that Act came into force. It may apply to John, but the facts are not clear on whether Rob has been registered as John's father. The other two ways in which an unmarried father can acquire parental responsibility are through an agreement with the mother or through a court order.

Parental responsibility is defined in *Children Act 1989 s 3(1)* as 'all the rights, duties, powers and responsibilities and authority which by law a parent of a child has in relation to the child and its property'. Thus the emphasis of the Act is on the obligations of parenthood, and the prime feature is that in questions of the child's upbringing, their welfare is of paramount importance: *s 1(1)*. In the present case, it would be wrong, therefore, to talk of Rob's rights to see his children; rather, the emphasis is on what is in the best interests of the children.

It is extremely unlikely that Nina would consent to Rob having parental responsibility in the present circumstances, and so he would need to apply to the court. This would be a question of the child's upbringing, and therefore the child's welfare is the paramount consideration, not the feelings of Nina or Rob (*Re G (A Minor) (Parental Responsibility Order) (1994)*). The usual attitude of the court is to grant parental responsibility to fathers who have demonstrated an attachment and commitment to their children (*Re E (Parental Responsibility) (1995)*). Whilst Nina's feelings about Rob are understandable, he did have a relationship with his children, and if he shows remorse and is unlikely to be violent again, then it may be possible for him to obtain the order. In *Re T (A Minor) (Parental Responsibility: Contact) (1993)*, parental responsibility was refused to a father who had been guilty of serious violence to the mother and cruelty to the child. In the present case, Rob has not been violent to Nina or the children, nor has he ill-treated the children.

In *Re P (Parental Responsibility) (1998)*, it was suggested that the correct test should be to examine the level of commitment and attachment the father has demonstrated to the child and his reasons for seeking the order. In the present case Rob has shown attachment and commitment and does not appear to be seeking the order so that he can interfere unnecessarily in the children's lives, as was the case in *Re P (Parental Responsibility) (1998)*. It may be in the child's best interests to know that his or her father had sufficient commitment to seek the order, *Re M (Contact) (1998)*.

The effect of an order is to give him a say in the upbringing of his children, but it would not allow him to 'interfere in matters within the day to day management of the child's life' *Re P (A Minor) (Parental Responsibility Order) (1994)*. In *Re S (A Minor) (Parental Responsibility) (1995)* it was held that a father who has had involvement in the upbringing of his children and is committed to their welfare can have parental responsibility, but that this does not automatically mean he will have contact with the children if the mother opposes this. Then the court will consider whether to make a contact order.

Rob, as the natural father of the children, can apply as of right, for one of the s 8 orders: *s 10(4)*. These orders are residence orders, determining where the child should live, contact orders, determining whether and how frequently a child should see a particular person, prohibited steps orders, which forbid the taking of a measure, and specific issues orders, which resolve a particular dispute over the upbringing of the child. It is obviously not appropriate for Rob to seek a residence order, as he is not in a position to care for his children at present. However, he might seek a contact order which, if granted, would allow Tara and/or John to visit their father.

When considering whether to grant an order, the court must bear in mind the non-interventionist policy: *s 1(5)*. This requires the court to make orders only where to do so is better than making no order at all. If no order is made in the present case, it is extremely unlikely that any agreement will be reached amicably between the parties. The circumstances of the breakdown in the relationship and subsequent homicide have ensured animosity and bitterness which are not conducive to the co-operation sought by the Act. There would obviously need to be a court-imposed settlement to this problem.

Clearly, any delay in resolving the problem would be prejudicial to the children's welfare, and the court is required to bear this in mind (s 1(2)), and draw up a timetable for the future conduct of the case to ensure that delay is kept to a minimum (s 11). This issue of contact between the children and their father concerns their upbringing and the s 1(3) checklist must be considered by the courts in making any contested s 8 order. The paramount principle is that of the child's welfare (s 1(1)) but, in deciding how best to promote it, the court must have regard to the factors in s 1(3). These include the ascertainable wishes and feelings of the child concerned (in the light of his age and understanding); his physical, emotional and educational needs; the likely effect on him of any change in circumstances; his age, sex, background and other relevant characteristics; any harm he has suffered or is at risk of suffering; how capable his parents and any other relevant person are of meeting his needs, and the range of powers available to the court under the Act.

Here, Nina will clearly have the children living with her, and the court needs to consider the issue of contact only. Both children are very young, and it is unlikely that John, aged 2, can articulate any wishes, and he probably has no recollection of his father. Tara is aged 5, and will almost definitely remember her father, and may want to see him, since she will find it difficult to understand the enormity of what he did. However, Tara is considerably younger than the age at which the court tends to view the child's wishes as decisive; this is normally around the teenage years (*Stewart v Stewart (1973)*). She will have little awareness of the long-term consequences of her decisions, and so her views would be treated with caution. If she expressed a vehement opposition to visiting her father, the court would discount this if it were felt to be the result of pressure from Nina: *Re S (Infants) (1967)*.

By examining the physical, emotional, educational needs of the children, the court usually recognises the desirability of maintaining or establishing contact with a natural parent: *Re H (Minors) (Access) (1992)*. Rob is the natural parent of the two children concerned, and in normal circumstances contact would be inevitable. However, there is the difficulty caused by the crime he has committed. The courts are reluctant to expose children to persons of extreme depravity or criminality: *Scott v Scott (1986)*. Rob has not been violent to the children, and has otherwise been a good father. It is arguable that the child's need for contact, especially Tara who had an established relationship with her father, outweighs any moral judgement on the behaviour of Rob. This is easier to sustain if Rob exhibits genuine remorse and regret at what has occurred. If, however, he is unrepentant, the court might be concerned that the children will receive wrong messages about crime from their father, thereby doing them moral harm.

This issue of harm and the risk of it would count against Rob if there was any moral danger to the children through contact, or any risk that they would be exposed to physical danger. Much will depend, therefore, on the attitude Rob has exhibited towards his crime, and possibly to Nina. It might not be in the children's interests to have contact with their father if he is threatening and aggressive towards their mother. It seems likely that if a contact order is made, it will be made in respect of both children. Although John has no recollection of his father, it would be divisive to treat these siblings differently, as they have to live as a single family unit (*S v S (1988)*), and both ultimately have the same need to maintain blood relationships. This contact could be by way of visits to prison, letters, phonecalls, etc. The court can specify the steps that Nina has to take to ensure contact is maintained, such as requiring her to read out Rob's letters to the children (*Re O (Contact: Imposition of Conditions) (1995)*). If, however, Nina is deeply opposed to the idea of contact, and it can be shown that this causes her great distress, then the child's interest in seeing its natural parent may have to give way to its interests in maintaining a happy and healthy caring parent. Consequently, if contact is genuinely damaging to Nina's mental or physical health, then no order will be made: *Re B (A Minor) (Access) (1992)*. However, Nina must comply with any order that the court makes, or else she faces being sent to prison for contempt, *A v N (Committal: Refusal of Contact) (1997)*.

Regardless of the issue of contact with Rob, Nina must also deal with the issue of contact with Jean, Rob's mother, and the children's grandmother. Jean is not entitled to apply for a s 8 order as of right; instead she must seek leave from the court, *s 10(2)*. In granting leave, the court will consider the factors in s 10(2), namely the type of order being sought, the relationship between the applicant and child and the risk of the application disrupting the child's life, thereby causing harm. Here, Jean would be seeking a contact order which would enable her to have a relationship with her son's children. Rob and Nina were never married, and so Rob has no parental responsibility which would enable him to arrange contact. Whether leave would be granted, would depend on the kind of relationship Jean had with the children previously. If she had formed an integral part of their lives, playing the role of grandmother, it is likely that she would be given leave. She would be seeking to reinforce an existing relationship and would not be seeking merely to interfere and disrupt.

If leave is granted, then the usual principles of non-intervention (s 1(5)), delay (s 1(2)), and welfare being paramount (s 1(1)) apply. The statutory checklist in s 1(3) would require the court to consider the children's wishes, but, as mentioned earlier, this will not carry much weight. The desirability of maintaining relationships with close blood relatives is an established principle, and it is difficult to see that it would be in the best interests of the children to be deprived of the love and affection of a grandmother because of the actions of their father. This assumes that Jean has played a part in their lives, and does not seek to disrupt or upset the children. There does not seem to be risk of harm, and Jean's ability to care and cope with the children might determine the kind of contact permitted. This could be by way of telephone calls, letters, visits or possibly even staying visits to their grandmothers. Only if such contact could be demonstrated to be damaging to Nina's health, given the exceptional circumstances of the case, would contact be denied: *Re B (A Minor) (Access) (1992)*.

Question 37

Oliver and Penny lived together for eight years, during which time two children, Abigail, aged 6, and Beatrice, aged 4, were born. There is a very strong bond between Oliver and the two children, as he works from home and has spent a great deal of time with them. Penny has been a successful journalist, travelling all over the world to cover assignments. She has recently met and fallen in love with Jimmy, an out of work hippy who has an ambition to hitchhike throughout the world. Penny has announced to Oliver that she might go to join Jimmy and she would then be taking the girls with her. She has also said that whilst Abigail is Oliver's daughter, Beatrice is the result of an affair she had with another journalist, Neil.

Oliver is distraught at the prospect of losing the girls, both of whom he loves very much. He does not believe Penny's story about Beatrice, but, even if it is true, he says it does not change the way he feels about Beatrice.

Advise Oliver.

Answer plan

- Parental responsibility for both girls must be considered, who has it and how it may be exercised;
- it will be necessary to consider Beatrice's status as Oliver's child;
- then consider whether Oliver needs leave to apply for a s 8 order;
- explain the range of s 8 orders, the general non-interventionist policy and need to avoid delay;
- then look at the welfare of the children in the light of the s 1(3) checklist, and the difficulty faced if they are taken abroad.

Answer

Oliver's position regarding the two children, Abigail and Beatrice, is somewhat complicated as he is not married to their mother, Penny, and there is a possible dispute over Beatrice's paternity. It is not doubted that he is Abigail's father, but whilst he may have a financial responsibility for her upkeep under the *Child Support Act 1991*, he does not have parental responsibility under the Children Act 1989. Under *Children Act s 2(1)*, parental responsibility is borne by the natural mother of the child and by the natural father if he is married to the mother at the time of the child's birth or conception. Therefore, only Penny has parental responsibility for Abigail and Beatrice. Oliver could only have parental responsibility for Abigail if he married her mother, or by formal agreement, or by court order: Children Act 1989 s 4. in respect of Beatrice, Oliver could have parental responsibility if he was registered as Beatrice's father but on the facts this seems unlikely.

Consequently, Penny has parental responsibility for both girls, and this is defined in *Children Act 1989 s 3(1)*, as 'all the rights, duties, powers and responsibilities and authority which by law a parent of a child has in relation to the child and its property'. Penny can therefore choose where her daughters should live, and she is under no legal obligation to involve Oliver in these decisions. If Oliver wishes to be involved in the future upbringing of the two girls, he will need to apply for a court order under *s 8* of the *Children Act 1989*.

A natural father of a child can apply for a s 8 order as of right, and so Oliver can definitely make an application in relation to Abigail. The position regarding Beatrice is more complex. If she is Oliver's child then he has the right to apply for a s 8 order (*s 10(4)*) *Children Act 1989*, but if she is not his child then his right to apply must be based on the fact that Beatrice has lived with him for at least three years (*s 10(5)*). This permits an application for a residence or contact order, but not for a prohibited steps order or a specific issues order, where leave would be required. *Section 10(9)* provides the criteria to be applied in deciding whether to grant leave. In the present case, Oliver has a close relationship with Beatrice and she is not likely to be harmed by any disruption, and therefore he would probably be given leave to make his s 8 application. Leave will usually be granted to those with a genuine interest in this child's welfare, and would be refused to those who were merely seeking to meddle and interfere.

As well as the issues relating specifically to a s 8 order, it may be desirable to deal with the issue of Beatrice's paternity. As Oliver and Penny were never married, there is no assistance from the presumption of legitimacy. Therefore, Beatrice's paternity will need to be settled by way of blood tests or DNA genetic testing. These can be ordered by the court (*Family Law Reform Act 1969 s 20(1)*), and if Penny refuses to comply without good reason then adverse inferences can be drawn (*FLRA 1969s 23(1)*). In the present case, it seems likely that testing would be ordered, as it is usually in the child's best interests to know who his or her father is: *S v S (1972)*.

In determining Oliver's application for a s 8 order, it must be borne in mind that the welfare of the child is the paramount consideration in issues concerning its upbringing: *s 1(1) Children Act 1989*. Thus, the court will consider what is in Abigail's and Beatrice's best interests, not necessarily what the parties want. There are a number of different orders available under s 8, namely a residence order, determining where the children should live; a contact order, dealing with the arrangements for contact and visits; a prohibited steps order, which can be used to prohibit the taking of a particular step; and a specific issues order, which can be used to seek the courts assistance on a particular issue. The last two orders should not be sought if the matter could be dealt with by way of a residence or contact order (*Children Act 1989 s 9(5)*), and so Oliver would be best advised to seek a residence or contact order initially. Any unresolved issues could then be dealt with by way of a prohibited steps or specific issues order.

In dealing with an application for a s 8 order, the court must have regard to the non-interventionist policy in *s 1(5)* of the Act. This provides that the court should not make an order, unless the making of an order is better than not making one. The policy of the Act is to encourage consensus and agreement wherever possible, but unfortunately Oliver and Penny seem unlikely to agree where the children should live, and so a court order may be necessary.

Having become involved, the court must recognise that delay will often prejudice the welfare of the children (*s 1(2)*) and, with this in mind, a timetable for the future conduct of proceedings must be set (*s 11*). The welfare of the children is the paramount consideration (*s 1(1)*), and the statutory checklist in *s 1(3)* of the Children Act provides a list of factors to be considered.

The first factor is the ascertainable wishes of the child in the light of their age and understanding. Both Abigail and Beatrice are quite young, and are well below the age where their opinions would be viewed as decisive: this is usually around the teenage years (*Stewart v Stewart (1973)*), where the child is able to appreciate the long-term consequences of their decisions. Most children of 6 and 4 will wish to have contact with both parents, but may be unable to grasp the implications of a choice of residence. If the girls have been coached or pressurised, then their views will be disregarded: *Re S (Infants) (1967)*.

The court will then consider the physical, educational and emotional needs of the children. Here the children are both young girls, and traditionally there has been a preference for keeping young girls with their mother: *Re W (A Minor) (1983)*. In *Plant v Plant (1982)*, it was stressed that usually there are obvious advantages in leaving young children in the care of their mother, unless she is incapable or unsuitable. This would in the past have favoured Penny but, in *Re H (A Minor) (1980)*, it was emphasised that times had changed and that many fathers were as capable as mothers of looking after small children. Ultimately, it is a question of the welfare of the children, and there are obvious advantages to young girls being with their mothers, especially through puberty. However, in the present case, the mother has been frequently absent, and the girls have been cared for predominantly by their father. There is nothing to suggest that he has been unable to minister to their needs, and so it should not necessarily be assumed that the girls will go to their mother.

It is obviously necessary to provide the children with a caring, stable upbringing, and Oliver would be able to do this. Penny, on the other hand, has had a busy career and is proposing to join her new boyfriend, hitchhiking around the world. This lack of a stable home base and the possible educational disadvantages may well count against Penny; *May v May (1986)* shows the importance attached to a good education.

The court will try to ensure that Abigail and Beatrice remain together, as siblings derive considerable support from one another: *Adams v Adams (1984)*. The likely effect of change must also be considered, as the tendency is to preserve the status quo and avoid unnecessary disruption: *J v C (1970)*. The girls have been used to their home and being looked after by Oliver, whilst Penny was away working. To uproot them from this, remove Abigail from school, and subject them to the peripatetic existence that Penny has in mind, would arguably be detrimental to their welfare. Oliver is able to provide greater continuity of care and, in *Riley v Riley (1986)*, the court expressed a preference for the children living with a parent who could provide continuity of care in one place as opposed to the parent who was constantly on the move.

The age, sex and background and any other relevant characteristics of the children are considered, together with the risk of harm to the children. There is no suggestion that Jimmy is an unsavoury character or would harm the girls, but the travel plans of Penny and Jimmy seem unconventional and possibly hazardous for such small children.

Lastly, the capabilities of the parents and any other relevant person of meeting the child's needs must be considered. There is often an advantage if a parent can show that they have an established and suitable relationship with a parent substitute, as the child's interests are often better served in a two-adult household. Here, Jimmy and Penny's relationship is very new, and Jimmy is an unconventional person who does not seem to fit the stereotype of the replacement father. Oliver has no partner that we are told of, but he has been a loving and caring parent to the girls and has a good chance of obtaining a residence order.

However, if the court grants a residence order in favour of Oliver, then he must also be given parental responsibility to enable him properly to care for the girls: *s 12(1)*. The parental responsibility of Penny will not end just because a residence order has been made in favour of Oliver. Penny should still continue to play an important part in her daughters' lives, and it is likely that she would be given generous contact with the girls. In *Re H (Minors) (Access) (1992)*, the court stressed that it would usually be in the child's best interests for contact to be maintained with natural parents.

In the unlikely event of Penny being granted the residence order, then again it is probable that Oliver would be granted generous contact with the girls. A person in whose favour the residence order is granted, cannot remove a child from the jurisdiction for more than one month without the written consent of everyone with parental responsibility or leave of the court: *s 13(1)*. Therefore, Oliver could not remove the children if he had a residence order, but it would seem that Penny could if she had the order, as no one other than she would have parental responsibility for the children. It would therefore be necessary to seek a prohibited steps order under s 8 if Oliver wished to prevent Penny subsequently taking the children overseas. The courts would, however, usually allow the children to accompany an emigrating parent who has a residence order in their favour: *Chamberlain v de la Mare (1982)*. However, Penny is not remarrying, nor is her way of life overseas going to be settled or stable and so the court might feel that the disruption of contact with Oliver is not in the children's interests, given that they are so fond of him: *Re K (A Minor) (1992)*.

To conclude it would seem that Oliver should seek a residence order to enable the two girls to live with him, and this, in the circumstances, should be forthcoming. In the course of this application, it may be that Beatrice's paternity will be resolved. In any event, Oliver should be allowed generous contact and should seek to prohibit the taking of the children overseas, by way of a prohibited steps order.

CHAPTER 8

CHILDREN ON DIVORCE

▌INTRODUCTION

When parties divorce, it may be that they can reach agreement on where the children should live and how frequently they should have contact with their other parent. The Children Act 1989 seems to encourage parents to adopt a responsible attitude towards these issues and to agree these matters where possible. It is important for the adults involved to remember that divorce ends the husband/wife relationship, but that both continue to be parents of the children.

If there is a dispute over the children, then it is resolved by the same method as other disputes over a child's upbringing and welfare, namely by the making of a s 8 order. The general non-interventionist policy, the need to avoid delay and the welfare principle, and s 1(3) checklist will apply, as in the previous chapter.

Question 38

Mike and Laura are getting divorced, but they are having difficulty making arrangements for their two children, Kate, aged 13, and Julia, aged 6. Laura has set up home with Ian in his small house, which she admits will be cramped if both girls join her. Kate does not like Ian and is refusing to join her mother, complaining that Ian is bossy and makes her life a misery. Kate has a good relationship with Mike and wishes to stay with him. Mike is remaining in the former matrimonial home, having managed to raise enough cash by way of a mortgage to buy out Laura's share. Laura is unhappy with Kate being with Mike; she feels Kate is too young to make a decision and has been swayed by Mike's promises of a puppy if she stays with him.

Mike has agreed that Julia can live with Laura, as she is disabled and he would find it difficult to give her the care she needs. However, he is anxious to be able to see her each weekend and during the week if he can. Laura is opposed to this, claiming that it would be disruptive and she is keen that Julia looks on Ian as her new father. Mike has heard rumours that Laura is encouraging Julia to use Ian's surname instead of his.

Advise Mike.

Answer plan

- Introduction should explain parental responsibility and the procedure for filing arrangements for children on divorce. Then consider the non-interventionist policy and need to avoid delay;
- continue by outlining the various s 8 orders available to deal with these problems, namely where the child should live, the issue of contact and change of surname;
- take each issue in turn and look at the child's welfare in the light of the s 1(3) checklist;
- where Kate should live will be affected by her wishes as well as the parties' respective abilities to care for her;
- contact with Julia is usually viewed as desirable; explain why;
- then deal with the special provisions on change of surname.

Answer

Since Mike and Laura were married, they both have parental responsibility for their children: *Children Act 1989 s 2(1)*. This is defined in *s 3(1)* as 'all the rights, duties, powers and responsibilities and authority which by law a parent of a child has in relation to the child and its property'. Both Mike and Laura will continue to have parental responsibility after divorce, as the Children Act 1989 emphasises the continuity of parental care, and the emphasis is also on the obligation of the parent to meet the needs of the child, rather than the outdated concept of parental rights. Consequently, the important and paramount issue here is the welfare of the children (s 1(1)) rather than the wishes of the parties.

There are three issues that need to be resolved, namely, where Kate should live; the extent of Mike's contact with Julia; and the use of a different surname for Julia. The Children Act 1989 tries to encourage consensus between the parents where possible, and the non-interventionist approach is enshrined in the Act: s 1(5). On divorce, the parties are required to file a statement of arrangements for the children, detailing the measures that have been agreed and the areas of disagreement. If the parties have reached agreement then there will be no need for the court to intervene, but if, as here, there are unresolved issues then the court will need to make the decision as to what is best for the children.

The court has jurisdiction on divorce to make one or more of the s 8 orders, namely a residence order; a contact order; a prohibited steps order; and a specific issues order. The first issue concerns where Kate should live and this should be dealt with by way of a residence order. Delay is usually prejudicial to the welfare of the child (*s 1(2)*) and therefore it is necessary for the court to draw up a timetable for the conduct of the case (s 11) in order to minimise delay.

In determining where Kate should live, the court will have regard to the s 1(3) checklist bearing in mind that Kate's welfare is the paramount consideration: s 1(1). The factors in *s 1(3)* include the ascertainable wishes and feelings of the child (in the light of their age and understanding); the physical, emotional and educational needs of the child; the likely effect of any change in circumstances; the child's age, sex, background and other relevant characteristics; any harm which she has suffered or is at risk of suffering; how capable the parents and any other relevant person are of meeting the child's needs.

Kate's parents cannot agree where she should live and Kate herself has exhibited a preference for staying with her father, Mike. Kate is aged 13, an age where her wishes are likely to be given weight by the courts: *Stewart v Stewart (1973)*. Assuming Kate is reasonably intelligent and articulate, she is likely, at 13, to appreciate the long-term consequences of her decision. She has a good rapport with her father, but does not have a good relationship with Ian. There seems to be genuine difficulty, given Ian's forceful behaviour, and it may be argued that the attitude displayed by Ian and Laura in relation to Kate's sister, Julia, illustrates a somewhat heavy-handed attempt to replace Mike in the children's affections. This could be upsetting for Kate, and it does not seem that she has reasons when she says she wants to stay with her father. Laura's view that Kate is too young to decide would probably not be shared by the court, and in *Marsh v Marsh (1977)* a child of 12 was able to state her preference.

The only concern might be that Mike's promise of a puppy might be viewed as a bribe or pressure (*Re S (Infants) (1967)*), but given Kate's age and prior good relationship with her father, it is unlikely that this influenced her decision. Kate's physical, emotional and educational needs must be considered, and it is usual for teenage girls to live with their mother, who are often better equipped to deal with the problems of puberty: *Re W (A Minor) (1983)*. However, in *Re H (A Minor) (1980)*, this view was not given great weight by the Court of Appeal who recognised that in many cases a father may be in a position to provide better care for a particular child than its mother. Kate has a better rapport with her father, and her relationship with her mother may be very strained if forced to live there. Both Mike and Laura can provide Kate with a home, although Mike's position is more comfortable than Laura's cramped house. Whilst material advantages get little weight (*Stephenson v Stephenson (1985)*), it does seem that the situation for Kate would be better if she lived with her father. The usual position of keeping siblings together for the mutual support they give each other (*Adams v Adams (1984)*) might not apply so strongly here, given the large age gap between the children, and the fact that Julia is disabled may mean that the needs of the individual girls should be considered separately (*B-T v B-T (1990)*).

At present, Kate has been staying with her father, and the court will consider the effect of changing this. There is generally a reluctance to disturb the established status quo (*J v C (1970)*) but, in the instant case, it would be difficult to argue that Kate's presence with Mike is so established that it cannot be varied (*Allington v Allington (1985)*), especially since Laura has maintained contact. However, the desirability of a stable upbringing is very important, and working fathers often experience difficulty when faced with bringing up a child. The courts have frequently preferred the continuous care of the mother: *Re K (1988)*. However, in such cases, the children have been very young, whereas here Kate is 13 and would be at school for most of the time that Mike was at work, and would presumably be happy with after-school activities and care until her father returned home.

There is no suggestion that Kate would be at risk of harm with either parent, and they both seem to have been loving and capable parents. However, Kate has a better relationship with her father, and her antagonism towards Ian may be difficult to overcome. It would seem, therefore, that Kate's welfare would best be served by making a residence order in favour of Mike, with generous contact between Kate and Laura and Julia. Laura's parental responsibility for Kate would continue, despite the residence order.

The situation concerning Julia raises two controversial issues, that of contact and change of surname. The parties are agreed that Julia should reside with Laura, and consequently there will be no need for a residence order, based on the non-interventionist policy in s 1(5). However, the degree of contact is not agreed and so the court will need to consider making a contact order under s 8. Mike, as a parent, can apply as of right (*s 10(4)*) and the problem will be resolved by the use of the *s 1(3)* checklist to ascertain what is best for Julia since her welfare is paramount (s 1(1)).

Julia is only 6 years old, and the nature and extent of her disability are unknown. Not a lot of weight would be attached to her wishes, as given her age she is unlikely to have the understanding of the long-term implications of a decision: *Stewart v Stewart (1973)*. However, it is generally recognised that it is in the interests of her emotional needs to have contact with her natural parent: *Re H (Minors) (Access) (1992)*. Mike has been a good father to Julia and contact would only be denied if it were damaging to Julia. The court would not be sympathetic to Laura's desire to replace Mike with Ian as Julia's father; this is generally viewed as being confusing and upsetting for a child. Julia has had a relationship with Mike for the past six years, and it would be in her interests for this to be maintained. Contact by telephone or letter may be difficult, and it seems likely that Mike will be allowed to visit Julia. Whether it will be practicable for him to take her out or have her stay with him will depend on the extent of her handicap. It is desirable for there to be generous contact between parent and child but it may be necessary to restrict Mike's contact with Julia to certain periods. This provides a degree of certainty for Laura and Ian, who are trying to build a family life together, without being interrupted at unpredictable times by Mike wishing to see Julia. It would also enable Julia to be better prepared, and so some kind of formalised contact may be ordered.

A contact order, like a residence order, does not usually extend beyond the child's sixteenth birthday. However, in exceptional circumstances, it may do so (Children Act 1989 s 9(6)) and, if Julia's disability is profound, then a longer order may be necessary.

The problem of Julia's surname has caused Mike some concern since Laura seems to want Julia to adopt Ian's surname. It is not possible to change a child's surname without permission from all those with parental responsibility or with leave from the court: *s 13(1)*. It is unlikely that the court would order a change of surname, as it usually is in the child's interests to preserve this link with her father: *W v A (1981)*. The change would only be permitted if the child had actually been using the changed name for a long time: *R v R (1982)*.

If there is no residence order in force in relation to Julia, then Mike could apply for a prohibited steps order to prohibit the use of the new surname, or raise as a specific issue order the question of what name Julia should be known by. As indicated earlier, the court tends to preserve the child's real name, and in *Re PC (Change of Surname)* (1997) the court stressed that one parent with parental responsibility cannot change a child's surname without the consent of the other parent with parental responsibility.

Question 39

Felicity and George married seven years ago, and they have two children, Henry, aged 4, and Harriet, aged 3. Last year, the marriage experienced difficulties and George agreed that Felicity could go and spend some time with her sister, who lives on a remote Scottish island, in order to 'recharge her batteries'. However, Felicity stayed longer than the three weeks she had agreed with George, and during her time away she was uncontactable by phone and never responded to any of George's letters. George initially found looking after the children difficult, but he found an excellent nanny, Jo, with whom he has now fallen in love. George and Jo are now sharing the former matrimonial home, and the children seem contented.

Felicity heard of this in a letter from her mother, and returned to collect her children and take them to Scotland with her, where she hopes to marry Fergus, a sheep farmer she has just met.

George refuses to let the children go, saying that they are happy where they are. Advise Felicity, who is divorcing George, on whether she will be able to take the children with her.

Answer plan

- Begin by explaining the basic concepts of parental responsibility and the availability of s 8 orders on divorce;
- the non-interventionist policy and the need to avoid delay must be stated;
- how the residence order will be determined by reference to what is in the child's best interests and the s 1(3) checklist must be explained as relevant to the case;
- the issue of contact must also be considered.

Answer

Felicity and George both have parental responsibility for their children as they are married (*Children Act 1989 s 2(1)*), and each can exercise this independently of the other (*s 2(7)*). This means that both Felicity and George can individually exercise 'all the rights, duties, powers and responsibilities and authority which by law a parent of a child has in relation to the child and its property' (s 3(1)). The emphasis in the Act is on the parental obligation to nurture and care for the child, and the child is not to be regarded as the property of the parents. Thus, the child needs a home and day-to-day care, which both parents have provided in the past. However, George and Felicity now have opposing views as to by whom and where such care should be provided. Obviously, it will not be possible for them both to exercise their contradictory plans for the children, and so the court will need to be involved.

Section 8 of the Children Act 1989 enables the court to make four different kinds of order in relation to children. These are residence orders, which determine where and with whom the child should live, which is clearly an appropriate order in the present case; contact orders, which determine who the child should be able to have contact with and the basis for such contact; prohibited steps orders; and specific issues orders. Particular problematic issues can be resolved by seeking a prohibited steps order to prevent the taking of certain measures or a specific issues order to deal with a particular point concerning the upbringing of the child.

A *s* 8 order can be sought on divorce or other family proceedings (*s 10(1)*), but it is also possible to make a free-standing application without other proceedings taking place (*s 10(2)*). In determining the application, the court will view the welfare of the children as its paramount consideration (s 1(1)), and both Felicity and George, as parents, can apply as of right for such an order (*s 10(4)*). However, in line with the non-interventionist policy of the *Act* (*s 1(5)*), the court will only make an order if that is preferable to not making one. There are no longer routine residence orders made on divorce, as the parties are encouraged to agree their arrangements for the children. However if, as in this case, no agreement can be reached, then the court will need to be involved.

It is important to settle the issue of where the children should live as soon as possible, to give stability to the children and avoid any unnecessary disruption. The Children Act 1989 recognises that delay is often prejudicial to the welfare of the children (s 1(2)) and so the court will provide a timetable for the conduct of the case (s 11).

In determining the issue of where the children should live, the court will look at the statutory checklist of factors contained in s 1(3) to come to the result that is in the best interest of the children's welfare. First, the ascertainable wishes and feelings of the children given their age and understanding must be considered. The children in the present case are very young, and it is unlikely that they have sufficient understanding to make any rational decision. They are apparently happy with their father, but there is nothing to indicate that they would be unhappy with their mother, and so no assistance will be derived from the wishes of the children.

Next, it is necessary to look at the physical, emotional and educational needs of the children, and this ties in with the other factor of the child's age, sex, background and other relevant characteristics. In the present case, the two children are young, pre-school children, and there has traditionally been a tendency to the view that such children are usually better off in their mother's care: *Re W (A Minor) (1983)*. It is not clear how long ago Felicity left her children, but there are cases where fathers have brought up children in the absence of the mother, only for her to be given the care of the children on her return (for example, *Greer v Greer (1974)*). This strong link between mothers and young children could be broken if there was evidence that Felicity would be an unsuitable or incapable parent, but there is insufficient evidence of this on the facts. The Court of Appeal in *Re H (A Minor) (1990)* recognised that this should not be regarded as akin to a presumption, but that in reality it was frequently the mother who was in the best position to provide for young children's day-to-day needs. George has managed to care for the children, but given the age of the children, he will have to put up a strong argument that his arrangements with Jo enable him to meet their needs better than Felicity and Fergus.

The children should usually be kept together (*Adams v Adams (1984)*), as they can derive support from one another, and so the fact that Harriet is a girl and Henry a boy would not point to their being separated, and cared for by the parent of the same sex. Both parents seem able to provide adequate homes for the children and the court will not be overly concerned with material advantages: *Re F (1969)*.

The court will also consider the likely effect of change on the children, as disruption can be prejudicial to their welfare. If the children are well-established in satisfactory living conditions then the court will be loath to disrupt this: *J v C (1970)*. George will argue that the children have become settled with him and Jo, and they are happy in their familiar surroundings. Certainly, Felicity's plans would involve moving them from an area that they are familiar with to new and different surroundings. However, she could argue that the children have not been with their father for very long (*Allington v Allington (1985)*), although she has not kept much contact with them. She could also argue that moving to be with Fergus will provide the children with a better quality of life in a rural area, near other members of their family as her sister lives there. Also in her favour is the fact that she does not need to work, and so can provide her children with the continuity of care that the court finds desirable: *Re K (1988)*. George cannot do this, and would need to rely on Jo, with whom he does not necessarily have a stable relationship.

There is no suggestion that the children have been harmed by Felicity or George or are at risk of this in the future. Neither Jo nor Fergus appears to be an unsuitable character and so this factor will not be decisive. The capacity of the parents and other relevant persons, namely Jo and Fergus, to meet the children's needs must finally be considered. It is not a question of judging which parent has been the better person (*Re K (1988)*), but rather which one can best look after the children. Therefore, Felicity's behaviour is irrelevant unless it sheds light on her ability to care for the children. Neither parent has remarried, although both have new partners and it basically seems that Felicity's strongest arguments are based on her ability as a full-time mother to best care for her young children. George's strongest point is the fact that he has cared for the children since Felicity left but, in view of the relatively short time, it may be that the residence order would be granted to Felicity.

However, it is important for the children to maintain contact with their father, as preserving blood ties is usually in their best interests: *Re B (Minor) (Access)* (1992). There are two ways in which this can be achieved: either by a split residence order allowing the children to live part of the time with their mother, and part with their father (*s 11(4)*), or by making a contact order in favour of George. If the children are going to live at least part of the time with Felicity, the remoteness of their home will make regular contact with George difficult. He may be able to see them at weekends, or possibly for longer in holiday periods, but he will not have day-to-day contact, and so the court will probably make an order for reasonable contact, leaving the parties to work out the finer details. It may be better for the children if a split residence order was avoided, as the appearance of two very distant homes may be disruptive.

In conclusion, therefore, it would seem likely that Felicity would obtain a residence order so that the children live with her and have contact with their father, George. George's parental responsibility continues despite the divorce and residence order, and he should still continue to play an important role in his children's lives.

Question 40

Victoria and Albert are married and are both aged 45; they have three children, Edward, aged 14, Alice, aged 10, and Eugenie, aged 2. The couple have recently separated, after Eugenie made certain remarks that Victoria construed as being allegations of sexual abuse against Albert. Albert has vigorously denied that anything improper occurred between himself and Eugenie, and states that Victoria was just looking for an excuse to leave him. Victoria has since moved into a large house owned by Alexandra, her lesbian lover, taking the children with her. Victoria wants the children to live with her, and does not want them to see Albert, whereas Albert is unhappy about the children being with Victoria and Alexandra.

Advise Victoria on what approach the court would take concerning the children, if she were to divorce Albert.

Answer plan

- Begin by explaining the procedure for determining what should happen to the children on divorce and the availability of s 8 orders if there is a dispute;
- briefly outline parental responsibility, the non-interventionist policy and need to avoid delay;
- determine the residence order by looking at what is in the child's welfare by reference to the s 1(3) checklist. The important issue is the effect of Victoria's lesbianism on her ability to care for her children;
- then examine the problem the allegation of child abuse causes in relation to contact between the children and their father.

Answer

If Victoria were to divorce Albert, then she would need to file a statement of arrangements for the children, indicating what areas of agreement there are. If there are unresolved areas, then it is possible for her to apply for one or more of the orders in s 8 Children Act 1989 (*s 10(1)*) at the same time as taking these family proceedings. Nevertheless, it is possible to make a free-standing application for a s 8 order without seeking any other relief from the courts (*s 10(2)*), and this would be the sensible step to take if she is unsure about divorce.

Section 8 provides for four types of order, namely, a residence order, a contact order, a prohibited steps order, and a specific issues order. The first two orders seem relevant here, and it is not possible to obtain a prohibited steps order or specific issues order if a residence or contact order is more appropriate: *s 9(4)*. As parents, both Victoria and Albert can apply for a s 8 order as of right: *s 10(4)*.

Since Victoria and Albert were married at the time of the births of their children, they both have parental responsibility for the children: *s 2(1)*. This is defined in *s 3(1)* as 'all the rights, duties, powers and responsibilities and authority which by law a parent of a child has in relation to the child and its property'. The emphasis is on the parental obligation to care for the children, and this parental responsibility continues, even after divorce or the making of a s 8 order. This parental responsibility can be exercised by each parent independently of the other (*s 2(7)*), and there is no longer any automatic parental veto of the other parent's actions. Obviously though, the parents in this case have completely opposing views as to what should happen to the children, and so there is an unacceptable stalemate that will need to be resolved.

The court will only intervene if absolutely necessary, and there is a non-interventionist policy (s 1(5)) of only making a s 8 order if this would be better than not making one. Since Victoria and Albert are implacably opposed to each other's proposals, an order will be necessary. To avoid delay, which is viewed as prejudicial to the welfare of the child (s 1(2)) once an application has been made for a s 8 order, the court will lay down a timetable for the future stages of the case: s 11.

A residence order determines where and with whom a child should live; whereas a contact order enables contact between a child and another person, in this case, a parent. The prime and paramount importance is the child's welfare (*s 1(1)*), not the wishes of the parents, and the court will apply the statutory checklist in s 1(3). This contains various factors, namely, the ascertainable wishes and feelings of the child; its emotional, physical and educational needs; the likely effect of any change in circumstances; the age, sex, background and other relevant characteristics; the risk of harm; and the capability of the parents and any other relevant person to meet the child's needs.

In the present case, the two older children will be able to articulate their views, whereas Eugenie, at two, will have little or no understanding of what is happening. Edward, at 14, is of the age where a great deal of weight would be attached to his views. He is likely to be 'Gillick competent' in the sense that he has the intelligence and maturity to make decisions with an awareness of the long-term consequences: *Stewart v Stewart (1973)*. Alice is 10 and, whilst her views will be considered, the weight accorded them will depend on her intelligence and maturity. In *Marsh v Marsh (1977)* the views of a 12 year old and a 9 year old were adhered to, and so Alice's views may well be taken into account. On the facts, nothing is mentioned as to the views of either child but, given the sensitive nature of Victoria's relationship with Alexandra, the ability of the children to accept this and not be unduly embarrassed by it will be important.

Looking at the physical, emotional and education needs of the children, together with their age, sex, background and other relevant characteristics, there are arguments both for and against Victoria. Eugenie is a young child, and there is a tendency to view young children as being better cared for by their mother: *Greer v Greer (1974)*. Likewise, for older girls it might be argued that the problems of puberty are best dealt with by the mother: *Re W (A Minor) (1983)*. Whereas for older boys, there is a somewhat weaker argument that they would be better served by being with their father, who can provide a role model for them in their adolescence: *W v W and C (1968)*. However, these are now recognised as being generalisations, rather than presumptions, by the Court of Appeal in *Re H (A Minor) (1990)*. The crucial question will be to look at the child's needs and see which parent can best meet those needs. There would need to be pressing arguments that Victoria's ability to provide care for her children should be overridden, and the main argument of Albert will be that Victoria's lesbianism prevents her from adequately caring for the children. In the past, this might have prevented the children from living with their mother, but now this is not necessarily so. In *Re P (A Minor) (1983)*, the court stressed that it was not about to moralise on sexual practices of parents, but instead to examine what effect this might have on the children. Where the mother was a caring mother, then her lesbianism would be a disadvantage because it could expose her children to embarrassment and ridicule. In *Re P (A Minor)* (1983) the children lived with the mother because the only other alternative was for them to go into local authority care, which the court felt was unacceptable. If Albert is not proposing to care for the children himself, then it is doubtful that the court would prevent Victoria from gaining a residence order. However, if Albert was prepared to offer the children a home, then the court would look at the nature of the relationship. In *C v C (A Minor) (1991)*, the court stressed that lesbianism was not an automatic disqualification of a mother from looking after her children. It is, however, an unusual background, but a sensitive, loving lesbian relationship can often be a more satisfactory environment for a child than a less sensitive or loving heterosexual have had.

There have been cases where mothers such as Victoria have been given residence orders, since they were in a better position to provide continuity of care for their children (*Re K (1988)*), whereas the father who had to work could not. The living conditions of both Albert and Victoria seem adequate, and the court is not overly concerned by material advantage: *Stephenson v Stephenson (1985)*. However, it is usually desirable to keep brothers and sisters together (*Adams v Adams (1984)*) because of the mutual support they derive from each other. The two older children in the present case are reasonably close in age and their interests could better be served by being together.

The possible effect of change is unlikely to be influential here, as the current living arrangements are recently arrived at (*Allington v Allington (1985)*), so there is really no status quo to disrupt. However, the risk of harm will play a part here. Victoria's lesbianism could cause embarrassment, but it could also subtly harm the children if she were too indiscreet or militant: *B v B (Minors) (1991)*. This does not seem to be the case, and so it would be necessary to consider whether there is any risk of harm from Albert. There are the allegations supposedly made by Eugenie, which have been strongly denied. Allegations of child abuse are very easily made, and a chance remark by a child can easily be misconstrued. There does not seem to be any evidence to support Victoria's allegation, and it might be difficult to convince the court that Albert was a risk to the children. Even if there had been sexual abuse, there is no absolute rule prohibiting contact between a child and the abusing parent (*H v H (1989)*); much will depend on the circumstances of the case. Without wanting to trivialise sexual abuse of children, if the assault were not of the most serious nature and there was no lasting harm and genuine regret by the abuser, then the child may suffer more from a cessation of contact with the parent. Supervised contact may be in the child's best interests.

Looking at the ability of the parents to meet the children's needs, it seems that Victoria is more able to provide the day-to-day care that is usually desirable, and if Alexandra is a caring partner, this will improve her case, and consequently she may well obtain a residence order. It is nevertheless considered to be in a child's best interests to maintain contact with its father (*Re B (Minor) (Access) (1984)*), and there would need to be pressing reasons for terminating such contact. There is no evidence that Albert has harmed Alice or Edward and the evidence of harm to Eugenie is not strong. Consequently, there is likely to be a contact order enabling the children to see their father, unless they do not wish to do so. Even then, the court would be mindful of the possibility that they had been pressurised by Victoria.

CHAPTER 9

CHILDREN AND THE LOCAL AUTHORITY

■ INTRODUCTION

On occasion, it will be necessary to consider whether a local authority obtain a court order to protect a child's interests when that child is at risk. In addition, the local authority has a duty to support a child in need by providing services. This duty is exercisable with the consent of the child's parent if the child is voluntarily accomodate and the child's parent is free to remove the child at any time. This is to be contrasted with the compulsory nature of the powers that can be exercised when the child is at risk from harm. The Children Act 1989 made fundamental changes to the relationship between the child, their parents and the local authority. The power that the local authority used to have to compulsorily take a child into care without a court order has been abolished, and there is no automatic right to take a child into care compulsorily where the child has been voluntarily placed in local authority accommodation.

Once again, the welfare of the child is the paramount consideration and the need to avoid delay (s 1(2)), and the non-interventionist policy in *s 1(5)* are applicable to such cases. It is important to be aware of the large range of powers available to the local authority and to realise that the rationale of the Children Act 1989 is that children are usually happier and their welfare best promoted within their own family. Removing a child from its family should be an exceptional measure when there is no other way of adequately protecting the child from harm. The emphasis is on the local authority seeking the co-operation of the child's parents where possible.

The taking of compulsory steps in relation to a child is a very serious step, and the local authority should carefully consider whether its compulsory powers should be used. The litigation itself can be very stressful for the child and their parents, and so the local authority should proceed with caution: *Lancashire County Council v A (2000)*. The concept of parental responsibility is still important and the exercise by the local authority of its powers does not terminate the parental responsibility of the child's parents. If the local authority is concerned about a child's welfare, then it is under a duty to make enquiries: *s 47*. If these enquiries are frustrated by the parents, then there is the power to apply for a child assessment order under *s 43*. If this discloses cause for concern, in that there is a likelihood of the child suffering significant harm, then an application may be made for a care order under *s 31*. This vests parental responsibility with the local authority who must then take steps to promote the child's welfare. If the situation is appropriate, then a supervision order may be made instead. This provides for a supervising officer to be appointed to befriend the child and family and promote the child's welfare within the family. More speedy protection may be available through an emergency protection order (s 44), which enables a child to be temporarily removed from his home.

The *Family Law Act 1996 (Sched 6)* makes changes to *Children Act 1989 s 38* relating to interim care orders and *s 44* relating to emergency protection orders. Under the Act it is possible to make an exclusion requirement in respect of a person living with the child if this would mean that the child will cease to suffer, or cease to be likely to suffer, significant harm. Another person living in the house, whether or not the child's parent must be able and willing to give the child the level of care that it would be reasonable to expect a parent to give, and that person must consent to the exclusion requirement.

The various criteria for these orders must be detailed and an examination conducted of whether the evidence satisfies the criteria. The threshold criteria in section 31 must be satisfied before a case order or a supervision order can be obtained. Then the child's welfare and the welfare checklist must be considered.

Remember to discuss methodically and sensibly the powers available to the local authority, and not to be too draconian. The emphasis is on keeping the child within the family where possible.

As well as the compulsory powers of the local authority, you should be aware of the duty to assist a family in need voluntarily: ss 17–20 of the Act are relevant here. In considering whether to make a compulsory order, the court should ask the local authority if the child's welfare could be better served by supporting the child and their family with the voluntary assistance provided for by the duties in ss 17–20, *Oxfordshire County Council v L (Care and Supervision Order) (1998)*. If local authorities provide support where required, it will often render compulsory intervention unnecessary. It can be very expensive to take a child into care, and the decision of whether or not to act is for the local authority. Family law orders under Children Act 1989 s 8 cannot be used to try to force the local authority to take a child into care, *Re J (Specific Issue Order) (1995)*. Nor can a local authority be sued in tort for its failure to take a child into care if that child subsequently suffers harm, *X v Bedfordshire County Council (1995)*. The only option would be judicial review, which only rarely succeeds, *Re T (Accommodation by Local Authority) (1995)*.

Question 41

Harry and Isobel have two children, Jessica, aged 12, and Jack, aged 14. The local authority has received letters from the children's school, expressing concern over the well being of the children. Jack is an unruly child and does not respond to discipline at school. He frequently does not attend school, and is making poor progress in his studies. The school is also concerned at reports that Jack spends time in the local shopping centre in the company of much older youths, who have reputations for shoplifting and mugging.

Jessica has previously appeared to be a happy child but over the past few months she has become increasingly withdrawn and has occasionally been found weeping in the classroom. She refuses to talk to anyone about what is bothering her and will not undress for PE classes in front of anyone. Matters came to a head when Jessica fled in tears from a biology class on human reproduction. The school is concerned that Jessica may be suffering from sexual abuse.

The local authority's social worker has visited Harry and Isobel, who do not seem overly concerned, saying that 'boys will be boys, and Jessica's just moody'. Advise the local authority on the options open to it in respect of Jessica and Jack.

Answer plan

This question involves a consideration of the compulsory powers of the local authority to safeguard the well being of the two children of the family. Both Harry and Isobel have parental responsibility, but there are concerns about their ability to properly to discharge it. Mention the duty to investigate under s 47, and then consider each child separately.

In relation to Jack, the possible options are an education supervision order (s 36) or a care order (s 31). The basis for each order must be explored, as must the threshold criteria of likelihood of suffering significant harm. The child's welfare is paramount and the s 1(3) checklist should be discussed. The possibility of a supervision order should be considered.

Jessica's problem appears more serious, and needs to be investigated. The possibility of obtaining a child assessment order (s 43) or, if necessary, an emergency protection order (s 44) should be explored, together with the statutory basis for making such orders. Once Jessica's true situation has been assessed, then the option of a care order (s 31) should be explored.

Answer

Since Harry and Isobel are married both have parental responsibility for Jessica and Jack. Parental responsibility is defined as 'all the rights, duties, powers and responsibilities and authority which by law a parent of a child has in relation to the child and its property': *Children Act 1989 s 3(1)*. The emphasis of the Act is on the parents' obligation to care for their children and promote their children's welfare. Clearly, concerns are expressed in the instant case as to whether Harry and Isobel are properly fulfilling their parental responsibility. Just as the Children Act 1989 imposes duties on parents, it also imposes duties on the local authority. Section 47 of the Children Act 1989 requires the local authority to investigate cases where there is reasonable cause to suspect that the child or children. Concerned is suffering or is likely to suffer significant harm. The Act requires the local authority to act, wherever possible, in partnership with the parents of the children. Encouraging co-operation between parents and local authority and maintaining wherever possible the care of the child within the family are the guiding philosophies of the Act. It would appear that Harry and Isobel are unconcerned about the problems that their children may be experiencing. However, it does not seem feasible for the local authority to ignore the concerns expressed by the children's schools.

In relation to Jack he is not attending school and is associating with undesirable persons. The local authority has two real options open to it. It may apply for an education supervision order under s 36 of the Act or, if the case warrants it, it may apply for a care order under s 31 of the Act. (The wardship option which may have been available in the past is no longer available to local authorities since the passing of the Children Act 1989.) Any application made under the Children Act 1989 will have the child's welfare as the paramount consideration (*s 1(1)*) and the court will be reluctant to intervene unless it can be shown that the making of an order is better than leaving things as they are (s 1(5)). An education supervision order is made on application, usually to the Family Proceedings Court where the local education authority acts in consultation with the social services. Section 36 of the Children Act 1989 requires children of compulsory school age to attend school or else an education supervision order may be made. Jack is of compulsory school age and it does seem that he is not being properly educated according to his needs, age, and ability, given the amount of time during which he is absent from school. Section 36(5) creates a presumption that a pupil at a school who is not attending regularly is not being properly educated. Thus, it would seem that it would be possible to show to the court that Jack is not being properly educated. If the court was satisfied of this, it could appoint a supervising officer to ensure that the child attends school. This supervising officer takes responsibility for guiding and assisting both the child, Jack, and his parents, Harry and Isobel, in understanding the importance of education and laying down certain guidelines to ensure that Jack does attend school.

The order will usually last for one year but it can be extended or conversely it can be discharged on application by the child, Jack, or his parents or, if all is going well, by the education authority. If however the supervision order does not succeed in getting Jack to attend school (and it may be that his undesirable associates play a part in this) then the local authority may need to consider the more drastic step of seeking a care order. A care order is available under *s 31* of the *Children Act 1989* and is only available once the local authority has carried out preliminary investigations to see if any action is necessary to safeguard or promote Jack's welfare: *s 47(1)*. Ordinarily, the local authority must consult both Jack and his parents but if the case is an urgent one or consultation may prejudice Jack's welfare then the local authority may act without consultation. In any application for a care order, both Jack and his parents must have notice and be made respondents to the application. Since Jack is a child it is usually necessary to appoint a children's guardian to act to safeguard his interests. The children's guardian will talk with Jack and try to ascertain Jack's feelings and wishes in regard to the present position. As a 14-year-old child he is obviously entitled to be consulted and clearly his co-operation will be essential for the smooth running of any future plans concerning him. The statutory grounds for a care order are found in *s 31* of the *Children Act 1989.*

The Family Proceedings Court must be satisfied that the child is suffering or is likely to suffer significant harm. This does not require proof on the balance of probabilities that there will be harm in the future; it is enough to show a real, significant likelihood of harm (*Newham London Borough Council v AG (1993)*). Harm includes ill-treatment or impairment of health and development. In the present case it does not appear that Jack is being ill-treated at home, but his lack of attendance at school, his association with somewhat undesirable individuals, and his parents' apparent unconcern at this, do seem to indicate that maybe his health and development are being impaired. The second criterion under s 31 is that the harm or likelihood of harm is attributable to the care being given to the child or likely to be given to him if the order is not made, not being what it would be reasonable to expect a parent to give him or secondly the child being beyond parental control. This is an objective standard based on what a reasonable parent could or could not do, *Lancashire County Council v A (2000)*. In *Re O (A Minor) (Care Order) 1992* the persistent truancy of a child was deemed suitable for a care order to be made and this would be the case here. Since neither Harry nor Isobel is able to control Jack to ensure that he attends school, or they do not particularly concern themselves over his attendance, this would show that it is not reasonable for them to behave in that way concerning the education of their 14-year-old son. Again, as with any Children Act 1989 order, the child's welfare is the paramount consideration (s 1(1)) and, in order to determine what would be in Jack's best interest, the *s 1(3)* checklist would be examined.

The first consideration in the checklist would be the wishes of the child, given his age and understanding. Jack is 14-years-old and definitely at the age where the court would consider his wishes. However, this does not mean that he would be able to dictate to the court what he wished to do. Definitely, his disinclination to attend school would not result in the court deeming any care order unnecessary. In fact, his inability to behave maturely in respect of his education may indicate that his wishes will not carry a great deal of weight. The second criterion on the checklist is the child's physical, emotional and education needs. Clearly Jack is in need of some guidance, and the fact that he is not attending school and is associating with somewhat dubious characters indicates that he is a child who seems to be drifting through life. The apparent unconcern of his parents seems to indicate that something must be done for Jack. However, whether this would necessarily require him to leave his home and be taken into the care of the local authority is another matter. The court may decide that a less draconian measure would be more suitable. Jack will have been consulted by his children's guardian as to his wishes and his views about remaining with his parents or leaving home to enter local authority care. If Jack wishes to remain at home it may be that the shock of being threatened with removal will be enough to make him mend his ways. If the court is of the view that Jack and his parents may be able to correct the defects with a little assistance from other persons, then maybe the education supervision order discussed earlier, or a supervision order will be more appropriate. The supervision order under the s 31 criteria requires the threshold of harm in section 31 to be satisfied. However, the effect of a supervision order is very different. A supervision order does not vest parental responsibility in the local authority; instead a supervising officer, either a local authority officer or a probation officer, is appointed to assist and befriend and advise the child and his parents (s 35(1)). The supervising officer will do what is necessary to ensure that the child is guided and that his welfare is promoted. Usually a supervision order lasts for one year but it can be extended up to three years by one application; to continue beyond the three year period another application would be necessary. The supervising officer will try to give directions to Jack: telling him to attend school; possibly also requiring him to participate in certain activities; and imposing obligations with the consent of Harry and Isobel to help them deal with Jack and promote his welfare. *In Oxfordshire County Council v L (1998)* a supervision order was considered appropriate for six children. This was because the parents wanted to meet their obligations to their children, and with help from the local authority they were likely to be able to do so.

The position regarding Jessica is somewhat more complex. The incidents at school give considerable cause for concern over Jessica's health and well being. However, it is not clear that there is any actual abuse and the local authority should proceed with caution in this very delicate area. As with Jack, a case conference should be held in which the child's welfare and situation should be discussed.

However, in the instant case there is the concern that consultation with the parents and with Jessica may increase Jessica's unease and could be detrimental by causing delay. Therefore, the local authority needs to act to get to the bottom of the problem and to find out exactly what it is that is concerning Jessica and how if at all she has been abused. The usual first course in such a situation is to apply to the court for a child assessment order. Such an order is available to the local authority and will enable it to find out exactly what is going on in relation to the child. However, full notice must be given by the local authority to both the child and the child's parents and, at the hearing, the court must be satisfied that the local authority has reasonable cause to suspect that Jessica is suffering or is likely to suffer significant harm, and that an assessment of Jessica's health and development is required in order to establish whether or not she is suffering harm, and that it is unlikely that an assessment will be made or made satisfactorily without a child assessment order.

In the instant case the school report of Jessica's behaviour does give rise to concern that Jessica has suffered some kind of harm. Her responses do not seem to be those of the average 12-year-old in such a situation. Whilst most 12-year-olds go through periods of modesty whilst changing, and also possibly show concern over learning the facts of life, Jessica's reaction appears extreme. It is also combined with a significant change in personality, all of which gives cause for concern. There is no need to show on the balance of probabilities that Jessica is likely to suffer significant harm, just that there is a real likelihood. Harry's and Isobel's response is somewhat dismissive and it does not seem likely that the local authority will be able to assess Jessica without a child assessment order. Such an order, if made, will only last for seven days and it does not affect Harry and Isobel's parental responsibility. The local authority have no parental responsibility during the lifetime of this order; the order merely requires Harry and Isobel to produce Jessica so that she can be assessed. This may mean that Jessica continues to live at home although it is possible for her to be assessed as an in-patient in hospital. If Jessica is to remain in hospital, then contact will usually be allowed under *s 43* between Jessica and her parents. There is the possibility that a child of sufficient age and understanding may refuse to consent to the assessment. Clearly, Jessica is a disturbed and upset child, but hopefully, with proper explanation and reassurance, she will be happy to comply with the order. If the local authority are frustrated in their enforcement of the child assessment order or if concern exists that more immediate protection is required for Jessica, then an emergency protection order under *s 44* of the Act may be sought. The basis of such an application is, first, that the local authority may apply if it has reasonable cause to believe that Jessica is likely to suffer significant harm if either she is not removed to accommodation provided by the local authority or she does not then remain in the place where she is being accommodated. A further option open to the local authority is to apply under *s 44(1)(b)*, on the basis that enquiries are being made with respect to the child and that those enquiries are being frustrated by access to Jessica being unreasonably refused by the parents, and the applicant will also need to show that they have reasonable cause to believe that access to the child is required as a matter of urgency.

The emergency protection order is a very draconian measure; it gives the local authority parental responsibility for the duration of the order (s 44(4)) and the local authority can take such action as is reasonable to safeguard or promote Jessica's welfare. The court will authorise the child's removal to local authority accommodation or it will order that the child remains in any hospital or other place where the child is being accommodated prior to the order being made. The court will consider whether contact should be allowed between Jessica and her parents and also whatever medical and psychiatric assessment is necessary. Usually the child will have contact with her parents but if it is considered that this would be detrimental to her welfare then contact can be refused and this refusal cannot be challenged. An emergency protection order lasts for eight days (s 45(1)) although it can be extended once more for a further seven days (s 45(6)) if the court has cause to believe that, if it is not extended, Jessica will suffer significant harm. The emergency protection order can be challenged by the child and her parents and anyone else having parental responsibility for her, after 72 hours have expired. However, a challenge is not possible if the parties were given notice of the hearing and were present at it (s 45(11)). Since the emergency protection order is a very dramatic step to take, the court will consider long and hard whether it is in the child's best interest for such an order to be made.

Under the Children Act s 44A, it is possible for the court to make an exclusion requirement in respect of Harry if this would mean that Jessica would no longer suffer significant harm or be at risk of it. This would exclude Harry from the home as part of an interim care order or emergency protection order, provided that Isobel was able to care for Jessica and consented to the making of the order. This would mean that Jessica could remain at home if Harry were not there. As well as ordering this, the court can accept an undertaking from Harry that he would leave until matters were finally sorted out.

Clearly, in the present case there are concerns as to what is occurring to Jessica and it would seem that the parents' attitude is somewhat ambivalent, given the concerns expressed by the local authority. Whether this is sufficiently significant to give rise to the need for an emergency protection order is debatable. Concern has frequently been expressed at the hasty removal of children from their parents' care by local authorities; therefore it may be that the local authority would be best served by making an application for a child assessment order in the instant case, since the evidence of abuse is not sufficiently overwhelming to justify the application for the emergency protection order. An emergency protection order should only be sought if the child assessment order is being thwarted by Harry and Isobel, Jessica's parents. If either the child assessment order or the emergency protection order produces evidence that Jessica is in fact being abused, then the local authority will need to consider more long-term measures. The appropriate measure to take would be the care order under s 31 of the Act. The local authority may apply for a care order if they can establish the threshold criteria in s 31. They must satisfy the court that Jessica is suffering or is likely to suffer significant harm and, second, that the harm or likelihood of harm is attributable to the care being given to Jessica or likely to be given to her if the order is not made, not being what it would be reasonable to expect a parent to give her or, second, that the child is beyond parental control. The evidence of Jessica's distress at school and her change in personality, coupled with the findings of the investigation, either under the child assessment order or emergency protection order, may substantiate the claim that Jessica is suffering significant harm. Harm under the Act means ill-treatment or impairment of health and development. Ill-treatment includes sexual abuse as well as physical and mental ill-treatment. If indeed Jessica has been sexually abused by either or both of her parents, then the criterion of harm will be satisfied and clearly, if nothing is done, Jessica will continue to suffer this significant harm. It is also necessary to show that the harm is because of the care being given to the child by her parents. If the parents are responsible for the abuse or are failing to act to protect Jessica from it, then their actions are not those of the reasonable parent and the s 31 criteria will be established. Jessica's welfare under s 1(1) of the Act is the crucial consideration and is paramount throughout. In cases of serious sexual abuse it will be necessary to remove the child from the family environment so as to ensure that the abuse does not continue. The s 1(3) checklist must be applied and Jessica's wishes must be ascertained. If she is being abused she will obviously have confused feelings about her parents and whether she wishes to remain with them or be removed into local authority care. This is not a case where the court can stand back and do nothing. The non-interventionist policy enshrined in s 1(5) of the Act will have to be put to one side as something needs to be done to ensure that Jessica's well being is safeguarded.

Any care order that is made will last until Jessica is 18 unless it is discharged earlier either on application by the child, by her parents or by the local authority. Even though a care order is made, the local authority should consider the question of contact, especially in relation to the parents of the child. Usually contact will be allowed even though a parent may have abused the child. It will usually always be possible for the other innocent parent to see the child. Even the abuser may have limited supervised access to the child since it is often in the child's best interest for the relationship to be given the opportunity to be repaired. However, it is crucial to try to ensure that any abuse is not repeated. If Jessica is taken into care by the local authority, the local authority has a duty under *s 22* of the Act to promote the child's welfare and to consider Jessica's wishes and those of her parents at all stages. The parental responsibility of Harry and Isobel does not end on the making of the care order and the local authority will still try to keep them involved in the upbringing of their child where this is still in the child's best interest. The local authority will consult Jessica to see how she wishes her future to unfold and it will also consult her parents if possible. In making any decisions about the child, s 22(5) of the Act requires the local authority to take into account the wishes and feelings of the child and her parents, and also to take into account the child's religion, racial origin and cultural background.

In conclusion, therefore, it can be seen that in relation to Jack the appropriate measures for the local authority are an education supervision order and, failing that, a care order or possibly a supervision order under s 31 of the Act. In relation to Jessica, however, more stringent measures may be needed. First, an investigation by way of child assessment order will be required or, in an emergency, an emergency protection order. If either of these measures discloses that Jessica is being abused then it will be necessary to make a care order under s 31 of the Act. In relation to both children any application must have their welfare as the paramount consideration, and consequently it will only be when the full facts are known about Jessica and Jack that the appropriate order can be sought.

Question 42

Molly has three illegitimate children by different men, and has struggled to bring them up. Two years ago, Molly had a mental breakdown and was admitted into hospital. The two eldest children, both boys, were accommodated by the local authority with temporary foster parents, whilst the youngest child, a girl, was looked after by Molly's mother, Connie.

When Molly was released from hospital, she demanded the return of her children, but was unable to cope with them, and severely neglected them. Again, the local authority and Connie stepped in to look after the children, at Molly's request, which they have done to date.

Molly has recently begun to live with Frank, who has a criminal record of violence and sexual offences. Molly has indicated to the local authority that as soon as she feels up to it, she wants the children to live with her and Frank.

Both the local authority and Connie are concerned about this, as Molly does not have a good record as a mother, and Frank's criminal record raises serious questions about his suitability as a substitute parent.

Advise the local authority.

Answer plan

Begin by explaining the concept of parental responsibility and the local authority's obligation to provide assistance to Molly and the children as being a family in need: ss 17–20. This is a voluntary arrangement and does not give the local authority parental responsibility or any compulsory powers over the children.

This would only be possible on an application for a care order (s 31), and the threshold criteria of likelihood of significant harm must be established. The child's welfare is paramount and it may be that having examined the s 1(3) checklist, the court is satisfied that there is sufficient risk to justify themaking of an order.

The possibility of speedy intervention by way of an emergency protection order (s 44) should be examined, and so should the possibility of the grandmother applying for a residence order under s 8.

Answer

In the instant case the local authority requires advice on what steps, if any, it should take in relation to the three children of Molly. Molly, as a single parent is the only person with parental responsibility over her children: *s 2* of the *Children Act 1989*. As Molly never married the fathers of her children, it is she, and she alone, who bears parental responsibility. Parental responsibility may be defined as 'all the rights, duties, powers and responsibilities and authority which by law a parent of a child has in relation to the child and his property' (s 3(1)). This parental responsibility places an obligation on Molly to promote her children's welfare and to provide for their everyday needs. However, in a case of a person such as Molly, where a parent experiences difficulty in coping with the demands that their children impose, the local authority has a statutory duty under the Children Act 1989 to assist parents and children in need. This general duty to children in need is contained in *s 17* of the Children Act 1989 and requires the local authority to safeguard and promote the welfare of children within their area who are in need, and, so far as is possible, to promote the upbringing of children by their families by providing a range and level of services to assist with those children's need: s 17(1). To supplement this duty the local authority is also under an obligation to provide accommodation to children in need, where the person who has been caring for the children is prevented whether permanently or not and for whatever reason from providing the children with suitable accommodation or care: *Children Act 1989 s 20*.

In the instant case Molly's mental breakdown has prevented her from providing her children with the care that they require and so it is quite clear that the local authority have voluntarily entered into a relationship with Molly, whereby they have provided accommodation for the children. The essential nature of this relationship, though, is a voluntary one; a relationship has taken place through the consent of the parent, Molly. The local authority acquires no parental responsibility in the present situation and instead all the parental responsibility remains with Molly. The local authority has, by virtue of s 22, a duty to safeguard and promote the children's welfare and it is required to take into account the wishes and feelings of the children and the children's parents under *s 22(4)*. This requires the local authority, when making decisions, to consider those wishes and feelings and also the child's religious, racial and cultural background. In the instant case, little is known of the ages of the children and, as such, not much can be said about the impact of the children's views on how the local authority will proceed. However, the local authority has a duty to promote contact between the child and its parent and it is quite clear that until any compulsory powers are exercised Molly has the right to contact with her children and she has the right to remove her children whenever she wishes without having to comply with any formal notice requirements. Thus, it would seem that Molly has the absolute right to remove her children from local authority care even though the local authority may be unhappy with her future living arrangements.

The only option available to the local authority in relation to the two children in its care is to take care proceedings under *s 31* of the *Children Act 1989*. In relation to the child who is living with Molly's mother, Connie, the local authority again has the option of care proceedings. However, there is the additional possibility that Connie, as a grandparent and someone with whom the child has had her home for a period of time, may possibly apply for a residence order in relation to the child under s 8 of the Children Act 1989. This residence order would enable the child to remain with her grandmother rather than return to her mother and her mother's new partner. There is the further possibility that Connie could apply for a residence order in relation to her other two grandchildren and each of these options will now be discussed in turn. The local authority cannot, as has previously been indicated, retain the two elder children in local authority accommodation without the consent of Molly. If Molly carries out her threat to remove the children from local authority care there is little that the local authority can do other than apply to the court in order to be able to exercise compulsory powers over the children. The long-term possibility is for the local authority to apply for a care order under s 31 of the Children Act 1989.

This application must be made to the Family Proceedings Court and the court must be satisfied, first, that the child is suffering or is likely to suffer significant harm. The two boys are at present suffering no harm but there is the likelihood that they may suffer significant harm if they return to their mother's care. Harm is defined in the act as meaning ill-treatment which can include, sexual, physical and mental ill-treatment and impairment of health and development. It does seem that if the children return to Molly, Frank's criminal record may pose a risk to them. Also, Molly's mental illness and her previous history indicate that the children's health and development may be impaired. It was held in *Newham London Borough Council v AG (1993)* that there is no need to prove the threshold criteria on the balance of probabilities; the court will be satisfied if there is a real significant likelihood of the child suffering harm. It is submitted that in the present case, given the seriousness of Frank's criminal record, that this will be made out.

The second part of the statutory criteria is that the harm or likelihood of harm is attributable to the care being given to the child or likely to be given to him if the order is not made, not being what it would be reasonable to expect a parent to give him or the child being beyond parental control. There is no evidence that the two elder children are beyond parental control, but the evidence does point to the level of care that the children might receive as not being at the level that it is reasonable to expect. If the statutory criteria are established, as in any Children Act order, the court must consider the child's welfare as its paramount consideration (*s 1(1)*), and in determining what is in the child's welfare the court will look at the s 1(3) checklist factors. The first of these factors is the ascertainable wishes of the children in the light of their age and understanding. As previously indicated, little is known of the age of these children, and if they are very young then the likelihood is that their wishes will not be given much weight. However, if the children are approaching teenage years then the court will give great credence to their wishes and to their fears about their future. If, as seems likely, the children are happy with the present arrangements and are concerned with returning to their mother the court will be reluctant to allow this to occur. Clearly, the child's educational and physical and mental needs are being met in local authority care and there is serious doubt as to whether their mother would be able to meet such a need. There is also considerable benefit derived from keeping siblings together and it is not clear that Molly will be able to cope with both children. It is likely that both children have also had contact with their sister whilst she has been with their grandmother. Looking at the range of powers available to the court, the court is probably going to be mindful of the fact that a care order does give a certain degree of control over the children's well being; whereas making no order at all would place the children at risk. This is not a case where the non-interventionist policy in s 1(5) would hold true.

However, care proceedings are usually taken after full notice is given to all the parties. This would require children's guardian to be appointed in relation to the children and it would also require Molly to be given notice as a parent. This could alert Molly as to the steps the local authority is planning to take and may result in her demanding the immediate removal of the children from local authority accommodation. In the event of this occurring, the local authority may decide to apply for an emergency protection order under *s 44* of the Act. An emergency protection order may be applied for on the basis in *s 44(1)(a)* that there is reasonable cause to believe that the child is likely to suffer significant harm if he does not remain in the place where he is presently being accommodated. This order is a somewhat draconian measure and it can authorise the child to remain in the place where he is presently being accommodated immediately prior to the order (*s 44(4)(b)*). This order gives the local authority parental responsibility for the children for its duration (*s 44(4)(c)*). However, the order only lasts for eight days (*s 45(1)*) although it can be extended once for a further seven days if there is reasonable cause to believe that if the order is not extended the children are likely to suffer significant harm.

If an emergency protection order is made, the court will give directions as to whether Molly is to be allowed contact with the children. There is little in the facts to require contact to be forbidden as Molly has not physically ill-treated the children. However, it is quite clear that contact with Frank should be prohibited. The emergency protection order can be challenged by the children or by Molly, the parent, under *s 45(8)*, but this cannot be challenged until 72 hours has elapsed and there will be no possibility of challenge if Molly was given notice of the hearing and was present at it (*s 45(11)*). This emergency protection order would give the local authority breathing space before a care order can be made. The care order under s 31 would probably need to be an interim order until the full facts can be put to the courts. If a care order is made, the local authority acquires parental responsibility for the children. Molly does not lose her parental responsibility but she will not be able to exercise it in a way that is inconsistent with the local authority's parental responsibility. By having a care order in relation to the children, the local authority can decide where the children should reside. This may be in local authority care or with foster parents or it may be that the local authority will arrange for the children to live with members of their family, either Connie, their grandmother, or maybe even Molly, provided she agrees not to reside with Frank. The care order will remain in force until the children are 18 unless it is discharged earlier either on application by the parent or by the child or local authority (*s 39(1)*) or, possibly, on the making of a residence order, for example, in favour of Connie, the grandmother. If a care order is made, contact is usually presumed to be in the child's best interest and, clearly, contact with Molly would not necessarily damage the children in any way. It is usually advantageous for children to maintain the relationship they have with their parents. However, it is not desirable for the children to develop any relationship with Frank and this is likely to be prohibited.

Turning to the child who is in the care of Connie, her grandmother, again the local authority could take care proceedings and seek an emergency protection order as indicated previously. However, there is the additional possibility that Connie, the grandmother, could seek a residence order under s 8 of the Children Act 1989. A residence order would settle the child's arrangements in so far as it would determine where the child should live and it would give Connie parental responsibility. This would not terminate Molly's parental responsibility but nevertheless, it would enable the child to remain with her grandparent. The difficulty here is that Connie, as a grandparent, will need leave in order to obtain a s 8 order. In deciding whether to give leave to Connie, the court will consider the nature of her application and her connection with the child. Clearly, she has a very close connection with the child and it does not seem that there would be any risk of her application disrupting the child's life. It is also quite clear that Connie's application would have the support of the local authority, in that the local authority has no desire for the child to return to her parent. However this application would contradict the wishes and feelings of Molly, the child's parent, but, as in any application, the court would probably allow leave since there is a genuine concern on the part of the applicant for the welfare of the child.

If an application is made for a residence order under s 8, the paramount consideration is the welfare of the child under s 1(1). In determining what was is the child's best interests, the court would have regard to the factors in the checklist (s 1(3)). The ascertainable wishes and feelings of the child, given their age and understanding, would be considered by the court. However, as before, little is known of the age of the child and therefore little can be said about the weight that would be attached to her views. Her educational, emotional and other needs have been satisfactorily met by her grandmother over the past few years and it seems likely that the grandmother would be in a better position to meet those needs than the mother and her new partner. Indeed the mother has a poor history in relation to mothering skills, albeit not through her own fault, and it does not seem that the living conditions with Molly and Frank would be conducive to the child's best interest.

Although the court does like to keep brothers and sisters together because of the mutual support that they derive from one another (*Adams v Adams (1984)*), the children in the present case have been used to living apart and therefore the mother's claim that she could accommodate them all together would have little weight. She has been unable to sustain in the past the obligation to care for all of her children together and it seems quite clear that the status quo would be disturbed if the child were removed from her grandmother's care to be given to her mother. Although generally there is an advantage in care being provided by a parent, the parent's conduct in the past has not been such to inspire confidence. The parent's new partner in the instant case does seem to pose a risk to the future well being of the children in that he has a violent record and a record that involves sexual offences. In *Scott v Scott (1986)*, the mother's partner had a history of violence and indecency and that off-set any advantages that living with a mother would normally involve.

In conclusion therefore, it would seem that this child's best interests might well be served by her remaining with her grandmother. In deciding whether to make a s 8 order, the court will have in mind the need to avoid delay (s 1(2)) and the need to avoid unnecessary intervention (s 1(5)). However, this is clearly a case where to allow the child to return to her mother may well wreak havoc with the child's welfare. Therefore the court will clearly have to consider whether to make a s 8 order in relation to the grandmother or whether to grant a care order in relation to the local authority. It seems clear that the local authority and grandmother are united in their concern about the well being of the child and it seems possible that either course of action could be employed for the welfare of the youngest daughter. However, in an emergency it may be necessary to couple either the care order or the s 8 residence order with an emergency protection order. However, it is important to note that only the local authority can apply for the emergency protection order. Connie, as a grandparent, would have no locus standi to make such an application if her daughter were to demand the return of the child.

Question 43

Sharon, aged 17, has one daughter, Jade, aged two, but has no idea who Jade's father is. The health visitor has contacted the local authority to express her concern about Jade. Sharon had failed to keep a number of appointments at the child health clinic, and when she had finally brought Jade, the child had a number of bruises. Jade is a boisterous and unruly child, and Sharon admits to finding her hard to handle.

When the health visitor asked Sharon about Jade's bruises, Sharon stormed out, telling the health visitor to mind her own business.

Advise the local authority on what steps, if any, they should take.

Answer plan

Again, this question requires an understanding of the relationship between the local authority's duty to assist families in need and the compulsory powers that may be exercisable after a court order for a child at risk. Sharon has parental responsibility for Jade and the local authority has a duty to investigate cases where it is suspected the child is suffering harm (s 47). Co-operation with the parent is desirable. Then explore the duty to assist and ss 17–20 under which Sharon could voluntarily seek local authority assistance in relation to Jade. If Sharon is unco-operative, then a child assessment order may be sought (s 43), and, in extreme cases, an emergency protection order (s 44). Both these options must be explored in detail. If there is a risk to Jade, then a care or supervision order should be sought (s 31).

Answer

Sharon, as an unmarried mother, is the one person who has parental responsibility for Jade. Parental responsibility is defined as 'all the rights, duties, powers and responsibilities and authority which by law a parent of a child has in relation to the child and its property': *Children Act 1989 s 3(1)*. This stresses that Sharon has the obligation to care for her child, and to promote the child's welfare.

The health visitor's concern over Jade's welfare must be sensitively handled by the local authority; whilst they must obviously act swiftly to employ their statutory powers for a child at risk, they must also ensure that careful consideration is given as to whether any intervention is necessary.

It is quite common for small children to have bruises without there being any abuse, and parents who are stressed or under pressure may over-react to questions such as those asked by the health visitor in the present case. The local authority need to determine whether Sharon is managing her parental responsibility without the need for interference, whether some action is required either to assist Sharon and Jade on a voluntary basis, or whether to protect Jade using compulsory orders from the court. Section 47 of the Children Act 1989 requires the local authority to investigate cases where there is reasonable cause to suspect that the child is suffering, or is likely to suffer, significant harm. The concern of an experienced health visitor should not usually be ignored, and these concerns, together with Sharon's youth do indicate that some kind of investigation may be called for. Initially, it would seem that the local authority should try to work in partnership with Sharon. The philosophy of the Children Act 1989 is to encourage co-operation between parents and the local authority, and to maintain, wherever possible, the care of the child within the family. A social worker should speak with Sharon, and relevant professionals, such as doctors and health visitors, can be consulted to obtain their views on the family.

It will be possible to gauge Sharon and Jade's position after talking with Sharon, and possibly holding a case conference. If, as seems likely, Sharon is experiencing difficulty coping with the demands of bringing up a two year old child, then the local authority may be able to provide assistance. There is a general duty on a local authority to safeguard and promote the welfare of a child in need, and to do this by promoting Jade's upbringing within the family by providing services to help meet the child's needs: *Children Act 1989 s 17(1)*. Jade will qualify as a child in need if she is unlikely to achieve, or maintain, or have the opportunity of achieving or maintaining a reasonable standard of health and development *(s 17(10))* unless the local authority provide services to facilitate this. Health includes both mental and physical health, *(s 17(11))*, and development includes the child's physical, intellectual, emotional, social or behavioural development.

Little is known about Sharon's socio-economic background, but it is likely that as a young single parent she is socially disadvantaged and not economically well-off. Her living conditions may be such that Jade is frustrated and bored, and might well qualify as a child in need. The local authority, in partnership with Sharon, could provide a range of services, including such things as nursery provision, clubs, etc to provide Jade with stimulation, and Sharon with some relief from the pressures of continuous child care.

The local authority could offer to accommodate Jade voluntarily under s 20 if Sharon is prevented (whether or not permanently and/or for whatever reason) from providing Jade with suitable accommodation or care. This can only take place if Sharon requests the local authority to assist her, and could be used to provide short-term care for Jade whilst Sharon sorts out other aspects of her life. Since this arrangement would be entirely voluntary, Sharon could remove Jade from the local authority's care at any time without having to comply with any formal requirements: *s 20(8)*. Before the local authority provides accommodation for such a child, it must ascertain the wishes of the child (*s 20(6)*) but, as Jade is only two, this will not be possible. Whilst Jade is being accommodated by the local authority, it has a duty to safeguard and promote her welfare (*s 22(3)*) and to consult Sharon and take into account Sharon's wishes and the religion, racial, cultural and linguistic characteristics of the child (*s 22(5)*). Sharon would be encouraged to keep close contact with Jade and to remain involved with her, so that when Sharon's position has stabilised she and her child can be reunited. The local authority does not acquire parental responsibility for a child voluntarily accommodated with them, and these measures are useful to help a family through difficult times.

However, it may be that, if Sharon persists in being evasive and abusive when asked about Jade, the local authority will need to satisfy itself that Jade is not suffering harm due to abuse or neglect. The most appropriate step in this instance would seem to be an application to the Family Proceedings Court for a child assessment order: *Children Act 1989 s 43*. This is a usual means of discovering what is happening to the child in circumstances where parental co-operation has not been forthcoming. The local authority must give notice of its application to Sharon, and the court will only grant an order if the applicant has reasonable cause to suspect that the child is suffering, or is likely to suffer, significant harm. Jade's bruising and Sharon's reluctance to take her to the clinic, and her aggressive reaction to the health visitor might suffice to establish this. In addition, it is necessary to show that an assessment of the child is necessary to establish whether she is suffering, or is likely to suffer, significant harm, and that it is unlikely that any satisfactory assessment will be made without a child assessment order. Sharon's unco-operative stance makes it likely that the grounds for an order have been established. However, as with all orders under the Children Act 1989, the child's welfare is the paramount consideration (*s 1*), and the court will wish to ensure that there is as little delay as possible (s 1(2)), once it determines that making an order is better than not making an order (s 1(5)).

An assessment order lasts for a maximum of seven days, and Sharon will be ordered to ensure that Jade turns up at the appropriate time and place for assessment. Jade would normally remain at home, unless the order specifies that she remain in another place, for example, a hospital (*s 43(9)*). The local authority does not acquire parental responsibility.

If Sharon fails to comply with the assessment order, then this may give grounds for the local authority to apply for an emergency protection order. Jade is not old enough to refuse her own consent to the assessment, and so if an order were made then it is likely that Jade's bruising could be examined and an opinion formed as to whether she was the victim of deliberate abuse or neglect or merely is a somewhat clumsy two year old, prone to cuts and bruising.

If Sharon refused to comply with the child assessment order, or the local authority formed the view that Jade was in immediate danger, then an application could be made for an emergency protection order. This is a more serious measure, and should only be taken in cases where there is a clear pressing need to protect a child at risk. The basis for granting an order under s 44 to the local authority is that there is reasonable cause to believe that the child is likely to suffer significant harm if she remains where she is and is not removed to local authority accommodation. The alternative is to show that enquiries are being made in respect of the child, and that those enquiries are being frustrated by Sharon unreasonably refusing access to Jade. There is then the need to show that access to the child is required as a matter of urgency. The emergency protection order lasts for eight days, although it may be extended for a further seven days: *s 45(6)*. The order can authorise the removal of Jade from her home, and gives the local authority parental responsibility for the limited time the order is in force. The court will decide whether Sharon should have contact with Jade during this time, and the order can only be challenged by Sharon, or Jade (*s 45(8)*), once it has been in force for 72 hours, provided they had no notice of the original hearing (*s 45(11)*).

If, after examining Jade, the local authority is still concerned about her well being, then there are two further options available; the care order or supervision order (s 31). The option of wardship is no longer available for local authorities. The local authority must apply to the Family Proceedings Court, or county court and High Court in complex cases, making Sharon, the parent, and Jade, the child, respondents in the case.

The basis for a care or supervision order may be found in s 31, and the court must be satisfied that the child is suffering, or is likely to suffer, significant harm, and this is attributable to the care being given to the child not being what it would be reasonable to expect a parent to give him, or the child is beyond parental control. There would be a need to establish significant harm which means ill-treatment, physical, sexual or mental abuse, or impairment of health and development. This must go beyond an occasional bruise, and it must be shown that the care being provided by Sharon falls short of what care can reasonably be expected.

CHAPTER 10

ADOPTION

▌INTRODUCTION

Adoption involves the severing of the legal relationship between a child and his or her natural parents and the establishing of a new relationship with the adoptive parents. The law on adoption has recently been amended with the introduction of the Adoption and Children Act 2002. This Act has extended the definition of who is able to adopt to include unmarried couples *(Adoption and Children Act 2002 ss 50, 114(4))* and to make the welfare of the child paramount whilst under the Adoption Act 1976 it was only the court's first consideration. Adoption procedure has also been amended.

Under the new Act, adoption can either be an agency adoption, where the child is placed by the adoption agency, or a non-agency adoption, where the child does not have to be placed by an adoption agency. The later category would include step-parent adoptions and adoptions of the child by a foster carer. Whatever the type of adoption, the child will need to be placed with the prospective adopters before the adoption order can be made. The length of this placement will vary depending on who is adopting the child *(Adoption and Children Act 2002 s 42)*. If the adoption is an agency adoption, students will need to be able to explain whether the child is placed with consent *(Adoption and Children Act 2002 ss 19–20)*, or under a placement order *(Adoption and Children Act 2002 ss 21–24)*. If the adoption is a non-agency adoption, prospective adopters will need to inform the local authority of their intention to adopt *(Adoption and Children Act 2002 s 44)*.

In deciding whether to make the adoption order the court is bound by the principle that the child's welfare is paramount and they will use the welfare checklist in *section 1(4)* to decide whether the child's welfare supports adoption. In addition, the consent of everyone with parental responsibility is needed before an adoption order can be made, although this can be dispensed with if the child's welfare demands it *(Adoption and Children Act 2002 s 52(1))*.

As well as reforming adoption law, the Adoption and Children Act 2002 also introduced special guardianship. Unlike adoption special guardianship does not completely remove parental responsibility from the birth parents, but most aspects of parental responsibility can be exercised solely by the special guardian *(Children*

Act 1989 s 14C). Students should be aware of special guardianship and should be able to consider it as an alternative to adoption or a residence order where appropriate.

Question 44

Anna and Bertie were married five years ago, and had a daughter, Carrie, who is now two. Bertie was a famous footballer, but the marriage encountered difficulties when he began to experiment with drugs. One night, whilst under the influence of drugs, Bertie became violent and assaulted Anna, breaking her nose. Bertie was horrified by what he had done and voluntarily entered a rehabilitation centre, but Anna divorced him on the basis of his behaviour. Anna subsequently married David, and Carrie lives with them. David adores Carrie and would like to adopt her. Bertie has tried to maintain contact with Carrie.

Advise Anna and David whether they will be able to adopt Carrie.

Answer plan

- Define adoption;
- examine who can be adopted and who can adopt;
- explain problem of step-parent adoption;
- look at issue of parental consent and dispensing with it;
- see if s 1 would permit the making of the order;
- consider alternatives to adoption.

Answer

Anna and David want David to adopt Anna's daughter Carrie. If the adoption is allowed this would mean that Carrie's birth father, Bertie, would be legally classed as a stranger to Carrie. Bertie is opposed to the adoption.

As Carrie is already living with Anna and David this is a non-agency adoption. The Adoption and Children Act 2002 has reformed the law so that a step-parent who wishes to adopt his step-child no longer need to adopt with that child's birth parent. As a result, in this case, it will just be David who is the adopter. David will need to inform the local authority that he intends to adopt Carrie. The reason for this is so that the local authority can visit the placement and prepare welfare reports to help the court decide whether the adoption is in Carrie's welfare. Under *s 42* of the *Adoption and Children Act 2002*, Carrie has to be placed with David for six months before he can apply to adopt her.

The court will only make an adoption order in favour of David if it is in Carrie's welfare to do so. The welfare of the child is now the court's paramount consideration – s 1(1) and the court will use the welfare checklist in *section 1(4)* to determine what is in Carrie's welfare. In this case, the main problem for the court is the fact that an adoption order would terminate the parental responsibility of Bertie and make him a legal stranger to his daughter. Although, the facts state that Bertie has been violent in the past, he has tried to maintain contact with his daughter and the court might well feel that it would not be in Carrie's interest to erase Bertie from her history. Furthermore, Bertie has tried to obtain help for his problem and it is far from clear that he would be violent again.

Furthermore, it should be noted that under the *Adoption and Children Act 2002 s 1(6)* the court does have to consider whether any alternatives to adoption could better promote the welfare of the child. It is unclear why David wishes to adopt Carrie but if it is because he wishes to strengthen his rights in relation to Carrie, this could also be done through a residence order which would give David parental responsibility whilst not removing that of Bertie. Alternatively, under section 4A of the Children Act 1989 it is now possible for a court to make a parental responsibility order in favour of the step-parent meaning that in this case the court could award David parental responsibility without removing the parental responsibility of Bertie.

On the facts given, it is unlikely that the court would consider an adoption order to be in Carrie's welfare, however, if they were to do so Bertie's consent to the adoption would be required. Under *s 52(1)* of the *Adoption and Children Act 2002* a birth parent's consent can be dispensed with if the welfare of the child demands it. The problem with this section is that once the court has decided that adoption is in the child's welfare, it is arguably very difficult for a parent to then argue that it is not also in the child's welfare for their consent to be dispensed with. As a result, if (and on the facts this is unlikely), the court decides that adoption is in the welfare of Carrie, it is very likely that they will dispense with Bertie's consent and the adoption order will be made.

Question 45

Georgia and Henry married in 1996 and had two children, Imogen and James, now aged 7 and 5 respectively. After James' birth, Henry left home, unable to cope with the demands of two young children, and had a nervous breakdown which has left him permanently mentally impaired. He how resides in a mental hospital. After Henry left, Georgia struggled to look after the children, but then felt unable to cope. She placed the children with the local authority voluntarily, saying that she needed time to work things out. Georgia then went to London where she initially worked as a waitress, but for the past three years she has worked as a prostitute. She has never gone to see the children, although she has sent them cards and presents at Christmas and for their birthdays.

The local authority placed the children with foster parents, Kate and Luke, with whom the children have lived for the past four years. Kate and Luke would like to adopt Imogen and James, and the local authority is supportive, feeling that they have taken excellent care of the children.

Advise on the prospects of Kate and Luke successfully adopting the children if Georgia and Henry do not consent.

Answer plan

- Explain concept of adoption; who can adopt and who can be adopted;
- look at issue of parental consent for both Henry and Georgia and how it may be dispensed with;
- explain the adoption procedure.

Answer

In the present case, Kate and Luke wish to apply to adopt the two children who have been in their care for the past four years. They will need to obtain a court order under the Adoption and Children Act 2002 which will have the effect of completely severing the legal relationship between the parents, Georgia and Henry, and the children, and establishing a new relationship between the children and Kate and Luke, the adoptive parents. Thus, an adoption order has permanent effect and is the only way of terminating the parental responsibility of Georgia and Henry.

Both Imogen and James are qualifying children, as they are under 18. Assuming Kate and Luke are over 21, they can adopt the children and because of reforms in the Adoption and Children Act 2002, they can adopt the children whether they are married or not.

As Imogen and James are already living with Kate and Luke this would be a non-agency adoption. Kate and Luke would need to inform the local authority that they intend to adopt the children, and the children would need to have been placed with them for a year before they could apply to court for an adoption order – Adoption and Children Act 2002 s 42(4).

The court would need to consider whether adoption is in Imogen and James's welfare. The fact that Kate and Luke have cared for Imogen and James for the last three years and that the local authority favour the adoption suggests that they are providing a good supportive environment for the children and it would support the children's emotional and physical well-being to be adopted. Although the court should consider alternatives to adoption under *s 1(6)* of the *Adoption Act* it is arguable that adoption is the most appropriate option. This is because adoption offers permenency.

As Georgia and Henry were married both their consents are needed to the adoption order. From the facts, it seems likely that Georgia would refuse her consent. However, under s 52(1) the court can dispense with consent if the welfare of the child demands it and it seems that this is a likely outcome in this case. Henry?

Finally, it is possible for the court to attach conditions to an adoption order. The court could make the adoption order but with a condition supporting indirect contact via cards and presents between Imogen and James and Georgia.

CHAPTER 11

AN OVERVIEW

INTRODUCTION

It is common to find examination questions, whether problem or essay questions, that span a number of issues. Consider very carefully exactly what is being asked of you and ensure that you cover all issues carefully. The following questions attempt to bring together the various topics from earlier chapters.

Question 46

Lucy and Richard are married and live with two children of their own, Caroline, aged 4, and David, aged 2, and Lucy's son from a previous relationship, John, aged 10. The marriage has encountered difficulties, and Richard has left home on a number of occasions, but returned within days. However, Richard left the home four weeks ago and is refusing to return, informing Lucy that he has found himself another woman.

(a) Advise Lucy, who does not want to divorce Richard, on how, if at all, she may obtain maintenance for herself and the children.

(b) Lucy is also concerned that Richard may attempt to raise money by mortgaging the matrimonial home, which is registered in his name only. The home was purchased by way of a deposit of £5,000 paid by Richard, with the outstanding £45,000 by way of mortgage. Richard paid the mortgage contributions for five years, but then Lucy won a competition and used all her prize money to pay off the outstanding mortgage of £40,000. What should Lucy do?

Answer plan

(a) This concerns maintenance for spouses and children where there is no divorce. The powers of the Magistrates' Court under the DP (MC) A 1978 for spouses, and for the child of the family who is not the natural child of both and for the child of the family

- explore ss 1 and 2 and the factors in s 3,
- then consider the County Court's powers under *MCA 1973 s 27* on the basis of failure to provide reasonable maintenance,
- maintenance for the natural children must be sought by reference to the Child Support Act 1991 and its provisions should be explained.

(b) This concerns property interests in the home and their protection:

- look at legal and equitable entitlement.
- consider implied, resulting, constructive trusts.
- protection through overriding interest.

Answer

(a) Lucy, as Richard's spouse, may apply either to the Magistrates' Court under the DP (MC) A 1978 or to the County Court under the MCA 1973 to ensure that she receives a reasonable level of financial support. The same jurisdiction may be used to obtain financial provision for John, as he is not Richard's natural child. Provision for Caroline and David will be obtained by reference to the Child Support Act 1991, since Richard is their natural biological father.

An application to the Magistrates' Court under the DP (MC) A may be made by Lucy for her own benefit and for that of John. John is a child of the family, defined in MCA 1973 s 52 as a child treated by both parties as a child of the family. An application for an order under s 2 can seek periodical payments, which are unsecured, in addition to lump sums up to a maximum of £1,000 per application. One of the grounds in s 1 must, however, be satisfied; namely that the respondent has failed to provide reasonable maintenance for the applicant and/or a child of the family, or has behaved in such a way that the applicant cannot reasonably be expected to live with him, or that the respondent has deserted the applicant.

The simplest option in the present case would be to rely on the failure to provide reasonable maintenance. Clearly, the present situation is that Richard is providing no maintenance for Lucy and John and this will obviously fall short of what the court would be likely to order. Therefore the ground will be made out.

In determining the level of maintenance to award, the court will consider the factors in DP (MC) A 1978 s 3(1), which closely mirror the factors in MCA 1973 s 25. The income, earning capacity and financial resources of the parties are not elaborated on in the question but it is likely that, with such young children, Lucy is in need of support from Richard. The needs and obligations of the parties must be considered (s 3(1)(b)), as must the standard of living enjoyed by the parties prior to Richard leaving. Both parties appear to have made their respective contributions to the marriage (s 3(1)(f)), and it is not clear whether Richard's conduct in leaving frequently is such that it would be inequitable to disregard it under s 3(1)(g).

In determining the provision for John, the court would look additionally at the manner in which he is being educated and any special needs he may have. Since John is not Richard's natural child, s 3(4) requires the court to examine whether Richard assumed responsibility for John, and on what basis. It does seem that Richard has cared for John for some years knowing that John is not his child. Finally, the liability of any other person to maintain the child is considered, but little is known of John's natural father and whether he can be traced and made to contribute to his child's upkeep.

Although the Magistrates' Court is quicker and cheaper than the county court, an application under MCA 1973 s 27 may be made on the basis that Richard has failed to provide reasonable maintenance for the applicant and/or child of the family. The factors to be considered mirror those in DP (MC) A 1978 s 3, but the advantage to a county court application is that secured periodical payments and unlimited lump sums may also be awarded. Unlike an order from the Magistrates' Court, the County Court order is not terminated automatically by continued cohabitation of more than six months. This may be useful in light of Richard's tendency to come and go from the family's life, and Lucy's unwillingness to consider divorce.

Provision for the two natural children of Lucy and Richard will be by reference to the *Child Support Act 1991*. This Act applies wherever the caring parent is in receipt of State benefits, and also if the parents in non-benefit cases are unable to agree on the level of provision that should be provided. The court no longer has any power under the MCA 1973 to make provision for children in a disputed case.

The Child Support, Pensions and Social Security Act 2000 has replaced the complex Child Support Act formula with a percentage method of assessment. Richard would be termed a non-resident parent and he would pay 20 per cent of his net income for the support of his two children. Lucy's income would be ignored, and there are no allowances for Richard's housing costs, and so on. However, this figure may be adjusted downwards if Richard acquires a second family or if the children spend time living with him.

(b) The matrimonial home is registered in Richard's name only, and, in the absence of fraud, this declaration of legal entitlement is absolute: *Goodman v Gallant (1986)*. There is no evidence of any written declaration of a beneficial interest for Lucy and so her only option of obtaining an interest will be by way of implied, resulting or constructive trust, which does not require any formalities. If Lucy can establish an interest, this may protect her from Richard's financial manoeuvering.

Any such interest for Lucy is determined by reference to the strict rules of property law (*Pettitt v Pettitt (1970)*), with no discretion for the court to do what seems fair in the circumstances. The courts do not tend to emphasise the strict distinctions between the different types of trust, and would look to see if there was a common intention to share, together with detrimental acts by Lucy.

Although Lucy did not contribute to the deposit or the initial mortgage contributions by Richard, she did use £40,000 of her prize money to pay off the outstanding mortgage. Such an enormous contribution is unlikely to be made without an intention that, by so doing, Lucy would acquire an interest in the home. It is not clear whether the parties intended the amount of the share to be reflected by their respective contributions, as is usually the case (*Cowcher v Cowcher (1972)*), or whether equal shares were intended but, either way, Lucy clearly has a beneficial entitlement to a share of the home. In *Midland Bank v Cooke (1995)*, it was stated that in determining the extent of the interest, the court could take into account the parties' intentions as evidenced by the whole history of the marriage, not just contributions that would suffice to create the original interest.

She is presently concerned about her position should Richard attempt to mortgage the home. Since Lucy is in occupation of the home, which does not need to be continuous or exclusive (*Kingsnorth Finance v Tizard (1986)*), she has an overriding interest by virtue of *Land Registration Act 1925 s 70(1)(g)*. This means that even if her interest is not registered, she will be protected against mortgage or sale to a third party (*Williams and Glyns Bank v Boland (1981)*). Her interest can only be overreached if Richard appoints another trustee for sale and payment is made to Richard and the other trustee: *City of London Building Society v Flegg (1987)*.

It is probably best for Lucy to register her interest in order to be protected and then, as a co-trustee, she can refuse her consent to any mortgage. If, however, she is not a trustee she will have no automatic veto over the mortgage, and so she could seek an injunction preventing the mortgage and seeking the appointment of a second trustee so that her interests can be safeguarded.

Question 47

Nancy and Bill are lovers and are cohabiting in Bill's small flat. However, Bill has a drink problem and frequently returns home drunk, when he subjects Nancy to violent attacks. Nancy has just discovered that she is pregnant and is concerned about her well being and that of her child if she stays with Bill. However, she has nowhere else to go, and is finding it difficult to obtain a job.

Advise Nancy:

(a) whether, and on what basis, Bill may be excluded from the flat;

(b) what measures can she take to ensure that Bill is not violent to her in the future and

(c) if she remains with Bill, whom she still loves, what steps could the local authority take in relation to her child?

Answer plan

(a) Look at provisions for occupation orders under Family Law Act 1996; Nancy is a non-entitled applicant.

(b) Look at non-molestation orders under s 42 Family Law Act 1996;

(c) Concerns local authority powers:

- mention duty to investigate (s 47),
- duty to assist voluntarily (ss 17–20),
- consider care order (s 31) and the criteria for the making of such an order,
- emergency protection order (s 44).

Answer

(a) In advising Nancy on whether and on what basis Bill may be excluded from the flat it is necessary to realise that the flat is owned or rented by Bill, and he would seem to be an entitled respondent within the Family Law Act 1996. Nancy, however, appears to have no right to occupy the flat by virtue of a beneficial interest or contractual entitlement or by virtue of any enactment. Since she is Bill's lover, she has no matrimonial home right to occupy either and so she would be a non-entitled applicant within the Family Law Act 1996.

The Court nonetheless has jurisdiction to entertain her application for an occupation order if she and Bill have lived together as husband and wife and are accordingly cohabitants within s 62. Nancy is a non-entitled applicant and Bill seems to be an entitled respondent and so s 36 will apply. This would require the court to first consider the making of an occupation rights order, giving Nancy the right to occupy the home, which she would not otherwise have, and then to make a regulatory order excluding Bill.

In making an occupation rights order the court will take all the circumstances of the case into account including the housing needs and resources of the parties and any relevant child; the financial resources of the parties; the likely effect on the health, safety and well being of the parties and relevant child of any order or no order being made; the conduct of the parties in relation to each other and otherwise; the length of time they have lived together as husband and wife; whether there are any children; the time that has passed since they lived together; and the existence of any proceedings between the parties under the Children Act or in relation to ownership of property (s 36(6)).

In the present case Nancy has nowhere to live and has no job or financial resources. Since she is pregnant she is physically more vulnerable and clearly needs somewhere to stay. However, the flat is Bill's and he also needs somewhere to stay. His drink problem means that he is also vulnerable, but his behaviour towards Nancy has been blameworthy, and his violence could clearly put her and the unborn child at risk. Even though the couple are cohabitants, the facts would seem to suggest that Nancy should be allowed to occupy the flat for a short period of time. This might, then, see her through her pregnancy, and once she has a baby, she will be a greater priority housing need for local authority accommodation.

If an occupation order is made, then the court can make a regulatory order excluding Bill from the home or restricting his occupation. The factors influencing the court in determining whether to make such an order are the housing needs and resources of the parties; their financial resources; the effect of any order or failure to make an order on the health, safety or well being of the parties or relevant child; the conduct of the parties in relation to each other and otherwise; the likelihood of significant harm to the applicant or child if no order is made; and the likelihood of significant harm to the respondent if an order is made. With non-entitled cohabitants, unlike the position with entitled applicants, there is no compulsion to make an order on the basis of a risk of significant harm. This puts cohabitants at a disadvantage over spouses, who will usually be entitled applicants by virtue of their matrimonial home rights.

However, in the present case there have been significant violent episodes, which would clearly continue if Bill were allowed to remain in the flat. He is a single male whose behaviour has been blameworthy and violent. The court is likely to be prepared to exclude him from the home. Such orders are of limited duration, however, and are for an initial six month period, with the possibility of one further six month extension. This would, nevertheless, be sufficient to see Nancy through the difficult period of her pregnancy.

Since there has been violence in the past, it seems likely that Nancy would be allowed to occupy the flat and exclude Bill for a limited period of time.

(b) Second, the measures that Nancy could take to protect herself from Bill's violence in the future would be to seek a non-molestation order under

Family Law Act 1996 s 42. Nancy would need to show that she and Bill are associated persons within s 62. This could be satisfied by showing that they were living together as husband and wife, and were cohabitants, or that they lived together in the same household. Once the baby is born, they will also be associated since they are the parents of the same child.

It is then possible for Nancy to apply for a non-molestation order on its own or as an adjunct to other family proceedings, such as an occupation order. The court has a discretion whether or not to make the order and will look at all the circumstances of the case, including the need to secure the health, safety and well being of the applicant and the relevant children. There is no requirement that the respondent has to have been violent, and the order can be widely drafted to afford protection, not just from violence, but from pestering and harassment. In the present case there have been several violent episodes which look likely to continue, posing a grave risk to Nancy's health and that of the unborn child. The court will almost inevitably grant a non-molestation order, and given the history of violence and its continued threat, no undertaking would be accepted, and a power of arrest is likely to be attached (s 47).

The order can be for a limited time or until further order (s 42(7)), and here it is likely to be a continuing order.

(c) Nancy is concerned that if she remains with Bill, whom she still loves, the local authority may take steps in relation to her child once it is born. If Nancy and Bill do not marry then only Nancy will have parental responsibility: *s 2* of the *Children Act 1989*. This imposes on her an obligation to act for the welfare of her child: *s 3(1)* of the *Children Act 1989*. The local authority have a duty to investigate cases where they have reasonable cause to suspect the child is suffering, or likely to suffer harm: s 47 of the Children Act. The local authority will, through its social workers, consult with the family and try to work in partnership to assess the needs of the child. If Nancy's child is deemed to be a child in need, then the local authority has an obligation to provide services for that child under s 17 and, in extreme circumstances, to provide accommodation for the child under s 20. These are exercised on a voluntary basis in cooperation with the parent, and so it is important for Nancy to realise that, even if she tries to patch up her relationship with Bill, the local authority will be there in the future to help her and her child should she turn to them. However, the real problem lies in that the local authority may decide that their cause for concern is sufficient to justify them applying to the court to exercise compulsory powers over Nancy's child.

There is a power for the local authority to apply to the Family Proceedings Court for a care order under *s 31* of the *Children Act 1989*. In order to grant a care order, the court must be satisfied that the child is suffering, or is likely to suffer, significant harm. Harm is defined in the Act as including ill-treatment or impairment of health and development. The concept of ill-treatment includes sexual abuse and physical and mental ill-treatment. There is no evidence that Bill will necessarily ill-treat the child. However, his violence and alcoholism raises serious concern about his ability to control himself whilst drunk. Although Nancy's child will not, at birth, be suffering significant harm, there is obviously the argument that it is likely to do so: in *Newham London Borough Council v AG (1993)* it was stressed that the standard of proof in such a case is not based on the balance of probabilities, since the court is trying to predict the likelihood of harm. Therefore, the local authority will be able to satisfy the threshold criteria if they can show there is a real significant likelihood of harm. Clearly, Bill's alcoholism, the extent to which he is able to control it, and his willingness to try to reform so as to assist with the upbringing of his child, will be crucial in determining the likelihood of harm. The time for assessing the likelihood of harm is the time at which the local authority intervene to assist the child. It is not necessarily the case that harm must be shown at the time of the hearing. This was the outcome of *Re M (A Minor) (1994)* in which the House of Lords held that the time when the child is actually suffering, or is likely to suffer, significant harm is the point at which the local authority first takes protective steps.

This harm or likelihood of harm has to be attributable to the care being given to the child or likely to be given to him if the order is not made, not being what it would be reasonable to expect a parent to give him; or the child being beyond parental control. Obviously, it is the first of these that is applicable in the present case. There is nothing on the facts to indicate that Nancy will be an unsuitable parent. She is expressing concern over the welfare of her child and she does not have any previous history of bad parenting. However, the concern is expressed over Bill and his violent and unpredictable nature. Clearly, his violence, if it is directed against the child, is unacceptable and unreasonable. The court will not necessarily make an order just because the threshold criteria are satisfied. The non-interventionist policy of the *Act (s 1(5))* means that the court will only make an order if this is better than leaving things as they are. The court recognises the need to act without delay (*s 1(2)*) and the paramount consideration is, as ever, the welfare of the child (*s 1(1)*).

The welfare, then, of Nancy's unborn child will, once it is born, be the paramount consideration and will determine whether or not a care order will be made. Clearly, the child's welfare is usually best served by its upbringing in a family environment but, whilst Nancy remains determined to live with Bill, serious concern will be expressed over the ability of herself and Bill to promote their child's welfare. Since the child is a newborn child there is no real status to maintain and it may be that the court will take the view, that a care order does enable the local authority to have a wider discretion as to what to do to promote the child's welfare. Clearly, the philosophy of the Act is that compulsory measures are a last resort and that children are better off with their natural families. However, where there is serious concern over the natural ability to care for the child, it may be that a care order is the best option. This care order does not mean that the child will necessarily be taken away from Nancy and Bill, but it does give the local authority the opportunity to keep a close eye on the child's progress. Consequently, it seems likely that the local authority may seek to obtain a care order. Care orders are obtainable on notice being given to the parents in the case and also by the guardian *ad litem* being appointed for the child.

If the local authority decides that more speedy measures are needed, they can apply for an emergency protection order under the Act. An emergency protection order is available under s 44 if the local authority can show that there is reasonable cause to believe that the child is likely to suffer significant harm if he is not removed from the accommodation where he is, to accommodation provided by the local authority. It is also possible that the local authority may apply for an emergency protection order if it is making enquiries with regard to the child under s 47, and those enquiries are being frustrated by access to the child being unreasonably refused, and there is reasonable cause to believe that the access to the child is required as a matter of urgency. Therefore, if, after the child's birth, Bill appears to be violent or, for example, Nancy does not co-operate with the local authorities enquiry, then the local authority may seek an emergency protection order.

Such an order is a significant measure and it gives the local authority parental responsibility for the duration of the emergency protection order. The order only usually lasts for eight days (s 45(1)), although it can be extended for a further seven days. The emergency protection order will authorise the child's removal to local authority accommodation and the court will direct whether contact is to be permitted between the child and any other person. It is likely that Nancy would still be able to see her child because she is not abusing it but Bill may have contact restricted or refused. The emergency protection order can be challenged after 72 hours have passed by the parents or by the child unless they were present and were heard at the hearing. This emergency protection order is obtainable very speedily without notice and could help the local authority prepare its application for the care order.

The effect of the care order if made would be to vest the parental responsibility in the local authority who would need to exercise it in the child's best interests. Nancy would not lose her parental responsibility if the local authority acquire it under a care order and the local authority are under an obligation to work in partnership with the parents, consulting them where possible and taking their views and the views of the child into account (*s 22* of the *Act*). Thus, it seems that the local authority could possibly obtain a care order and may need an emergency protection order should Bill remain violent.

The Family Law Act 1996 introduces reform to the Children Act 1989 in that it permits a local authority to make an application for a short-term emergency exclusion requirement. The court can make an interim care order under s 38 of the

Children Act 1989 if it appears that the threshold criteria in s 31 will be satisfied. Should it appear that if Bill is excluded from the home the child will cease to suffer or cease to be likely to suffer significant harm, and if Nancy is able and willing to care for the child, and consents to Bill being excluded, then an exclusion requirement can be made requiring Bill to leave the home, or the area the home is in, and prohibiting him from entering the home. A power of arrest can also be attached to this. This exclusion requirement is also an option if the local authority apply for an emergency protection order, but it is only going to be possible if Nancy agrees to Bill's exclusion.

Question 48

Amy and Benedict went through a ceremony of marriage four years ago, when Amy was 16 and Benedict was 20. Amy's parents were unhappy with the marriage, and so refused their consent. Amy and Benedict eloped and were married in a country church one month later. The banns were read using Amy's middle name, Louise, instead of Amy, and Benedict shortened his name to Ben, as he was commonly called.

Twins were born subsequently, and are now aged two and a half. However, the marriage has broken down, and Amy wishes to end the marriage.

Advise Amy:

(a) on what basis her marriage to Benedict may be ended;

(b) on the status of the two children of the marriage;

(c) whether Benedict is liable to pay maintenance for the children and, if so, on what basis;

Answer plan

(a) Look at possible ways of ending marriage:
- nullity on basis that void under s 11 (used false names; parental consent irrelevant),
- nullity on basis that voidable under s 12 (no real evidence).

(b) status of children and their legitimacy:
- s 1 Legitimacy Act (belief that marriage is valid renders children legitimate).

(c) liability to pay maintenance under the Child Support Act 1991:
- explain the statutory formula.

Answer

(a) The marriage between Amy and Benedict may be ended by an application for nullity if the marriage is void under s 11 of the Matrimonial Causes Act 1973 or if the marriage is voidable under s 12 of the Matrimonial Causes Act 1973. An application for divorce is also possible under *s 1* of the *Matrimonial Causes Act 1973*.

A void marriage is one that is a complete nullity: *De Renville v De Renville (1948)*. Technically, there is no need to apply for a decree of nullity in the case of a void marriage; however, Amy would be advised to do so in order to achieve certainty, and in order to avail herself of the provisions for financial security in the Matrimonial Causes Act 1973.

Examining the criteria which make a marriage void in s 11, it can be seen that these defects occur if the parties have married within the prohibited degrees: if either party is under 16, which does not apply here; or if they have married in disregard of certain formalities under the Marriage Acts. In the present case, the marriage took place according to the rites of the Church of England and there is serious concern as to whether the banns have been duly published. The purpose of calling banns is to ensure publicity and to enable those with objections to object to the marriage. It is possible to marry in an area in which the couple do not live, provided they have established residence for the qualifying period, as is the case for Amy and Ben. The banns have been read using somewhat different names from those of the couple's legal names. In the case of Benedict he is usually known as Ben and so there could be an argument that he did not intend to deceive anyone by the use of his abbreviated name, as in *Dancer v Dancer (1948)*. However, Amy, by the use of her middle name, could arguably have been said to have deceived and to have removed the possibility of persons objecting to her marriage. Much might depend upon how frequently Amy was known by the name of Louise, but it does seem that there may be an intention to deceive here.

The couple have also married without parental consent. In the case of Amy, she is under 18 and parental consent is required. However, the lack of consent is not a defect that renders the marriage void: *s 48(1)(b)* of the *Marriage Act 1949*. It does seem here that Amy and Ben have married in church without objections being made and therefore, subject to the fact that the banns may not have been duly published because of the concealment, the marriage may nevertheless be valid. The marriage will only be void if the banns were not duly published and both parties knowingly and wilfully married in disregard of this. It is somewhat contentious as to whether both Ben and Amy married in disregard of this: if they did, the marriage is void and a nullity decree should be sought under s 11.

If, however, the marriage is valid, then the only other options open to Amy are to apply for nullity on the basis of the marriage being voidable under s 12 of the

Matrimonial Causes Act or to apply for a divorce under s 1 of the Matrimonial Causes Act. There is insufficient evidence on the facts of this case to indicate what has gone wrong with the relationship after the marriage. However, if it can be shown that either the basis for declaring the marriage to be voidable exists or the basis for a divorce exists, then the marriage between Amy and Benedict may be ended.

(b) Second, the status of the two children of the marriage depends upon *s 1* of the *Legitimacy Act 1976*, as amended. Historically, children of a void marriage would have been deemed illegitimate and this somewhat harsh consequence could flow after many years of the marriage and even after the death of both parties to the marriage. Section 1 of the Legitimacy Act 1976 mitigates this rule by deeming a child to be legitimate if either or both parents believe that the marriage was valid at the time of conception or the time of the marriage, whichever is the later. Section 1 only applies if the father is domiciled in England and Wales at the date of the birth, which appears to be the case here. The question then turns on whether either Amy or Ben or both of them reasonably believed that their marriage was valid. It is already established that the marriage is void if they realised that the banns had not been duly published. However, it is not clear under s 1 whether any mistake of law that they may make can ever be reasonable. Thus, it could be argued that if Amy and Ben, whilst realising that they had used different names, reasonably believed that that did not effect the validity of their marriage, then their children will be legitimate. This is a somewhat unsatisfactory position. The status of the two children in the present case will depend, therefore, upon whether the marriage was void; if so, there is the additional uncertainty of s 1 of the Legitimacy Act.

The consequence of this may be that the children in the present case are legitimate, in which case both Amy and Ben have parental responsibility under *s 2(1)* of the *Children Act 1989*. If however, the children are illegitimate, then only Amy will have parental responsibility under the Act. If the marriage, however, was merely voidable or was ended on divorce, both of the children will be legitimate.

(c) Ben's liability to pay maintenance will lie under the *Child Support Act of 1991*. This Act applies by imposing a maintenance requirement on the natural father of the children. These two children have been born in wedlock and are presumed to be the natural children of Amy and Benedict. Benedict may dispute paternity, in which case paternity will need to be established before he can be held liable under the Child Support Act.

The first step is to assess whether there are qualifying children, and both twins are qualifying children under the Act.

Benedict would be termed a non-resident parent and he would pay 20 per cent of his net income for the support of his two children. Amy's income would be ignored, and there are no allowances for Benedict's housing costs, etc. However, this figure may be adjusted downwards, if Benedict acquires a second family, or if the children spend time living with him.

Question 49

Felicity and Greg married in February 1997, and have a son, Edmund, who is now 7. When they married, Felicity agreed that Greg's widowed mother, Iris, could come and live with them if she ever became unable to look after herself, and Greg agreed that the same would apply to Felicity's mother.

Three months ago, Greg's mother, Iris, became ill and moved in with Felicity and Greg to convalesce. Iris has often been difficult, criticising the way Felicity and Greg bring up Edmund, and often taking sides in the increasingly frequent matrimonial rows. Felicity finally confronted Greg, telling him that either his mother should leave, or she, Felicity, would leave. Greg responded by saying that Felicity had over-reacted, at which point Felicity stormed out.

Advise Felicity:

(a) Whether she can divorce Greg;

(b) whether she can exclude Greg's mother from the matrimonial home, in the event of there being no divorce;

(c) whether she can prevent Iris seeing Edmund.

Answer plan

(a) Basis for divorce:
- irretrievable breakdown and the five facts,
- only real possibility is behaviour,
- problem as to behaviour,
- could separate and wait two or five years.

(b) Seek occupation order under s 33 Family Law Act 1996 as entitled applicant

(c) Contact between grandmother and child:
- parental responsibility and ability to act independently,
- need to apply for s 8 order,
- welfare and the s 1(3) checklist.

Answer

(a) In order to divorce Greg, Felicity must establish that their marriage has broken down irretrievably: MCA 1973 s 1(1). This must be done by reference to one of the five facts in MCA 1973 s 1(2): *Richards v Richards (1972)*. In the present case, it may be argued that, even if one of the five facts were established, Felicity would have difficulty in establishing irretrievable breakdown, as in *Biggs v Biggs (1977)*. The couple appear to have experienced temporary difficulty during the stay of Iris, rather than a permanent breakdown in their relationship. However, if Felicity established one of the facts, then the court will grant the decree (*s 1(4)*) unless it is satisfied that the marriage has not irretrievably broken down.

Felicity has no evidence that Greg has committed adultery (s 1(2)(a)) and the couple have not been separated for long enough to allow a petition on the basis of two years desertion (s 1(2)(c)), or two years or five years living apart (s 1(2)(d) and (e)). The only possible basis for an immediate divorce is to present a petition based on s 1(2)(b), that is, that the respondent, Greg, has behaved in such a way that she cannot reasonably be expected to live with him. There needs to be some behaviour or conduct on Greg's part that is referable to the marriage. Felicity's complaint appears to centre on Iris' behaviour, and this cannot form the basis of a petition based on Greg's behaviour. Instead, Felicity would have to argue that his uncaring response to her problem is symptomatic of his neglect and lack of concern. This does seem somewhat flimsy, and it would then be necessary to show that, given the individual characteristics of the spouses (*Ash v Ash (1972)*), it would be unreasonable to expect Felicity to continue to live with Greg (*Livingstone-Stallard v Livingstone-Stallard (1974)*). The mere fact that Greg is unconcerned or undemonstrative in the face of his wife's demands for attention may well not suffice: *Pheasant v Pheasant (1972)*. However, given the special procedure for obtaining a divorce, it is possible that Felicity's petition would not face much scrutiny.

She could, however, continue to live apart from Greg, that is, in two separate households: MCA 1973 s 2(6). Felicity must also recognise that the marriage is at an end (*Santos v Santos (1972)*), although this does not need to be communicated to Greg. If this continues for two years, and Greg consents to the granting of the petition, then a divorce may be obtained under MCA 1973 s 1(2)(d). If Greg refused consent, then Felicity will not be able to argue constructive desertion as she did not have good reason to leave. Instead, she will need to wait until she and Greg have been separated for five years, and petition under MCA 1973 s 1(2)(e).

(b) In order to exclude Greg's mother, Felicity will need to make an application for an occupation order under the provisions in the Family Law Act 1996. Felicity is an entitled applicant within s 33 as she has matrimonial home rights in relation to the dwelling house, which has been her home and the home of her spouse, Greg. She may also have some other entitlement to occupy, either by virtue of a legal or beneficial entitlement.

Accordingly, Felicity can apply for an order under s 33 against a respondent who is an associated person within s 62. Greg's mother is an associated person since she is a relative by virtue of being Greg's mother, and she is also an associated person by virtue of living in the same household as Felicity.

The order can require the respondent to leave the home or otherwise regulate the occupation of the home by the parties. In determining whether and what regulatory order to make, the court will take into account the circumstances of the case, including the housing needs and resources of the parties; their financial resources; the likely effect of any order or failure to make an order on the health, safety or well being of the parties or relevant child; and the conduct of the parties in relation to each other and otherwise. The court can then exercise its discretion over whether to make an order. Felicity will argue that she and her child need to remain in the house, and that, since Iris has not given up her own home, she could return there without difficulty. She will also argue that Iris' behaviour is having a detrimental effect on her health and the well being of the family. However, the position is slightly complicated by the fact that Iris is in the home with the agreement of Greg, and, initially, of Felicity herself. In addition to this, Iris is sick, although it is not clear how severe her illness is.

If, however, under s 33(7) it appears that the applicant or relevant child is likely to suffer significant harm attributable to the conduct of the respondent if the order is not made, then the court must make an order, unless the respondent or relevant child is likely to suffer equal or greater significant harm if the order is made. This requires the court to first consider whether there is the likelihood of significant harm, and then balance the harm of making an order with the harm of not making an order.

Harm is defined in s 63 to mean ill-treatment or impairment of mental or physical health with the additional criteria of impairment of development for a child. Ill-treatment includes both physical and sexual abuse in relation to a child, and development is widely defined to include physical, emotional, intellectual, social or behavioural development. The concept of 'significant' is likely to mean considerable or important, if guidance in earlier cases on the meaning of such wording in other statutes is followed: *Humberside County Council v B (1993)*.

It is difficult to see how, on the facts, Felicity would be able to sustain such an argument, so there would be no statutory presumption in favour of the order being made. It seems rather harsh to exclude Iris from the home, since she is only there temporarily until she recovers, but much would depend on the nature of her behaviour towards Felicity. This is a case where the court might be prepared to accept an undertaking from Iris that she will do her best not to interfere in Felicity and Greg's domestic arguments and to stop her criticism.

(c) The issue of Iris' contact with the child Edmund will be affected by whether Edmund has remained with his father and grandmother in the matrimonial home, or whether he has left and is staying with his mother. Since Felicity and Greg are married, they both have parental responsibility for Edmund: Children Act (CA) 1989 s 2(1). This is defined as 'all the rights, duties, powers and responsibility that a parent has by law in relation to the child and its property': CA 1989 s 3(1). However, both parents are entitled to act independently in the exercise of their parental responsibility, and this means that there is no automatic veto.

Consequently, if Edmund has remained with his father, Felicity will be unable to prevent her son seeing Iris, unless she seeks a residence order to enable Edmund to live with her, or a prohibited steps order to prevent Iris having contact with Edmund: s 8 CA 1989. If, however, Edmund is living with Felicity, she can prevent contact in the immediate future, but should be advised that Iris might apply for a contact order under s 8.

In any application for a s 8 order, the child's welfare will be the paramount consideration (s 1(1)), and must be determined by reference to the checklist in s 1(3). The court will be aware of the risk of prejudicing welfare by unnecessary delay (s 1(2)), and will only intervene if necessary (s 1(5)).

In the instant case, Felicity, as a parent, can apply for a s 8 order as of right, whereas Iris, as a grandparent, will require leave. However, given that Iris has a good relationship with her grandson, it is likely that the court would recognise her genuine concern and grant leave. There are two possible issues here: namely, where Edmund should live; and whether there should be contact with his grandmother. Advice has been sought on this latter issue only, and this advice would be given, first, on the basis that Edmund lives with Felicity, and, second, that he lives with his father.

If Edmund lives with Felicity, then she should be advised that the courts tend to view contact with other members of the family with whom the child has a good relationship, as being in the child's welfare. The *s 1(3)* checklist would require the court to take into account the ascertainable wishes and feelings of the child in the light of his age and understanding. Edmund is seven, and will almost definitely have a view as to whether he wishes to continue to see his grandmother. Although this view would not be conclusive, since he is only seven, it will be taken into account. Edmund's needs can be met by his grandmother, and since he has an existing relationship, he may be disturbed at any enforced change. There is no evidence that Edmund is at any risk of harm from Iris, and it may be that she has love and guidance to give that would be of benefit to Edmund. It seems likely that contact would be allowed, unless it was genuinely upsetting and distressing for Felicity, so as to be detrimental to Edmund's welfare.

Likewise, it is extremely unlikely that the court would regard it as in Edmund's welfare to prohibit contact with Iris should Felicity seek a prohibited steps order. This seems to be a vindictive action on Felicity's part, and she should be wary of making such an application, since it does not give the impression that she has her son's welfare at heart.

Question 50

In matters of the family, the child should come first, last and always.

Discuss to what extent English family law provides for children's welfare.

Answer plan

Requires an examination of various areas of family law in which the welfare of a child could be affected:

- Children Act 1989, disputes over upbringing and local authority powers;
- adoption – Adoption and Children Act 2002 changed the law so welfare is now paramount;
- divorce – granting – no consideration of welfare;
- ancillary relief – welfare first consideration;
- Child Support Act 1991 and possible conflict with welfare;
- property disputes – no consideration of welfare;
- occupation of home – just one of a number of considerations.

Answer

Where a family contains children and problems are encountered, the children are inevitably affected by what their parents do. It is not just the obvious cases where the dispute concerns the upbringing of the child; many disputes which appear to be solely between the adults have effects that impinge on their children's welfare. It is necessary, therefore, to examine to what extent English family law takes into account the child's welfare, and whether it does so in an adequate manner.

The Children Act 1989 is a crucial piece of legislation which does a great deal to make family law child-centred and responsive to the child's needs. The Act covers both the child and their relationship with the parents, as well as the role of the State and local authority powers. As its cornerstone, it provides that in matters of the child's upbringing and welfare, the child's welfare is the court's paramount consideration: s 1(1). This removes any doubt that existed by the old phrase 'first and paramount', and it is clear that ultimately the court must rule in favour of the option that best promotes the child's well being and interests. The s 8 orders will only be made on the basis that they promote welfare, and local authority powers will only be exercisable under the Act if in the child's best interests. To assist the court in determining what is in the child's welfare, s 1(3) provides a checklist of factors. Importantly, this checklist begins with the need to consider the child's ascertainable wishes in the light of his age and understanding. This reinforces the *Gillick* concept that, as a child becomes more mature, they should have a greater say in their own lives, provided they have sufficient maturity and understanding.

There are two other general principles in the Act which highlight the importance of considering the child's welfare. The first, in s 1(2), provides that the court must be mindful of the fact that delay is often prejudicial to the child's welfare, and imposes a positive duty on the court to set a timetable for the conduct of the proceedings. The second is the non-interventionist policy in s 1(5), whereby the court should only intervene and make an order if doing so is better than not making an order. This discourages routine orders and tries to encourage the parties to reach a consensus on the upbringing of the children when possible.

There is a substantial body of case law which has shown how welfare may be promoted, and the Children Act 1989 has done much to bury the notion that parents 'own' their children and can do as they wish. The concept of parental rights has been replaced by the notion of parental responsibility, which emphasises that the parents have an obligation to nurture their child and promote its well being, rather than treat it as a possession.

As welcome as the provisions of the Children Act 1989 are, they do not extend to all disputes which affect children. Adoption is one of the most significant decisions that can be made about a child and it is dealt with in the Adoption and Children Act 2002 rather than the Children Act 1989. The *Adoption and Children Act 2002 s 1(1)* makes it clear that the child's welfare is paramount in decisions relating to adoption. This is a change from previous legislation where adoption was only the court's first consideration *(Adoption Act 1976 s 6)*. Moreover, both the adoption agency and the court must have the child's welfare as their paramount consideration. The Adoption and Children Act 2002 has set out a checklist that details how a child's welfare should be assessed. Whilst this is similar to the checklist in the section 3 of the Children Act 1989, it does have specific criteria that reflect the fact that adoption is a lifelong decision and that adoption severs the link between the child and his birth family.

When a couple divorce, the basis of divorce is irretrievable breakdown, as evidenced by one of the five facts: MCA 1973 s 1(2). There is no consideration of the effect on the children if their parents divorce. Critics have argued that the adults involved should have to face up to the effect their divorce is having on their children, and there are those who argue that divorce is detrimental to children's welfare. The majority argue that it is the breakdown of the relationship that is detrimental to the children and there is no legislation that can force couples to get along amicably. To complicate divorce and the breakdown of a relationship by introducing a consideration of the children's welfare could lead to a party who is denied a divorce on these grounds resenting his or her children.

When ancillary relief and property matters are determined on divorce, the child's welfare is merely the first consideration, and even then only whilst he is a minor. The financial implications of divorce and the rehousing of the parties can have important repercussions on a child, but his welfare is of first, not overriding, importance. The factors in s 25 must be considered, and a solution reached by taking into account those factors will not always be one that is in the child's best interest. Indeed the consideration of conduct, where it would be inequitable to disregard it, to reduce a spouse's financial entitlement, may have repercussions on the children if that spouse is the parent with care of the children.

In considering financial obligations for a child's maintenance, the provisions of the MCA apply to financial support for children of the family who are not the natural children of the payer. Again, their welfare is a first consideration, and although the court is directed to consider their needs, the manner of their education, any physical or mental disability, the court also considers the parties' needs and resources, and the extent and basis of their assumption of responsibility for the child. It is not possible aggressively to promote a child's welfare by awarding high levels of financial support if this would have the effect of economically ruining the payer.

Financial responsibility for natural children is governed by the *Child Support Act 1991*, and one of the criticisms of the Act is that it often disregards the welfare of the children involved. The obligation on the mother to name the father if she receives State benefits could be detrimental to the child's welfare if it puts the mother under pressure and causes her distress. It can also re-involve the father in the children's lives, which is not always to their advantage, especially if he has been abusive or a bad influence in the past. Contact disputes may well increase, as many payers feel they are entitled to see the child they are being forced to support, and this is not in line with the consensus approach of the Children Act 1989. Where a mother is in receipt of benefits, the child support payments do not actually benefit her or her child; instead there is a reduction in her benefit to match any child support received. There is often little financial benefit to the children, and the assessment has often had dire financial consequences for the payer. The children suffer if their father is impoverished by the payments with no corresponding benefit to the mother. In addition, the extra costs may make it difficult for some payers to afford to maintain contact with their children as such contact can involve travel expenses, etc which are not routinely taken into account under the Act but require a departure direction.

Where there are property disputes between couples that have to be resolved by reference to the normal rules of property law, the welfare of the children is not a consideration. If there is no divorce, there may be a situation where a parent and child have no interest in the home and cannot remain there. Cases like *Burns v Burns (1984)* illustrate that even where there has been a lengthy relationship with children, no account can be taken of the children's needs in determining equitable interests. This depends on a common intention to share, contributions and detrimental acts, for which caring for children does not suffice. However, *Sched 1* of the *Children Act 1989* does contain a provision whereby the court can allow occupation of a house and transfer of interests if that is for the welfare of the children. This is a relatively new area and it remains to be seen how frequently it will be used to promote welfare of the child.

In matters concerning the occupation of the home under the MHA 1983, the welfare of the children was just one consideration, and does not override the others: *Richards v Richards (1984)*. The Family Law Act 1996 contains important reforms in the area of domestic violence and the exclusion of persons from the home. These powers have strengthened the protection available for children, and it seems that the Act may have elevated the level of a child's interests beyond that in the previous law. Thus, it can be seen that whilst the welfare of the child is frequently considered in family law matters, it is not always an overriding consideration. Delicate balance has to be maintained between the welfare of the child and the rights of its parents, but English law has gone a long way to ensuring that the child's welfare is always borne in mind.

INDEX

harm, definition of *see under* ill-treatment or physical/mental impairment in s 63
Harman v Glencross (1986) 90
Harrington v Gill (1983) 124
Harthan v Harthan (1949) 9, 10–11, 16
Hazell v Hazell (1972) 123
Hepburn v Hepburn (1989) 99
Hepplethwaite, Ros 71
Herbert v Herbert (1819) 4, 8, 10, 12
High Court 18, 159, 161, 205
Hirani v Hirani (1982) 9
Hopes v Hopes (1949) 26, 39
Horton v Horton (1947) 6, 9, 43
Horton v Horton (1948) 14
House of Lords, the 19, 75–76, 95, 164, 220
Housing Acts 145
Human Rights Act 1998 121, 130, 154
Humberside County Council v B (1993) 135, 139, 145, 227
Hussain v Hussain (1982) 5, 11
H v H (1975) 102
H v H (1989) 186
Hyde v Hyde (1866) 4, 8, 12

ill-treatment or physical/mental impairment in s 63 135, 139, 145, 198–199, 227
Inheritance (Provision for Family and Dependants) Act 1975 106, 122–124
intended matrimonial home, law of 3–4

Jane v Jane (1983) 158
J (HD) v J (AM) (1980) 59
Jones v Jones (1975) 59, 91, 92
Jones v Maynard (1951) 115
J v C (1970) 163, 172, 178, 182

Katz v Katz (1972) 25, 30, 33, 38
Kaur v Singh (1972) 9
Kilner v Kilner (1939) 119
Kingsnorth Finance v Tizard (1986) 121, 127, 216
K v K (Ancillary relief: pre-nuptial agreement) (2003) 76

Lambert v Lambert (2002) 76, 109
Lancashire County Council v A (2000) 187, 191
Land and Appointment of Trustees Act 1996 113, 118, 121, 122, 124, 125, 127
Land Registration Act 1925 113; s 70 of 120; s 70(1)(g) of 113, 118, 121, 124, 125, 127, 216
Lang v Lang (1953) 35
Law Commission 4–5, 45, 104, 130–133; recommendations on non-molestation orders 133; report on the ground for divorce 46–48

Law of Property Act 1925, s 53(1)(b) of 119, 122, 126
Law of Property (Miscellaneous Provisions) Act 1989, s 2 of 119, 122, 126
Law Reform (Miscellaneous Provisions) Act 1970 113; s 3 of 114, 115
Leadbeater v Leadbeater (1985) 86–87
Le Brocq v Le Brocq (1964) 26
Lee v Lee (1984) 82
Legal Aid Fund 95
Legitimacy Act 1976 224
Livesey v Jenkins (1985) 102
Livingstone-Stallard v Livingstone-Stallard (1974) 25–26, 30, 33, 39, 226
Lloyds Bank v Rosset (1991) 113, 116, 117, 120, 123, 126, 127
Lord Penzance 4, 8, 12
Lord Scarman 129, 130, 136

Macey v Macey (1981) 98, 101
Macfarlane v Macfarlane 76
McHardy & Sons v Warren (1994) 119–120
magistrates court 51, 52, 54, 56, 58, 60, 62, 65–67, 69, 132, 213–215
Maintenance Enforcement Act 1991 69
Marriage Act 1949 1–2, 10, 42; s 25 of, for Anglican weddings 8; s 48(1)(b) of 223; s 49 of 8, 16; sched 1, 5
Marriage Act 1970 1–2, 42
Marriage (Prohibited Degrees) Act 1986 5
marriages: and decree of presumption of death 12, 44; and English domicile 4, 5, 8, 10, 11; and Pakistani domicile 5; and place of domicile 3–6; and pregnancy 12; definition of 4; effect of polygamy 4, 5, 7, 13; issue of capacity 3–6, 11–14; issue of consummation in 6, 16, 18, 43; issue of formalities under s 11(a) 1–2, 7, 8, 17; petition under s 12(f) pregnancy per alium 14, 43; problem of s 11(c) 2, 15; prohibited degrees, problem of 1–2, 4, 8, 12, 13, 15, 42, 223; s 12 of 2; s 13 of 2; transsexuals and consummations 18–19; validity of, question and answers 2–19; void, under s 11(b) 2, 7, 10, 12, 15, 17; void, under s 11 MCA 1–2, 7, 8, 29, 41, 223; void, under s 12 MCA 1, 2, 6, 7, 10, 12, 13, 16, 29, 41, 42, 43, 223–224; *see also under* divorce; Marriage (Prohibited Degrees) Act 1986; Matrimonial Causes Act 1973
Married Women's Property Act 1964, s 1 of 113
Marsh v Marsh (1977) 157, 177, 185

Routledge•Cavendish Questions & Answers Series

Family Law
2007–2008

RACHAEL STRETCH

Routledge·Cavendish
Taylor & Francis Group

Fourth edition first published 2007
by Routledge-Cavendish
2 Park Square, Milton Park, Abingdon, Oxon OX14 4RN

Simultaneously published in the USA and Canada
by Routledge-Cavendish
270 Madison Ave, New York, NY 10016

*Routledge-Cavendish is an imprint of the Taylor & Francis Group,
an informa business*

© 1994, 1998, 2001 Tracey Aquino

© 2007 Rachael Stretch

Previous editions published by Cavendish Publishing Limited
First edition   1994
Second edition   1998
Third edition   2001

Typeset in Garamond by
Newgen Imaging Systems (P) Ltd, Chennai, India
Printed and bound in Great Britain by
MPG Books Ltd, Bodmin, Cornwall

British Library Cataloguing in Publication Data
A catalogue record for this book is available
from the British Library

Library of Congress Cataloging in Publication Data
A catalog record for this book has been requested

ISBN10: 1–85941–737–X (pbk)
ISBN13: 978–1–85941–737–9 (pbk)